QUICKEN® 6
FOR WINDOWS®

FOR

DUMMIES®

4TH EDITION

QUICKEN® 6 FOR WINDOWS® FOR DUMMIES®

4TH EDITION

by Stephen L. Nelson

IDG Books Worldwide, Inc.
An International Data Group Company

Foster City, CA ♦ Chicago, IL ♦ Indianapolis, IN ♦ Southlake, TX

Quicken® 6 For Windows® For Dummies®, 4th Edition

Published by
IDG Books Worldwide, Inc.
An International Data Group Company
919 E. Hillsdale Blvd.
Suite 400
Foster City, CA 94404
www.idgbooks.com (IDG Books Worldwide Web Site)
http://www.dummies.com (Dummies Press Web Site)

Library of Congress Catalog Card No.: 96-77702

ISBN: 0-7645-0036-8

Printed in the United States of America

10 9 8 7 6 5 4 3 2 1

4A/SU/QZ/ZW/IN

Distributed in the United States by IDG Books Worldwide, Inc.

Distributed by Macmillan Canada for Canada; by Contemporanea de Ediciones for Venezuela; by Distribuidora Cuspide for Argentina; by CITEC for Brazil; by Ediciones ZETA S.C.R. Ltda. for Peru; by Editorial Limusa SA for Mexico; by Transworld Publishers Limited in the United Kingdom and Europe; by Academic Bookshop for Egypt; by Levant Distributors S.A.R.L. for Lebanon; by Al Jassim for Saudi Arabia; by Simron Pty. Ltd. for South Africa; by Pustak Mahal for India; by The Computer Bookshop for India; by Toppan Company Ltd. for Japan; by Addison Wesley Publishing Company for Korea; by Longman Singapore Publishers Ltd. for Singapore, Malaysia, Thailand, and Indonesia; by Unalis Corporation for Taiwan; by WS Computer Publishing Company, Inc. for the Philippines; by WoodsLane Pty. Ltd. for Australia; by WoodsLane Enterprises Ltd. for New Zealand. Authorized Sales Agent: Anthony Rudkin Associates for the Middle East and North Africa.

For general information on IDG Books Worldwide's books in the U.S., please call our Consumer Customer Service department at 800-762-2974. For reseller information, including discounts and premium sales, please call our Reseller Customer Service department at 800-434-3422.

For information on where to purchase IDG Books Worldwide's books outside the U.S., please contact our International Sales department at 415-655-3172 or fax 415-655-3295.

For information on foreign language translations, please contact our Foreign & Subsidiary Rights department at 415-655-3021 or fax 415-655-3281.

For sales inquiries and special prices for bulk quantities, please contact our Sales department at 415-655-3200 or write to the address above.

For information on using IDG Books Worldwide's books in the classroom or for ordering examination copies, please contact our Educational Sales department at 800-434-2086 or fax 817-251-8174.

For authorization to photocopy items for corporate, personal, or educational use, please contact Copyright Clearance Center, 222 Rosewood Drive, Danvers, MA 01923, or fax 508-750-4470.

is a trademark under exclusive license to IDG Books Worldwide, Inc., from International Data Group, Inc.

About the Author

Stephen L. Nelson

Steve Nelson is a CPA with a master's degree in finance. As corny as it sounds, Steve truly enjoys writing books that make using personal computers easier and more fun. In fact, a substantiated rumor says Steve has written more than 40 computer books.

Steve is the best-selling author on the Quicken product, having sold something like 400,000 books about Quicken.

Welcome to the world of IDG Books Worldwide.

IDG Books Worldwide, Inc., is a subsidiary of International Data Group, the world's largest publisher of computer-related information and the leading global provider of information services on information technology. IDG was founded more than 25 years ago and now employs more than 8,500 people worldwide. IDG publishes more than 270 computer publications in over 75 countries (see listing below). More than 90 million people read one or more IDG publications each month.

Launched in 1990, IDG Books Worldwide is today the #1 publisher of best-selling computer books in the United States. We are proud to have received eight awards from the Computer Press Association in recognition of editorial excellence and three from *Computer Currents*' First Annual Readers' Choice Awards. Our best-selling ...*For Dummies*® series has more than 25 million copies in print with translations in 30 languages. IDG Books Worldwide, through a joint venture with IDG's Hi-Tech Beijing, became the first U.S. publisher to publish a computer book in the People's Republic of China. In record time, IDG Books Worldwide has become the first choice for millions of readers around the world who want to learn how to better manage their businesses.

Our mission is simple: Every one of our books is designed to bring extra value and skill-building instructions to the reader. Our books are written by experts who understand and care about our readers. The knowledge base of our editorial staff comes from years of experience in publishing, education, and journalism — experience which we use to produce books for the '90s. In short, we care about books, so we attract the best people. We devote special attention to details such as audience, interior design, use of icons, and illustrations. And because we use an efficient process of authoring, editing, and desktop publishing our books electronically, we can spend more time ensuring superior content and spend less time on the technicalities of making books.

You can count on our commitment to deliver high-quality books at competitive prices on topics you want to read about. At IDG Books Worldwide, we continue in the IDG tradition of delivering quality for more than 25 years. You'll find no better book on a subject than one from IDG Books Worldwide.

John J. Kilcullen

John Kilcullen
President and CEO
IDG Books Worldwide, Inc.

Publisher's Acknowledgments

We're proud of this book; please send us your comments about it by using the Reader Response Card at the back of the book or by e-mailing us at feedback/dummies@idgbooks.com. Some of the people who helped bring this book to market include the following:

Acquisitions, Development, & Editorial

Project Editors: Barb Terry, William A. Barton

Assistant Acquisitions Editor: Gareth Hancock

Permissions Editor: Joyce Pepple

Copy Editors: Kelly Ewing, Diana R. Conover, Diane Giangrossi

Technical Editor: Kevin Spencer

Editorial Manager: Mary C. Corder

Editorial Assistant: Chris Collins

Production

Project Coordinator: Regina Snyder

Layout and Graphics: Cameron Booker, Dominique DeFelice, Jane E. Martin, Michael Sullivan, Gina Scott, Angela Hunckler

Proofreaders: Rachel Garvey, Nancy Price, Dwight Ramsey, Rob Springer, Karen York

Indexer: David Heiret

General & Administrative

IDG Books Worldwide, Inc.: John Kilcullen, President & CEO; Steven Berkowitz, COO & Publisher

Dummies, Inc.: Milissa Koloski, Executive Vice President & Publisher

Dummies Technology Press & Dummies Editorial: Diane Graves Steele, Associate Publisher; Judith A. Taylor, Brand Manager

Dummies Trade Press: Kathleen A. Welton, Vice President & Publisher; Stacy S. Collins, Brand Manager

IDG Books Production for Dummies Press: Beth Jenkins, Production Director; Cindy L. Phipps, Supervisor of Project Coordination; Kathie S. Schutte, Supervisor of Page Layout; Shelley Lea, Supervisor of Graphics and Design, Debbie J. Gates, Production System Specialist

Dummies Packaging & Book Design: Patti Sandez; Packaging Assistant, Kavish+Kavish, Cover Design

◆

The publisher would like to give special thanks to Patrick J. McGovern, without whom this book would not have been possible.

◆

Author's Acknowledgments

Hey, reader, a lot of people spent a lot of time working on this edition of the book to help make Quicken easier for you. You should know who these people are in case you ever meet them in the produce section of the local grocery store squeezing cantaloupe.

The editorial folks are Barb Terry, Bill Barton, Kelly Ewing, Suzanne Packer, Diane Giangrossi, and Diana Conover. Thanks also to the production staff of Dominique DeFelice, Angela Hunckler, Jane E. Martin, and Michael Sullivan.

Thanks to Kevin Spencer for his technical assistance and superb attention to detail.

Special thanks to Kaarin Dolliver for her able assistance in reshooting most (all?) of the figures for this book, for helping me keep track of all the great new features in Quicken 6 For Windows, and for helping me to get the manuscript in on time.

Contents at a Glance

Cartoons at a Glance

By Rich Tennant • Fax: 508-546-7747 • E-mail: the5wave@tiac.net

page 9

page 53

page 153

page 271

page 237

Table of Contents

Introduction

. . . .

*Y*ou aren't a dummy, of course. But, here's the deal. You don't have to be some sort of techno-geek or financial wizard to manage your financial affairs on a PC. You have other things to do, places to go, and people to meet. And that's where *Quicken 6 For Windows For Dummies,* 4th Edition comes in.

In the pages that follow, I give you the straight scoop on how to use Quicken For Windows, without a lot of extra baggage, goofy tangential information, or misguided advice.

About This Book

This book isn't meant to be read cover to cover like some John Grisham page-turner. Rather, it's organized into tiny, no-sweat descriptions of how to do the things you need to do. If you're the sort of person who just doesn't feel right not reading a book from cover to cover, you can, of course, go ahead and read this thing from front to back.

I can recommend this approach, however, only for people who have already checked the TV listings. There may, after all, be a "Baywatch" rerun on.

About the Author

If you're going to spend your time reading what I have to say, you deserve to know my qualifications. So let me take just a minute or so to tell you about Stephen Nelson.

I have an undergraduate degree in accounting and a master's degree in finance and accounting. I am also a certified public accountant (CPA).

I've spent the last dozen years helping businesses set up computerized financial management systems. I started with Arthur Andersen & Co., which is one of the world's largest public accounting and systems consulting firms. More recently, I've been working as a sole proprietor. When I wasn't doing financial systems work, I served as the controller of a small, 50-person computer software company.

Oh yeah, one other thing. I've used Quicken for my business and for my personal record-keeping for several years.

None of this information makes me sound like the world's most exciting guy, of course. I doubt you'll be inviting me to your next dinner party. Hey, I can deal with that.

But knowing a little something about me should give you a bit more confidence in applying the stuff talked about in the pages that follow. After all, we're talking about something that's extremely important: your money.

How to Use This Book

I always enjoyed reading those encyclopedias my parents bought for me and my siblings. You could flip open, say, the E volume, look up Elephants, and then learn just about everything you needed to know about elephants for a fifth-grade report: where elephants lived, how much they weighed, and why they ate so much.

You won't read anything about elephants here. But you should be able to use this book in the same way. If you want to learn about something, look through the table of contents or index and find the topic — printing checks, for example. Then flip to the correct chapter or page and read as much as you need or enjoy. No muss. No fuss.

If there's anything else you want to learn about, of course, you just repeat the process.

What You Can Safely Ignore

Sometimes I provide step-by-step descriptions of tasks. I feel very bad that I have to do this. So to make things easier for you, I highlight the tasks using bold text. That way you'll know exactly what you're supposed to do. I also often provide a more detailed explanation in regular text. You can skip the regular text that accompanies the step-by-step descriptions if you already understand the process.

Here's an example that shows what I mean:

1. Press Enter.

Find the key that's labeled Enter. Extend your index finger so that it rests ever so gently on the Enter key. In one sure, fluid motion, press the Enter key using your index finger. Then release the key.

Okay, that's kind of an extreme example. I never go into that much detail. But you get the idea. If you know how to press Enter, you can just do that and not read further. If you need help — say with the finger part or something — just read the nitty-gritty details.

Is there anything else you can skip? Let me see now. . . . You can skip the Technical stuff, too. The information I've stuck in those paragraphs is really there only for those of you who like that kind of stuff.

For that matter, I guess the stuff in the Tip paragraphs can safely be ignored, too. But if you're someone who enjoys trying it another way, go ahead and read the Tips, too.

What You Should Not Ignore (Unless You're a Masochist)

Don't skip the Warnings. They're the ones flagged with the picture of the 19th-century bomb. They describe some things you really shouldn't do.

Out of respect for you, I'm not going to put stuff in these paragraphs such as "Don't smoke." I figure that you're an adult. You can make your own lifestyle decisions.

So I'll reserve the Warnings for more urgent and immediate dangers — things akin to: "Don't smoke while you're filling your car with gasoline."

Three Foolish Assumptions

I'm going to assume just three things:

- You've got a PC with Microsoft Windows 95 or Windows 3.*x*.
- You know how to turn it on.
- You want to use Quicken.

How This Book Is Organized

This book is organized into five mostly coherent parts.

Part I: Zen, Quicken, and the Big Picture

Part I, "Zen, Quicken, and the Big Picture," covers some up-front stuff you need to take care of. I promise I won't waste your time here. I just want to make sure that you get off on the right foot.

Part II: The Absolute Basics

This second part of *Quicken 6 For Windows For Dummies,* 4th Edition explains the core knowledge you need to know to keep a personal or business checkbook with Quicken: using the checkbook, printing, balancing your bank accounts, and using the Quicken calculators.

Some of this stuff isn't very exciting compared to the Jenny Jones show or the Montel Williams show, so I'll work hard to make things fun for you.

Part III: Home Finances

Part III talks about the sorts of things you may want to do with Quicken if you're using it at home: credit cards, loans, mutual funds, stocks, and bonds. You get the idea. If you don't ever get this far — hey, that's cool.

If you do get this far, you'll find that Quicken provides some tools that eliminate not only the drudgery of keeping a checkbook, but also the drudgery of most other financial burdens.

While we're on the subject, I also want to categorically deny that Part III contains any secret messages if you read it backwards.

Part IV: Serious Business

The Serious Business section helps people who use Quicken in a business.

If you're pulling your hair out because you're using Quicken in a business, postpone the hair-pulling — at least for the time being. Read Part IV first. It tells you about preparing payroll, tracking the amounts that customers owe you, and other wildly exciting stuff.

Part V: The Part of Tens

By tradition, a . . . *For Dummies* book includes "The Part of Tens." It provides a collection of ten-something lists: ten things you should do if you get audited, ten things you should do if you own a business, ten things to do when you next visit Acapulco and so on.

Appendixes

It's an unwritten rule that computer books have appendixes, so I included three. Appendix A gives you a quick and dirty overview of Windows 95, for those new to it. Appendix B summarizes how Quicken's online banking stuff works. Appendix C is a glossary of key financial and Quicken terms.

Conventions Used in This Book

To make the best use of your time and energy, you should know about the following conventions used in this book.

When I want you to type something, such as **Hydraulics screamed as the pilot lowered his landing gear**, I'll put it in bold letters. When I want you to type something that's short and uncomplicated, such as **Gennifer**, it will still appear in bold type.

By the way, with Quicken you don't have to worry about the case of the stuff you type. If I tell you to type **Gennifer**, you can type **GENNIFER**. Or you can follow e. e. cummings' lead and type **gennifer**.

Whenever I describe a message or information that you'll see on the screen, I present it as follows:

```
Surprise! This is a message on-screen.
```

You can choose menus and commands and select dialog box elements with the mouse or the keyboard. To select them with the mouse, you just click them. To select them with the keyboard, you press Alt and the underlined letter in the menu, command, or dialog box. For example, the letter F in File and the letter O in Open are underlined so that you can choose the File⇨Open command by pressing Alt+F, O. (I also identify the keyboard selection keys by underlining them in the text.) You can choose many commands by clicking icons on the iconbar as well.

My Plug for Windows 95

This book assumes that you're running Quicken under Windows 95. So does that mean I've left Windows 3.1 users out in the cold? No way. In terms of using Quicken, there's really no difference between running Quicken with Windows 3.1 and running Quicken with Windows 95. Sure — the windows and dialog boxes look a little different. But in terms of program mechanics, everything *works* the same way no matter which operating system you're using.

Well, almost everything. The only things that are mechanically different about Windows 3.1 are that it doesn't necessarily start when you turn on your computer (Windows 95 does), you sometimes install programs in a slightly different way, and you don't use the Start button to start programs. However, I think that I'm pretty safe in assuming that, if you're already using Windows 3.1, you know how to start Windows 3.1 and you know how to start programs using Windows 3.1. (If you don't know how to do one of these tasks, do yourself a favor. Upgrade to Windows 95.)

Until you get around to upgrading to Windows 95, however, you might have a question or two about how Windows 3.1 works — especially when it comes to installing Quicken. So whenever some task works differently in Windows 3.1 — and as I said, there are only about three things that work differently — I'll stick in a little note that explains how you accomplish that task the Windows 3.1 way — plus a nifty little icon (see the following section). I do this in Chapter 1, for example, when I explain how you install and start Quicken.

Special Icons

Like many computer books, this book uses icons, or little pictures, to flag things that don't quite fit into the flow of things. ...*For Dummies* books use a standard set of icons that flag little digressions, such as:

This icon points out nerdy technical material that you may want to skip (or read, if you're feeling particularly bright).

Here's a shortcut to make your life easier.

This icon is just a friendly reminder to do something.

 And this icon is a friendly reminder *not* to do something ...or else.

 As mentioned in the preceding section, whenever something in Quicken functions differently under Windows 3.1 than it does in Windows 95, this little icon will flag the Windows 3.1 explanation. (But don't expect to see many of these.)

Where To Next?

If you're just getting started, flip the page and start reading the first chapter.

If you've got a special problem or question, use the table of contents or the index to find out where that topic is covered and then turn to that page.

Part I
Zen, Quicken, and the Big Picture

"THE IMAGE IS GETTING CLEARER NOW...I CAN ALMOST SEE IT...YES! THERE IT IS—THE GLITCH IS IN A FAULTY CELL REFERENCE IN THE FOOTBALL POOL SPREADSHEET."

In this part . . .

When you go to a movie theater, there are some prerequisites for making the show truly enjoyable. And I'm not referring to the presence of Sandra Bullock or Arnold Schwarzenegger. (Although Ms. Bullock certainly doesn't hurt.) Purchasing a bucket of popcorn is essential, for example. One should think strategically both about seating and about soda size. And one may even have items of a, well, personal nature to take care of — such as visiting the little boys' or girls' room.

I mention all this stuff for one simple reason. To make getting started with Quicken as easy and fun as possible, there are some prerequisites, too. And this first part of *Quicken 6 For Windows For Dummies,* 4th Edition — "Zen, Quicken, and the Big Picture" — talks about these sorts of things.

Chapter 1

Setting Up Shop

● ●

In This Chapter

▶ Installing Quicken

▶ Touring Quicken

▶ Setting up your bank accounts and credit card accounts if you're a first-time user

▶ Retrieving existing Quicken data files

● ●

*I*f you have never used Quicken, begin here. The next section tells you how to install Quicken (if you haven't already) and how to start the program for the first time.

You also find out how you go about setting up Quicken accounts to track banking activities — specifically, the money that goes into and out of a checking or savings account.

If you have already begun to use Quicken, don't waste any time reading this chapter unless you want the review. You already know the stuff it covers.

By the way, if you have Windows 95, I assume that you know a little bit about it. No, you don't have to be some sort of expert. Shoot, you don't even have to be all that proficient. You do need to know how to start Windows applications (such as Quicken). It'll also help immensely if you know how to choose commands from menus and how to enter stuff into windows and dialog boxes.

If you don't know how to do these kinds of things, flip to Appendix A. It provides a very quick and rather dirty overview of how you work in Windows 95. Read the stuff in the appendix, or at least skim it, and then come back to this chapter.

Installing Quicken

You install Quicken the same way you install any program in Windows 95. If you already know how to install programs, you don't need any help from me. Stop reading here, do the installation thing, and then start reading the next section, "Setting Up Your First Accounts."

If you do need help installing Quicken, let me give you the step-by-step instructions:

1. **Click the Start button.**

    Note: The Start button, as you may know, appears in the lower-left corner of the Windows desktop. (The desktop is what you see after you turn on your computer.) So that you can't possibly miss it, Windows 95 sometimes features a moving pointer that, after you've turned on your computer, repeatedly points to the Start button. The following message also flashes:

    ```
    Click here to start programs, click here to start programs.
    ```

    If you're using Quicken 6 for Windows with Windows 3.1, you install the Quicken application by first starting Windows 3.1. (You can do this by typing **win** at the DOS prompt.) Then you choose the Program Manager's File⇨Run command, type **a:install** (if you're installing Quicken from floppy disks in drive A) or **d: install** (if you're installing Quicken from a CD in the CD-ROM drive D) into the Run dialog box's text box, and press Enter. Follow the on-screen instructions that the Quicken installation program gives.

2. **Choose Start⇨Settings⇨Control Panel from the Windows 95 menu bar.**

    Windows 95 displays the Control Panel window. As you may know, the Control Panel provides a whole bunch of tools you use for fiddling with and fine-tuning your computer (see Figure 1-1).

Figure 1-1:
The Control Panel window.

3. **Double-click the Add/Remove Programs icon.**

    Windows 95 displays the Add/Remove Programs Properties tool (see Figure 1-2).

4. **Select the Install/Uninstall tab if it isn't already selected.**

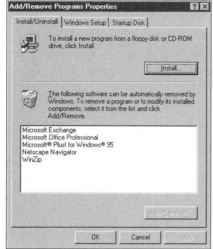

Figure 1-2:
The Add/
Remove
Programs
Properties
tool with the
Install/
Uninstall tab
showing.

5. **Insert the first floppy disk into the floppy drive (if your copy of Quicken comes on floppy disks) or insert the CD-ROM into the CD-ROM drive (if your copy of Quicken comes on a CD-ROM).**

   Is that business about a first floppy disk confusing? Maybe so. But here's the deal: The Quicken program and all the other stuff that comes with the Quicken program can't fit on just one floppy disk. (The program and all the stuff that comes with the program does fit on a CD-ROM, by the way.) So the folks who make Quicken must use several disks. One of these is labeled "Disk 1" or "Install Disk 1" or something. This disk is the first disk.

6. **Click the Install button.**

   Windows 95 displays a dialog box that tells you it's about to look for the program you want to install.

7. **Click the Next button.**

   Windows 95 looks at the floppy disk or CD-ROM and finds the Quicken installation program. Windows 95 displays another dialog box asking, basically, "Gee, what do you think I ought to do now?"

8. **Click the Finish button.**

   Windows 95 starts installing Quicken. Occasionally, the installation program asks you a question. Answer the question and click Next. After the installation is complete, click Finish, and Quicken restarts your computer. You're done.

If you're installing Quicken 6 for Windows under Windows 3.1, the installation program ends by displaying the Quicken program group window. (Basically, Windows 3.1 program group windows are the same as Windows 95 folder windows, in case you care. And you probably don't.)

Setting Up Your First Accounts

After Quicken is installed, you set up a bank account and tell Quicken how you want it to track your finances. This setup stuff isn't hard to do; you just need to find your most recent bank statement — or better yet — your last bank statement from the previous year.

You start Quicken the same way you start any Windows application. For example, click the Start button and then choose Programs⇨Quicken⇨ Quicken 6. (Or you can double-click the Quicken shortcut on the Windows 95 desktop.) Quicken starts, and you see the Quicken application window with the Quicken New User Setup dialog box showing (see Figure 1-3).

Figure 1-3:
The Quicken
New User
Setup dialog
box.

If you're starting Quicken and you use Windows 3.1, you start Quicken in a slightly different way. First, you start Windows by typing **win** at the DOS prompt. Then you display the Quicken program group window. You do this by double-clicking the Quicken icon that appears on your Program Manager. Then, after the Quicken program group window appears, you double-click the Quicken program item. By the way, if you don't know how to do this sort of stuff, you should upgrade to Windows 95. One of the biggest benefits of Windows 95 is that it makes starting and switching between programs easy. Really easy. And no, I don't own any Microsoft stock.

With your bank statement in hand and the Quicken New User Setup dialog box on-screen, follow these steps:

1. **Click the Next button so that Quicken moves to the second screen of the Quicken New User Setup dialog box.**

   Quicken displays a bunch of questions that you answer by clicking Yes and No buttons. Are you married? Do you have children? Do you own a house?, and so on. Answer the questions and then click Next.

2. Tell Quicken the name you want to use for the account.

You do this by typing a name into the Account Name text box (see Figure 1-4). By the way, you can be as general or as specific as you want. But it's a good idea to be as concise as you can. Brevity is a virtue. The reason is that Quicken uses your account name to label the tabs on the Quicken program window. (I'll show this to you in a minute.)

Figure 1-4:
The Quicken New User Setup dialog box with the account name text box displayed.

3. Click Next.

Quicken displays some new information that asks whether you've got the bank statement you'll use for setting up the new account.

4. Tell Quicken whether you've got the last bank statement.

This is pretty simple. If you do, click the Yes button and then click the Next button. If you don't, click the No button and then click the Next button. (If you click No, Quicken doesn't do any more setup stuff for the checking account.)

5. Enter the ending bank statement date, using your bank statement.

If you indicate that you have the bank statement handy, Quicken asks for the ending statement date, which is the date you start using Quicken. Enter the date in MM/DD/YY fashion.

"Geez, Steve," you're now saying to yourself, "What's MM/DD/YY fashion?" OK. Here's an example. If things are really going to be different starting July 1, 1997, enter **7/1/97**.

The best way to get started

Quicken wants you to use your last bank statement to set up the bank account you track. In this way, when you start using Quicken, your financial records are synchronized with the bank's records.

But I want to suggest something slightly different to you. Go back farther than just to the beginning of the previous month. (This is what you do when you use your last bank statement.) Go back to the beginning of the year and use the last bank statement of the previous

year — even if it's now several months after the beginning of the year. Now I'm not trying to waste your time. But let me point out two big advantages to having a complete year's data in Quicken. Tracking and tallying your tax deductions and planning your finances will be easier.

By the way, going back to the beginning of the year isn't as hard as you may think. Quicken provides a bunch of different tools to help you enter several months' worth of data in a very short time.

6. **Enter the ending bank statement balance, using your bank statement.**

This balance is whatever shows on your bank statement. This balance is also the amount of money in your account on the date you begin your financial record-keeping. If you have $4.16 in your checking account, type **4.16** into the Statement Ending Balance text box.

After you enter the bank statement balance, click Next. Quicken displays a message in the Quicken New User Setup dialog box that tells you that you just set up a bank account and asks whether you want to take a tour of Quicken's features. Click the Overview button to see the Quicken QuickTour (it's really pretty good). Or, if you'd rather not, click Done. Quicken removes the New User Setup dialog box and displays the Quicken application window (see Figure 1-5).

QuickTour in a nutshell

The Quicken QuickTour feature provides on-screen presentations that describe what Quicken does and how you use Quicken. I'm not going to describe here how you use the

QuickTour feature. Don't get me wrong — QuickTour is a great feature. It just seems sort of silly for me to write a tutorial about using a tutorial. To use QuickTour, all you do is read and click.

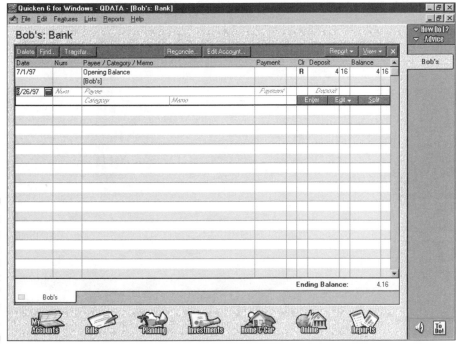

Figure 1-5:
The Quicken
application
window with
the account
register
window
showing.

A Quick SteveTour

You don't need to know much about the mechanics of the Quicken interface — the way its windows work — to begin working with Quicken. But I want to make a couple of quick comments.

Quicken changes the way document windows work

First, Quicken doesn't use document windows the way that other Windows applications do. Quicken basically turns document windows into pages that you leaf through by clicking the tabs that appear along the right edge of the application. Figure 1-6, for example, shows only a couple of tabs: Bob's, which is the register window for the account I named Bob's, and Accounts, which basically lists the bank accounts you've set up for Quicken. Not that you care, but these tabs are called QuickTabs.

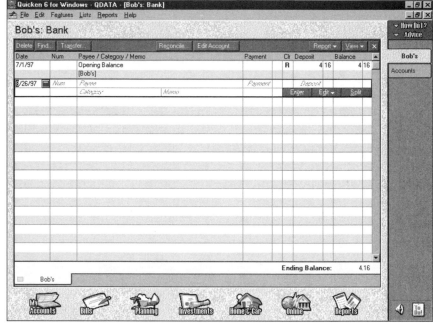

Figure 1-6:
The Quicken application window with the register window showing.

About the Activity Bar

Let me say a bit more about the Activity Bar icons, which appear along the bottom edge of the Quicken application window. Basically, the Activity Bar is just another menu system. Rather than organizing the Quicken commands into the usual Windows menus such as File, Edit, and so on, Quicken provides clickable icons — buttons, in effect — that you can click to open menus of commands grouped by financial management tasks. If you click the My Accounts icon, for example, Quicken opens up a menu of commands specifically related to working with accounts (see Figure 1-7).

About the iconbar

The *iconbar* is not a place where icons go to "tie one on." The iconbar is a set of command icons located at the top of the Quicken application window (see Figure 1-8). (Notice that when you add an iconbar to the Quicken application window, Quicken moves the QuickTabs from the right edge of the window to the bottom of the window.) You can easily choose a common Quicken command by clicking one of these icons with the mouse. I refer to the iconbar icons by their names in the pages that follow. (I also refer to an icon in the next paragraph — which is why I brought up the icon business here.) If you want to see a list of the iconbar icons along with descriptions of what they do, flip open the front cover of this book and look at the cheat sheet.

If you don't see an iconbar on your Quicken application window, right-click in the Activity Bar icons area and choose the Show Top Iconbar command from the Shortcuts menu.

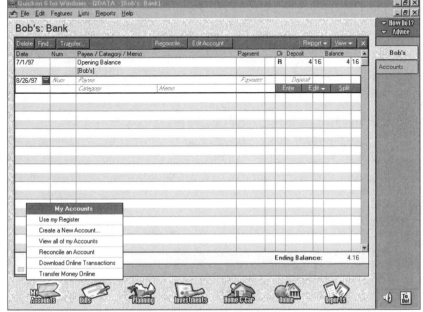

Figure 1-7:
The
Quicken
application
window
with the My
Accounts
menu
showing.

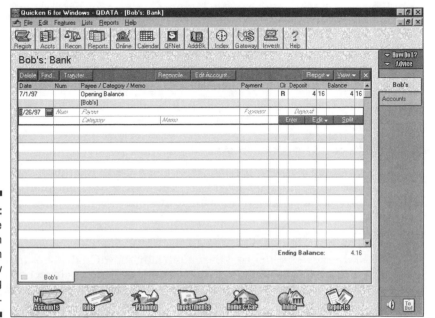

Figure 1-8:
The
Quicken
application
window
showing
the iconbar.

Account Register

After you get past the Activity Bar confusion and understand the iconbar — knowledge you've hopefully garnered in the past 20 or 30 seconds — you're pretty much on your way with Quicken. To see the account register window you'll spend most of your time working with, click the QuickTab for the register you want to open and look at or click the Registr icon. Quicken displays the account register (refer to Figure 1-8).

You basically use this account register to keep track of all your financial affairs.

Setting up Quicken if you've used Quicken before

Let's say that you're not new in town. Suppose that you're a Quicken veteran. An old hand. A longtime friend. Well, anyway, you get the idea.

Can you use the existing Quicken files you've been working on? Sure you can, as long as you've been using Quicken for DOS Versions 5.0, 6.0, 7.0, or 8.0 or Quicken for Windows Versions 1.0, 2.0, 3.0, 4.0 or 5.0. In fact, if the Quicken installation program can find a version of old Quicken files on your desk, it'll skip all the New User SetUp stuff and just begin using your existing files.

If Quicken doesn't find the old files, you need to specifically open the files. But if you have this problem, you should be able to solve it yourself. What's happened, if you find yourself in this boat, is that you've moved or messed around with the Quicken files with some other program, such as the Windows Explorer or the old File Manager. If you did that, presumably you had a reason. And, more to the point, you should know where you placed the files.

Using the File⇨Open command

Use File⇨Open to select and open your existing Quicken files. Here's how you do this:

1. **Choose File⇨Open from the menu bar.**

   Use your mouse or press Alt+F, O. Figure 1-9 shows the Open Quicken File dialog box that appears after you choose the command. Quicken uses this dialog box to ask the burning question, "Hey, buddy, what file you wanna open?"

2. **Tell Quicken in which folder the files are stored.**

   If the correct folder isn't the one already shown in the Look in box in the Open Quicken File dialog box, tell Quicken what the correct drive is. Click the down arrow at the end of the Look in box. After you do, Quicken drops down a list of the disk drives and folders your computer has. (This is why, as a point of fact, the little Look in box is called a drop-down list box. Get it?)

After the list of drives and folders appears, click the one where you've stored your Quicken files. Quicken closes the drop-down list box and displays your selection in the list box beneath the Look in box.

3. **Select the file from the list box.**

After you tell Quicken on which disk and in which folder you stored your data files, the Quicken files in that location appear in the list box. Just click the file you want.

Figure 1-9:
The Open
Quicken File
dialog box.

4. **Click OK after you find the file.**

Quicken opens the file and displays the active account in the register window. (Quicken also displays its Reminders window to show any unprinted checks or scheduled transactions.)

What if you can't find the Quicken file?

Uh-oh. This is a problem. But don't worry. You're not out of luck. What you need to do is to look through each of the folders on the disk. Or, if you've got more than one hard disk, look through each of the folders on each of the hard drives.

Bummer, huh? Maybe this is a reasonable place to bring up a point. If you're a new user, it's really best to just go with whatever an application (such as Quicken) suggests. If Quicken suggests that you use the QUICKENW directory — this is the suggestion for Windows versions of Quicken, by the way — just do it. If Quicken suggests that you use the drive C, just do it. If Quicken suggests that you take all your money, put it in a coffee can, and bury the can in your backyard . . . whoa, wait a minute. Bad idea.

Maybe there's a better rule. Hmmm. . . . How about this? Although you shouldn't follow suggestions blindly, you also shouldn't ignore Quicken's suggestions unless you've got a good reason. And "Just because," "I don't know," and "For the heck of it" aren't very good reasons.

Starting Quicken for the second time

The second time you start Quicken — and every subsequent time, too — things work pretty much the same way as the first time. Click the Start button. Then choose Programs⇨ Quicken⇨Quicken 6 for Windows. The only real difference is that you won't, of course, have to step through any of the new user setup stuff. Oh, and one other thing — if you installed Quicken in the usual way, it may display something called the Quicken Reminders window. What this window does, in effect, is show you half-completed transactions that you still need to do something with — such as checks you entered but still need to print. (I'll talk about the check printing in Chapter 5.)

Chapter 2

Introduction to the Big Picture

· ·

In This Chapter

▶ Boiling Quicken down to its essence

▶ Setting up additional bank accounts

▶ Adding categories

▶ Removing categories

▶ Modifying categories

▶ Understanding classes

· ·

*B*efore you spend a bunch of time and money on Quicken, you must understand the big picture. You need to know what Quicken can do. You need to know what you actually want to do. And, as a practical matter, you need to tell Quicken what you want it to do.

Boiling Quicken Down to Its Essence

When you boil Quicken down to its essence, it does five things:

✔ *It lets you track your tax deductions.*

This makes preparing your personal or business tax return easier for you or your poor accountant, Cratchit.

✔ *It lets you monitor your income and outgo either on-screen or by using printed reports.*

Usually, this stuff is great fodder for discussions about the family finances.

✔ *It lets you print checks.*

This device is mostly a time-saver, but it can also be useful for people who are neat-freaks.

✔ *It lets you track the things you own (such as bank accounts, investments, and real estate) and the debts you owe (such as home mortgage principal, car loan balances, and credit card balances).*

These things are really important to know.

> ✔ *It helps you make better personal financial planning decisions about such matters as retirement, your children's future college costs, and your savings and investments.*
>
> This stuff is really neat, I think.

You can do some of these things or all of these things with Quicken.

Tracking tax deductions

To track your tax deductions, make a list of the deductions you want to track. To do so, pull out last year's tax return. Note which lines you filled in. This tactic works because there's a darn good chance that the tax deductions you claimed last year will also be the tax deductions you'll claim in the future.

Just a little bit later in the chapter you'll read about Quicken's categories, which are used to track your tax deductions.

Monitoring spending

At our house, we (my wife Sue, and I, your humble author) use Quicken to monitor our spending on the mundane little necessities of life: groceries, clothing, baby food, cable television, and, well . . . you get the picture.

To keep track of how much we spend on various items, we also use the Quicken categories. (Is the suspense building?)

If there is a spending category you want to monitor, it's really easier to decide up front what it is.

Your list of spending categories, by the way, shouldn't be an exhaustive list of super-fine pigeonholes such as "Friday-night Mexican food," "Fast food for lunch," and so on. To track your spending or eating out, one category named something like "Meals" or "Grub" usually is easiest.

In fact, I'm going to go out on a limb. You can probably get away with half a dozen categories or less:

✔ Household Items (food, toiletries, cleaning supplies)

✔ Car

✔ Rent (or mortgage payments)

✔ Entertainment and Vacation

✔ Clothing

✔ Work Expenses

If you want to, of course, you can expand this list. Heck, you can include dozens and dozens of categories. My experience, though, is that you'll probably use only a handful of categories.

Do you want to print checks?

You can use Quicken to print checks. This little trick provides a couple of benefits: It's really fast if you have a lot of checks to print, and your printed checks look very neat and darn professional.

To print checks, you need to do just two things. First, look through the check supply information that comes with Quicken and pick a check form that suits your style. Then order the form. (The check forms that come with remittance advices — or check stubs — work well for businesses.)

You'll notice that the preprinted check forms aren't cheap. If you're using Quicken at home with personal-style checks (such as those that go in your wallet), using computer checks may not be cost effective. Even if you're using Quicken for a business and you are used to buying those outrageously expensive business-style checks, you'll still find computer checks a bit more expensive.

I'm pretty much a cheapskate, so I don't use printed checks at home (although I do use them in my business). I should admit, however, that I also don't write very many checks.

By the way, I've checked around. Although you can order Quicken check forms from other sources (such as your local office supplies store), they're about the same price from Intuit (the maker of Quicken).

Tracking bank accounts, credit cards, and other stuff

You must decide which bank accounts and credit cards you want to track. In most cases, you want to track each bank account you use and any credit card on which you carry a balance.

You may also want to track other assets and liabilities. *Assets* are just things you own: investments, cars, a house, and so on. *Liabilities* are things you owe: margin loans from your broker, car loans, a mortgage, and so on.

Shoot, I suppose that you could even track the things your neighbor owns — or perhaps just those things you especially covet. I'm not sure that this is a very good idea, though. (Maybe a healthier approach is to track just those things that your neighbor owns but you've borrowed.)

Planning Your Personal Finances

Your computer's computational horsepower makes it the ideal tool for doing complicated calculations. So maybe it's not a big surprise that Quicken comes with five powerful calculators that let you make smarter borrowing choices, better mortgage-refinancing decisions, more accurate saving and investment calculations, and extremely helpful retirement and college savings calculations.

I believe that these financial planning tools are the most valuable features offered by Quicken. I'm just sorry that I have to wait until Chapter 9 to talk about them.

Setting Up Additional Accounts

When you start Quicken for the first time, you set up a checking account. If you want to track any additional accounts — for example, a savings account — you must set them up, too.

Setting up another checking account

To set up a checking account, give the account a name and then its balance as of a set date. Here's how:

1. Click the Accts iconbar button.

You can either choose Lists⇨Account or click the Accts iconbar button. Quicken displays the Account List window, as shown in Figure 2-1.

2. Click the New button in the Account List window.

Quicken displays the Create New Account dialog box shown in Figure 2-2.

3. Select the type of account.

Tell Quicken which type of account you want to set up by clicking one of the account buttons. (I'm assuming that at this point you're just doing checking or savings accounts. I discuss why and when you use the remaining account types later in the book.) When Quicken displays the Checking Account Setup dialog box, click the Summary tab (see Figure 2-3).

Wondering about those other accounts? If the suspense is just killing you, you can look ahead. Chapter 10 describes how to set up and use Credit Card accounts. Chapter 11 describes how to set up and use Liability accounts. Chapters 12 and 13 describe how to set up and use Investment accounts. Chapter 14 describes how to set up and use a Cash account. And, finally, Chapter 16 describes how to set up and use Assets accounts. (Money market accounts work just like checking accounts.)

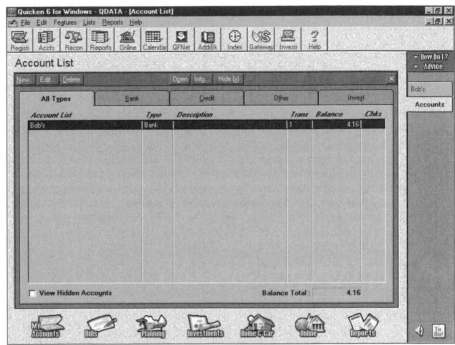

Figure 2-1:
The Account
List window.

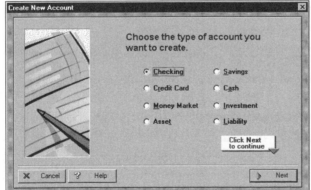

Figure 2-2:
The Create
New
Account
dialog box.

4. **Name the account.**

Move the cursor to the Account Name text box and enter a name.

5. **Move the cursor to the Description text box and describe the account in more detail if necessary.**

The name you give your accounts may be the only description you need. I only name my accounts; I don't describe them. However, if you've got a lot

Figure 2-3:
The
Summary
tab of the
Checking
Account
Setup dialog
box.

of different accounts or especially if you've got a lot of accounts at the same bank, you may want to provide a description of the account using the Description text box.

6. Click the Balance text box and enter the bank account balance.

Use the number keys to enter the balance. The folks at Intuit, by the way, really want you to use the balance from your bank statement. If you have terrible financial records — for example, you haven't reconciled your account since Ronald Reagan left office — this idea is probably good advice. If you have neat, accurate financial records, go ahead and use your check register balance.

By the way, if you do use the bank statement balance as your starting balance, be sure to enter all the transactions that cleared after the bank statement balance date. This should make sense, right? If a check or deposit isn't reflected in the bank statement figure, you must enter it later.

7. Enter the account balance date.

Enter the date you'll start keeping records for the bank account with Quicken. Move the cursor to the as of text box and type the month number, a slash, the day number, a slash, and the year number. If you start on January 1, 1997, for example, type **1/1/97**. Or, if this is way too complicated for you, click the button at the end of the as of text box so that Quicken displays a pop-up calendar. Then click the date. Use the << and >> buttons to move back and forth a month at a time.

8. Indicate whether you want to use the Quicken Bank Online or Pay Online features.

If you want to use the Online Banking or Online Bill Payment features, mark the appropriate check boxes. After you click one of these boxes, Quicken changes the name of the Done button to Next. Appendix B describes the online banking and bill-paying services that Quicken provides.

9. **Collect a bit more information if you want.**

   If you click the Info button, Quicken displays a dialog box into which you can record a bunch of other information about the bank account you're setting up: the name of the bank, your account number, the name of the person you deal with at the bank, and so on. You can fill in this stuff if you would like a reasonably convenient place to store this information.

10. **If the account's interest is tax-deferred, click the Tax button.**

    You may need to indicate whether an account's interest income is tax-deferred and whether transfers into or out of the account are tax-deductible. To do this, click the Tax button. Quicken displays the Tax Schedule Information dialog box, which lets you describe any tax implications of moving money to or from this account or of earning interest on the money in this account. Mark the Tax-Deferred Account check box to indicate that the interest earned on this account isn't taxable. Use the Transfers In and Transfers Out drop-down list boxes to describe which line of your tax return transfers into or out of this account should be reported. Just for the record, it's highly unlikely that this tax schedule stuff applies to a simple bank account.

11. **Choose Done or Next.**

    If you didn't choose to use the Quicken Online Banking or Online Bill Payment features, the Done button will be in the lower-right corner of the screen. After you click this button, Quicken redisplays the Account List window — just like the one shown in Figure 2-1. This time, however, the window lists an additional account — the one you just created.

    If you indicated in Step 8 that you will use the Online Banking or Online Bill Payment features, Quicken changes the name of the Done button to Next. After you click the Next button, Quicken displays a dialog box that asks for the name of the bank, its routing number, your account number, the bank account type, and your Social Security number. The sign-up and welcome letter that you received from your bank will provide the bank name and routing numbering information. (Hopefully, you'll know the account type you've just created — probably a checking account. And you should know your Social Security number, right?)

12. **Close the Account List window if you don't need it any longer.**

    You can do so by clicking the window's Close button.

Hey, Quicken, I want to use that account!

In Quicken, you work with one account at a time. The logic is quite simple: In Quicken, you record income and expenses for a particular account — a specific checking account, savings account, and so on.

You use the Account List window (refer to Figure 2-1) to tell Quicken which account you want to work with.

To display the Account List window, click the Accts button on the iconbar, choose Lists⇨Account, or click the Account List QuickTab if it shows. (If you're experiencing a sense of déjà vu right now, it's probably because I've already told you about these techniques earlier in the chapter.)

After you display the Account List window, select the account you want by using the up- and down-arrow keys or by clicking the mouse. Then press Enter or choose Open. Quicken selects the account and displays either the register window or the Write Checks window. (Chapter 4 describes how to enter checking account transactions using the Write Checks window.)

Let me see if there's anything else I should tell you at this point. Oh yes, I know. If the Account List window gets in your way after you display it, you can remove it from the application window by clicking the Close button.

Whipping Your Category Lists into Shape

When you set up Quicken, you tell it to use either the predefined home categories or both the home and business categories.

The predefined categories lists may be just what you want. Then again, they may not. Table 2-1 shows the home categories list, and Table 2-2 shows the business categories list. If you tell Quicken to use both the home and business categories, your actual category list combines the categories shown in Table 2-1 and those shown in Table 2-2.

Your categories list may vary slightly from the ones shown in Tables 2-1 and 2-2. Quicken may customize your starting categories list based on your answer to questions it asks in the New User Setup dialog box.

Take a minute to look through both lists. If you find categories you don't need, cross them off the list in the book. You'll be able to delete them in a minute or so on your computer. If you need categories you don't see, add them at the bottom of the list. You'll be able to add them in about two minutes or so. Remember that determining whether you need a category is pretty simple:

- ✔ To track a certain income or spending item for income tax purposes, you need a Quicken category.

- ✔ To track a certain income or spending item because you're just interested in (for example, renting VCR tapes), you need a Quicken category.

- ✔ Because you also budget by categories, you need a category for any income or spending item that you want to budget.

Table 2-1	The Predefined Home Categories
Categories	*Descriptions*
Income Categories	
Div Income	Dividend Income
Gift Received	Gift Received
Interest Inc	Interest Income
Invest Inc	Investment Income
Other Inc	Other Income
Salary	Salary Income
Salary Spouse	Salary Income of Spouse
Expense Categories	
Auto	Automobile Expenses
Fuel	Auto Fuel
Insurance	Auto Insurance
Service	Auto Service
Bank Charge	Bank Charge
Charity	Charitable Donations
Childcare	Childcare Expense
Clothing	Clothing
Dining	Dining Out
Education	Education
Entertainment	Entertainment
Gifts Given	Gift Expenses
Groceries	Groceries
Home Repair	Home Repair & Maintenance
Household	Miscellaneous household expenses
Housing	Housing
Insurance	Insurance
Interest Exp	Interest Expense

(continued)

Table 2-1 (*continued*)

IRA Contrib	Individual Retirement Account Contribution
IRA Contrib Spo	Individual Retirement Account Contribution of Spouse
Medical	Medical Expense
Doctor	Doctor & Dental Visits
Medicine	Medicine & Drugs
Misc	Miscellaneous
Recreation	Recreation Expense
Rent	Housing Rent
Subscriptions	Subscriptions
Tax	Taxes
Fed	Federal Tax
Medicare	Medicare Tax
Other	Miscellaneous Taxes
Property	Property Tax
Soc Sec	Social Security Tax
State	State Tax
Tax Spouse	Spouse's Taxes
Fed	Federal Tax
Medicare	Medicare Tax
Soc Sec	Social Security Tax
State	State Tax
Telephone	Telephone
Utilities	Water, Gas, Electric — and, oh yeah, the Cable
Cable TV	Cable television
Gas & Electric	Gas and Electricity
Water	Water
Vacation	Vacation Expenses
Lodging	Motel/Hotel Costs
Travel	Transportation Expense

Table 2-2	The Predefined Business Categories
Categories	***Descriptions***
Income Categories	
Gr Sales	Gross Sales
Expense Categories	
Ads	Advertising Expenses
Car	Car & Truck
Commission	Commissions
Insurance, Bus	Business Insurance (other than medical insurance)
Int Paid	Interest Paid
Late Fees	Late Fees and Finance Charges
Legal/Prof Fees	Legal & Professional Fees
Meals & Entertn	Meals & Entertainment
Office	Office Expenses
Rent on Equip	Rent — Vehicle, Machinery, Equipment
Rent Paid	Rent Paid
Repairs	Repairs
Returns	Returns & Allowances
Subscriptions	Magazine and Newsletter Subscriptions
Supplies, Bus	Business Supplies
Tax, Business	Business Taxes
Fed	Federal Business Taxes
Local	Local Business Taxes
Property	Property Taxes on Business Assets
State	State Business Taxes
Telephone, Bus	Telephone Business
Travel	Transportation Expenses
Utilities, Bus	Business Utilities
Wages	Wages & Job Credits

Subcategories . . . yikes, what are they?

One of the things I'm trying to do with this book is make Quicken easier for you to use. A big part of this goal is telling you which features you can ignore if you're feeling a bit overwhelmed. Subcategories are among those things I think you can ignore.

"Subcategories?" you say. "Yikes! What are they?"

Subcategories are categories within categories. If you look at the Taxes expense category in Table 2-1, for example, you'll notice a bunch of categories that follow the Tax category and are slightly indented: Fed (Federal Tax), Medicare (Medicare Tax), Other (Miscellaneous Taxes), Prop (Property Tax), Soc Sec (Social Security Tax), and State (State Tax).

When you use subcategories, you can tag a transaction that pays, for example, federal taxes; you can further break down this category into subcategories such as federal income tax, Medicare tax, and Social Security tax. If you want to see a list of the ways you've spent your money, Quicken summarizes your spending both by category and, within a category, by subcategory. On a Quicken report, then, you can see this level of detail:

Taxes

Federal Tax	900
Medicare Tax	100
Soc Sec Tax	700
Total Taxes	1,700

Subcategories are useful tools. There's no doubt about it. But they make working with Quicken a little more complicated and a little more difficult. As a practical matter, you usually don't need them. If you want to track a spending category, it really belongs on your list as a full-fledged category. For these reasons, I'm not going to get into subcategories here.

If you get excited about the topic of subcategories later on — after you have the hang of Quicken — you can peruse the Quicken documentation for more information.

If you do want to use the Quicken subcategories, don't delete the subcategories shown in Table 2-1. If you don't want to use the subcategories, go ahead and delete them.

Supercategories . . . double yikes!

Supercategories are a recent invention of the Intuit development people. (The supercategory feature appears only in the most recent versions of the DOS, Windows, and Macintosh products.) Supercategories combine categories into sets you can use in reports and in your budgeting. Sure. They're sort of cool. But you don't need to worry about them if you're just starting with Quicken.

Three tips on categorization

I have just three tips for categorizing:

✔ *Cross off any category you won't use.*

If you're a Canadian living in Canada, for example, get rid of the United States tax categories. Extra, unneeded categories just clutter your list. I think it's great if you can get down to just a handful of categories.

✔ *Don't be afraid to lump similar spending categories together.*

Take your utilities expense, for example. If you pay water, natural gas, electricity, and sewer, why not use a single Utilities category? If you pay different utility companies for your water, natural gas, electricity, and sewer, you can still see what you spend on just electricity, for example, even with a single, catch-all category for utilities.

✔ *Be sure to categorize anything that may be a tax deduction.*

Categorize medical and dental expenses, state and local income taxes, real estate taxes, personal property taxes, home mortgage interest and points, investment interest, charitable contributions, casualty and theft losses, moving expenses, unreimbursed employee expenses, and all those vague, miscellaneous deductions. (By the way, the foregoing is the complete list of itemized deductions at the time this book was written.)

Ch-ch-changing a category list

Okay, you should now be ready to fix any category list problems. Basically, you will do three things: add categories, remove categories, and change category names and descriptions.

Adding categories you'd love to use

Adding categories is a snap. Here's all you have to do:

1. **Choose Lists➪Category/Transfer.**

   Quicken displays the Category & Transfer List window (see Figure 2-4). This window lists the categories available and the accounts you've set up.

2. **Click the New button on the Category & Transfer List window.**

   The New button, by the way, is the first button on the left. Quicken, dutifully following your every command, displays the Set Up Category dialog box. It probably won't surprise you that you use this puppy to describe the new category.

   If you ever have a question about which button is which, move the mouse pointer so it rests just above the bottom edge of the button. Quicken displays a pop-up box with the button's name.

3. **Enter a short name for the category.**

   Move the cursor to the Name text box and type a name. Although you can use up to 15 characters, use as short a name as possible to clearly identify the category. Why? Because you'll need to use this category name every time you want to tag a transaction to fall into the category.

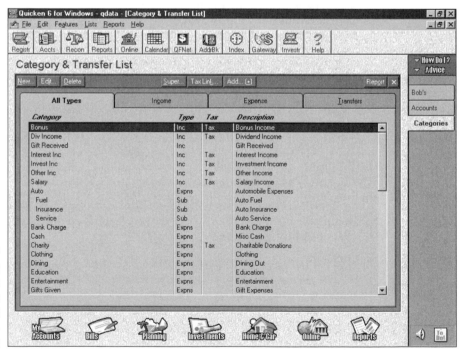

Figure 2-4: The Category & Transfer List window.

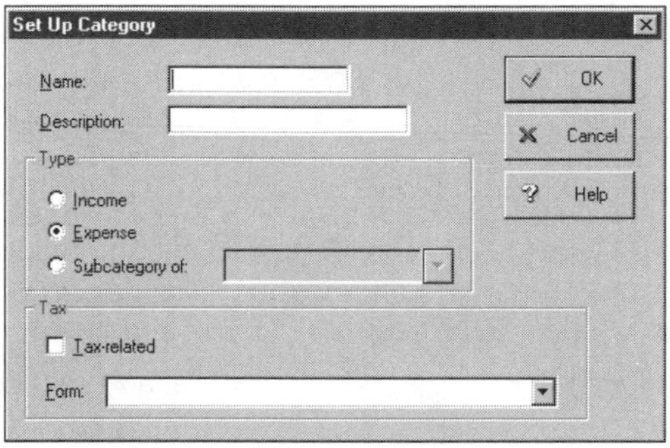

Figure 2-5:
The Set Up
Category
dialog box.

4. Enter a description for the category.

Move the cursor to the Description text box and then describe the category. (If you don't enter a description, Quicken uses the category name on reports that show the category.)

5. Indicate whether the category is an income category or an expense category.

Select the appropriate Income, Expense, or Subcategory of option button — just click your furry little friend, the mouse. If you've totally blown off my admonition not to use subcategories just yet, use the dialog box's drop-down list to indicate into which income or expense category a new subcategory falls.

6. Indicate whether the category tracks an amount you will use on an input line on next year's tax return.

By *line*, I mean the actual tax form line — such as the line on the 1040 form that tracks alimony.

Move the cursor to the Tax-related check box and then select the check box if the category is tax-related, or deselect the check box if the category isn't tax-related. Just to clear up any confusion, vacationing in Hawaii probably isn't a tax deduction — even if your neighbor promises it is. Then identify the form and line by opening the Form drop-down list box and selecting one of its entries.

7. Click OK.

Quicken adds the new category to the Category & Transfer List window shown in Figure 2-4 and then redisplays the window. Now that you understand the stuff in the Category & Transfer List window, note that it shows the category name, its type, the notation that a category is tax-related, and, golly darn, even its description.

Removing categories you loathe

Removing categories takes only a couple of keystrokes. With the Category & Transfer List window displayed, use the arrow keys or click the mouse to select the category you want to remove. Then click Delete. Quicken displays a message that asks you to confirm your decision. Assuming that you want to remove the selected category, click OK. Otherwise, press Esc or click Cancel.

Changing category names and descriptions

You can change a category name, its type, its description, and its tax-related setting if you later discover you've made some mistake, such as misspelling a word in a description.

To do so, display the Category & Transfer List window, as shown in Figure 2-4. Use the arrow keys or click your mouse to select the category you want to change. Then select the category and click the Edit button. Quicken displays a dialog box that has text boxes and option buttons describing the selected category's information: its name, description, type, and tax-related settings.

Make the changes you want by replacing text box contents or changing option button settings. Then click OK to save your changes and return to the Category & Transfer List window.

Do You Need a Little Class?

Categories aren't the only way you can summarize your financial records. Quicken provides a second tool, called *Classes*.

I have mixed feelings about classes, and I'll tell you why. I use them — with good success — to track the types of gross income that my business produces (writing, consulting, teaching, and so on) and the types of expenses my business incurs in these activities. (In fact, Writing, Consulting, and Teaching are the names of three of my classes.)

Classes present a couple of problems, however. First, you can't budget by classes. (Before you say, "Ah, Steve, I don't want to budget," please read the next chapter.) Second, you need to remember to tag transactions with their classes. (Quicken doesn't remind you to include classes but does remind you to include a category.)

Because I really don't think you'll use it now, I'm not going to describe how you use classes. But if you get really comfortable with the Quicken categories and you want a way to organize your financial information across categories, consider using the Quicken classes. You can flip to the Quicken documentation to get this information.

Chapter 3

Maximum Fun, Maximum Profits

* *

* *

I don't think a budget amounts to financial handcuffs, and neither should you. A budget is really a plan that outlines the way people need to spend their money to achieve the maximum amount of fun or the way businesses need to spend their money to make the most profit.

Should You Even Bother?

A budget, as you probably know, is just a list of the ways you earn and spend your money. And if you've created a good, workable categories list, you're halfway to a good, solid budget. (In fact, the only step left is to specify how much you earn in each income category and how much you spend in each expense category.)

Does everybody need a budget? No, of course not. Maybe at your house, you're already having a bunch of fun with your money. Maybe in your business, you make money so effortlessly you really don't plan your income and outgo.

For the rest of us, though, a budget improves our chances of getting to wherever it is we want to go financially. In fact, I'll stop calling it a budget. The word has such negative connotations. I know — I'll call it a *Secret Plan*.

Serious Advice about Your Secret Plan

Before I walk you through the mechanics of outlining your Secret Plan, I want to give you a few tips.

Your personal Secret Plan

You can do four things to make it more likely that your Secret Plan will work.

- *Plan your income and expenses as a family.*

  When it comes to this sort of planning, two heads are invariably better than one. What's more, though I don't really want to get into marriage counseling here, a family's budget — oops, I mean Secret Plan — needs to reflect the priorities and feelings of everyone who has to live within the plan. Don't use a Secret Plan as a way to minimize what your spouse spends on clothing or on long-distance telephone charges talking to relatives in the old country. You need to resolve clothing and long-distance charges issues before you finalize your Secret Plan.

- *Include some cushion in your plan.*

  In other words, don't budget to spend every last dollar (or if you're German, every last deutsche mark). If you plan from the start to spend every dollar you make, you undoubtedly have to fight the mother of all financial battles: paying for unexpected expenses when you don't have any money. (You know the sort of things I mean — car repairs, medical expenses, or that cocktail dress or tuxedo you absolutely *must* have for a special party.)

- *Regularly compare your actual income and outgo to your planned income and outgo.*

  This part of your plan is probably the most important and also what Quicken will help you with the most. As long as you use Quicken to record what you receive and spend, you can print reports showing what you planned and what actually occurred.

- *Make adjustments as necessary.*

  When you have problems with your Secret Plan — and you will — you'll know that your plan isn't working. You can then make adjustments, by spending a little less calling the old country, for example.

Your Business Secret Plan

These tips for personal Secret Plans also apply to businesses. But I've also got a special tip for small businesses using Quicken. (I'm going to write very quietly now so that no one else hears. . . .)

Here's the secret tip: Go to the library, ask for the Robert Morris & Associates Survey, and look up the ways that other businesses like yours spend money.

This survey is really cool. Robert Morris & Associates surveys bank lending officers, creates a summary of the information these bankers receive from their customers, and publishes the results. For example, you can look up what percentage of sales the average tavern spends on beer and peanuts.

Plan to take an hour or so at the library. It takes a while to get used to the way the Robert Morris & Associates information is displayed. The survey won't actually have a line on the tavern's page labeled "beer and peanuts," for example. It'll be called "cost of goods sold" or some similarly vague accounting term.

Remember to make a few notes so that you can use the information you glean to better plan your own business financial affairs.

Two things that really goof up Secret Plans

Because we're talking about you-know-what, let me touch on a couple of things that really goof up your financial plans: windfalls and monster changes.

The problem with windfalls

Your boss smiles, calls you into his office, and then gives you the good news. You're getting a bonus: $5,000! "About time," you think to yourself. Outside, of course, you maintain your dignity. You act grateful but not gushy. Then you call your husband.

Here's what happens next. Bob (that's your husband's name) gets excited, congratulates you, and tells you he'll pick up a bottle of wine on the way home to celebrate.

On your drive home, you mull over the possibilities and conclude that you can use the $5,000 as a big down payment for that new family van you've been looking at. (With the trade-in and the $5,000, your payments will be a manageable $200 a month.)

Bob, on his way home, stops to look at those golf clubs he's been coveting for about three years, charges $800 on his credit card, and then, feeling slightly guilty, buys you the $600 set. (Let's say that you're just starting to play golf.)

You may laugh at this scenario, but suppose that it really happened. Furthermore, pretend that you really do buy the van. At this point, you've spent $6,400 on a van and golf clubs, and you've signed up for what you're guessing will be another $200-a-month payment.

This turn of events doesn't sound all that bad now, does it?

Here's the problem: When you get your check, it's not going to be $5,000. You're probably going to pay roughly $400 in Social Security and Medicare taxes, maybe around $1,500 in federal income taxes, and then probably some state income taxes.

Other money may be taken out, too, for forced savings plans (such as a 401(k) plan) or for charitable giving. After all is said and done, you'll get maybe half the bonus in cash — say $2,500.

Now you see the problem, of course. You've got $2,500 in cold, hard cash, but with Bob's help, you've already spent $6,400 and signed up for $200-a-month payments.

In a nutshell, you face two big problems with windfalls. Problem one is that you never get the entire windfall — yet it's easy to spend as if you will. Problem two is that windfalls, by their very nature, tend to get used for big purchases (often as down payments) that ratchet up your living expenses. Boats. New houses. Cars.

Regarding windfalls, my advice to you is simple:

- ✔ Don't spend a windfall until you actually hold the check in your hot little hand. (It's even better to wait, say, six months. That way Bob can really think about whether he needs those new golf clubs.)
- ✔ Don't spend a windfall on something that increases your monthly living expenses without first redoing your budget.

About monster income changes

If your income changes radically, it becomes *really* hard to plan a budget.

Suppose that your income doubles. One day you're cruising along making $35,000, and the next day, you're suddenly making $70,000. (Congratulations, by the way.)

I'll tell you what you'll discover, however, should you find yourself in this position. You'll find that $70,000 a year isn't as much money as you might think.

Go ahead. Laugh. But for one thing, if your income doubles, your income taxes almost certainly more than quadruple.

One of the great myths about income taxes is that the rich don't pay very much or that they pay the same percentage. Poppycock. If you make $30,000 a year and you're an average family, you probably pay about $1,500 in federal income taxes. If you make $200,000 a year, you'll pay about $45,000 a year. So if your salary increases by roughly 7 times, your income taxes increase by about 30 times. I don't bring this fact up to get you agitated about whether it's right or fair to make the rich pay more; I bring it up so that you can better plan for any monster income changes you experience.

Another thing — and I know it sounds crazy — but you'll find it hard to spend $70,000 smartly when you've been making a lot less. And if you start making some big purchases such as houses and cars and speedboats, you'll not only burn through a great deal of cash, you'll also ratchet up your monthly living expenses.

Monster income changes that go the other way are even more difficult. If you've been making, say, $70,000 a year and then see your salary drop to a darn respectable $35,000, it's going to hurt, too. And probably more than you think.

That old living-expenses ratcheting effect comes into play here, of course. Presumably, if you've been making $70,000 a year, you've been spending it — or most of it.

But there are some other reasons why it's very difficult — at least initially — to have a monster salary drop. You've probably chosen friends (nice people, such as the Joneses), clothing stores, and hobbies that are in line with your income.

Another thing about a monster salary drop is sort of subtle. You probably denominate your purchases in amounts related to your income. Make $35,000 and you think in terms of $5 or $10 purchases. But make $70,000 a year and you think in terms of $10 or $20 purchases.

This observation all makes perfect sense. But if your income drops from $70,000 down to $35,000, you'll probably still find yourself thinking of those old $20 purchases.

So what to do? If you do experience a monster income change, redo your Secret Plan. And be particularly careful and thoughtful.

Monster income changes

To conclude this Secret Plan business, I'll make a philosophical digression.

If you've provided yourself and your family with the creature comforts — a cozy place to live, adequate food, and comfortable clothes — more stuff won't make the difference that you think.

I don't mean to minimize the challenges of raising a family of four on, say, $14,000 a year. But, hey, in my business I see a fair number of wealthy people. What continually surprises me is that when you get right down to it, someone who makes $300,000 or $600,000 a year doesn't live a better life than someone who makes $30,000.

Sure, they spend more money. They buy more stuff. They buy more expensive stuff. But they don't live better. They don't have better marriages. Their kids don't love them more. They don't have better friends or more considerate neighbors.

But you already know all this. I know you do.

Setting Up a Secret Plan

Okay, enough metaphysical stuff. Let's set up your budget — er, I mean, Secret Plan.

Budget window

To get to the window in which you'll enter your budget, click the Planning Activity Bar icon and choose the Budget My Spending command. Quicken displays the Budget window shown in Figure 3-1.

There's nothing very complicated about the window. The income and expense categories — including the ones you've created — appear along the left edge of the screen. There are subtotals for any categories with subcategories (if you have these), for the total inflows, and for the total outflows.

Across the top of the screen is a row of command buttons that makes your budgeting job easier. (I describe the more useful commands in a few paragraphs and provide brief descriptions of those that aren't quite as useful.)

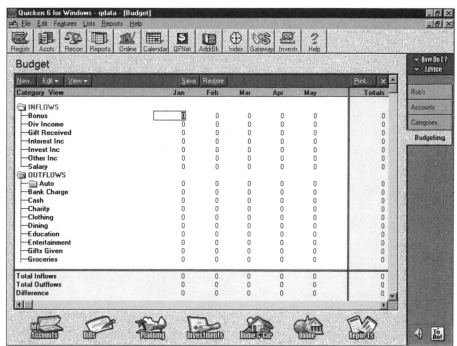

Entering budgeted amounts the simple way

Here's the two-step way to enter budgeted amounts — not to be confused with the Texas Two-Step:

1. **Select the amount you want to budget.**

   Select the budgeted income or expense amount you want to enter either by using the arrow keys or by clicking the amount with the mouse. For example, to select the January Salary budget field, click its number with the mouse. Or use the arrow keys to move the square and select the field. (You're doing this stuff so that you can enter the budgeted amount.)

2. **Enter the budgeted amount.**

   Type the amount you've budgeted and press Enter. Suppose that you've already selected the January Salary budget field and now need to enter a value. Say that you take home $3,000 a month. To use this figure as the January Salary budget, type **3000**.

After you press Enter, Quicken updates any subtotals and grand totals that use the salary income amount, as shown in Figure 3-2. For example, look at the Total Inflows subtotal at the bottom of the screen. And look at the Totals column along the right edge of the window. Notice the Edit button. (It's the second one from the left.) I talk more about all the cool things it lets you do later in the chapter.

You need to scroll the screen to the right to see months near the middle and end of the year. Unless you're using a really short categories list, you need to scroll down to see categories (usually expense categories) that aren't at the top of the list.

The easiest way to scroll is by using the mouse to click and drag on the scroll bars. If you don't already know how to do this, you can experiment (probably the most fun), or you can flip to Appendix A.

If you don't want to use the mouse or you just need to be different, you can use the old navigation keys, too. To scroll the screen right, just press the Tab key. To scroll the screen back, or left, press Shift+Tab. To scroll the screen up and down, use the PgUp and PgDn keys.

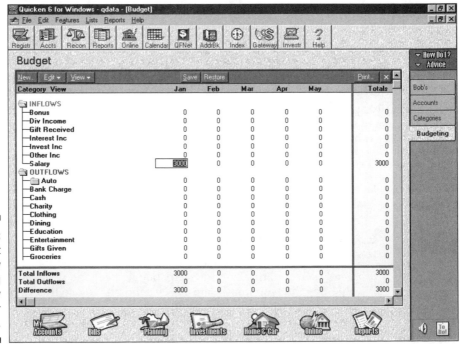

Figure 3-2:
The Budget window showing salary income for January.

The Category View and Totals columns don't scroll. You know what else? The months, Total Inflows, and Total Outflows rows don't scroll either. Quicken leaves these elements frozen in the window so that you can tell which column and row is which and how things are going.

Entering budgeted amounts the fast way

It just figures, doesn't it? There's the simple way and there's the fast way, and "never the twain shall meet."

If monthly budgeted amounts are the same over the year

Enter the first month's figures (as I described earlier). After you've done this step, click the Edit button. Quicken displays the Edit menu. Choose Fill Columns. If you choose Yes in the dialog box that appears, Quicken takes your January budget numbers and copies them into February, March, April, and through the rest of the year.

What if you make a mistake? What if you fill some row with a bunch of goofy numbers? No problem. Move the selection cursor to that row and choose Edit⇨Clear Row.

If budgeted amounts are the same as last year

If you used Quicken for record-keeping in the prior year, you can copy the actual amounts from the previous year and use these as part or all of the current year's budget.

To do so, click the Edit button and choose Autocreate. Quicken displays the Automatically Create Budget dialog box, as shown in Figure 3-3. You can then tell Quicken what it should copy from last year.

Here's how to use this dialog box:

1. **Indicate which months you want to copy.**

   Use the From and To text boxes to indicate from which months in the previous year actual category totals should be copied. If you want to copy the entire previous year's totals and it's now 1997, for example, specify these entries as **1/96** and **12/96**.

2. **Indicate whether the actual category totals should be rounded.**

   Want to round the actual category totals? No problem. Just use the Round Values to Nearest drop-down list box to indicate how much rounding you want: to the nearest $1, to the nearest $10, or to the nearest $100.

Figure 3-3:
The
Automatically
Create
Budget
dialog box.

3. Use category averages (optional).

To use the average actual spending in a category for the months identified in the From and To text boxes, indicate that you want to use averages for the period. To do so, select the Use Average for Period option button. If you leave the Use Monthly Detail option button selected, Quicken doesn't calculate and use averages; it just uses the actual monthly amounts from the previous year as the budgeted monthly amounts for the current year.

4. Limit the categories automatically budgeted (optional).

To tell Quicken you want only some of your categories automatically budgeted, click the Categories button. Quicken displays the Select Categories to Include dialog box (see Figure 3-4). Indicate which categories should be automatically budgeted by clicking them. To mark or unmark a category, click it. To mark all the categories, click Mark All. To unmark all the categories, click Clear All. After you've selected the categories you want to include as part of the automatic budget creation, click OK. Quicken closes the Select Categories to Include dialog box.

Figure 3-4:
The Select
Categories
to Include
dialog box.

5. Click OK.

Quicken uses the information entered on the Automatically Create Budget dialog box and the previous year's actual category totals to completely fill in the Budget window.

If a single category's monthly budget is the same over the year

Hey, you're on a roll now. So let's say that a single category's monthly budget is the same over the year.

To create a budget, enter the first month's budget figure as described earlier. Click the Edit button and choose Fill Row Right. If you choose Yes, Quicken takes the budget number for the selected category and copies it into the following months — probably February, March, April, and so on — through the rest of the year.

You can use Fill Row Right to copy budget amounts forward from months besides January. For example, if your rent runs $500 a month from January through June and then $600 from July through December, enter **500** into the January Rent field and use the Fill Row Right command to fill the rest of the year. Then enter **600** into the July Rent field. If you choose the Fill Row Right again, Quicken copies 600 forward to August, September, October, November, and December.

Budgeting biweekly amounts

Sometimes it doesn't make much sense to budget amounts on a monthly basis because you actually receive or spend on a biweekly basis. What if you're paid every two weeks? Or what if your bowling league meets every other Thursday? See the dilemma? You won't really know how many two-week periods there are in a month unless you look at a calendar and start counting with your fingers.

Lucky for you, Quicken provides a handy tool for budgeting those sorts of biweekly amounts: the 2-Week Command, which appears on the Edit button's menu. To use this command, select the category you want to budget biweekly and then choose the command. Quicken displays the Set Up Two-Week Budget dialog box. Coincidentally, this dialog box appears in Figure 3-5.

Figure 3-5:
The Set Up
Two-Week
Budget
dialog box.

Enter the biweekly amount in the Amount text box. Enter the first date you'll receive or spend the amount in the Every Two Weeks Starting text box, and then click OK.

After you finish entering your budget

After you enter your Secret Plan, either the simple way or the fast way (if you're the adventurous type), just click the Save button to save your work.

I should mention, too, that you can simply click the Close button if you don't want to save your work (in case you've been noodling around). If you want to revert to the previously saved version of the budget, click the Restore button.

I talk more about using the budget in later chapters (such as Chapter 6, for example). If you want to print a hard copy (Computerese for paper) of the budget, click the Print button (the fifth button from the left) and press Enter. If you have a printing question, go to Chapter 5.

Remember that you can have Quicken display a button's name by moving the mouse pointer so it points to the bottom edge of the button.

You're not going to use the budget for a while. But don't worry. In Chapter 5, I explain how to print reports, including a report that compares your actual spending with, ugh, your budget. Stay tuned. Same time. Same place.

The other button?

If you look closely at the Budget window, you can see that I haven't described the View button. Quick as a bunny, I want to describe what you do with this button, because it's pretty handy.

The View button

After you click the View button, Quicken displays the View menu. Because I thought you just might be interested in what this baby looks like, I include it as Figure 3-6. See? The bulleted list that follows describes what the mysterious commands do.

Chapter 3: Maximum Fun, Maximum Profits *51*

Figure 3-6:
The View
menu.

- *Months.* Tells Quicken you want to budget by the month. You don't need to use this command unless you've used one of the other commands; Quicken budgets by the month unless you tell it to do otherwise. Just choose the command or press Alt+M.

- *Quarters.* Tells Quicken you want to budget by the quarter. Just choose the command or press Alt+Q.

- *Years.* Tells Quicken you really are a Big Picture person (or business) and that you'll be budgeting by the year. (If you flip-flop between months, quarters, and years, Quicken automatically converts the budget figures for you.) To work with the Big Picture, just choose the command, or press Alt+Y.

- *Supercategories.* Tells Quicken either you do want to budget by super-category or you don't want to budget by subcategory. You can turn the command off and on by choosing the command or by pressing Alt+U.

- *Transfers.* Tells Quicken whether you want to budget account transfers. The only problem here is that you probably don't know what account transfers are (yet!). I talk about account transfers in the next chapter.

- *Zero Budget Categories.* Hides all the budget categories that show zero.

- *Other Budgets.* Displays the Manage Budgets dialog box, described in the next section.

The Budgets command

When you choose the Other Budgets command, the Manage Budgets dialog box appears (see Figure 3-7). The Manage Budgets dialog box is pretty neat. It lets you create more than one budget. To do so, you display the Manage Budgets dialog box, click the Create button, and then, when prompted, give the new budget a unique name. Something really clever. Whenever you want to use that budget, you display the Manage Budgets dialog box, click the budget you want to work with, and then click the Open button.

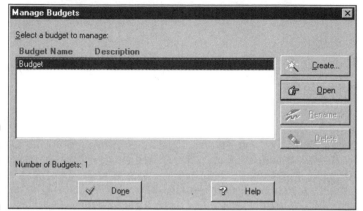

Figure 3-7:
The Manage
Budgets
dialog box.

Wanna budget with a spreadsheet?

Using the Edit menu's Copy All command — remember the Edit menu appears when you click the Edit button — you can copy the budget information shown in the Budget window to the Clipboard. After the budget information is there, you can start a Windows spreadsheet program such as Excel and use Edit⇨Paste to paste the budgeting stuff stored on the Clipboard into the spreadsheet. If you're familiar with a Windows spreadsheet, such as Excel, go ahead and try it. You might like it — if you want to use the spreadsheet program to analyze the data.

Part II

The Absolute Basics

In this part . . .

Okay, you're ready for the show to start. Which is good. This part — "The Absolute Basics" — covers all the nitty gritty details of using Quicken to keep your personal and business financial records.

If you're just starting to use the Quicken program or if you've just come from Part I, you'll find the stuff covered here dang important — dare I say essential — to using Quicken in even the most basic way.

Chapter 4

Checkbook on a Computer

● ●

In This Chapter

▶ Recording checks

▶ Recording deposits

▶ Recording transfers

▶ Splitting categories

▶ Deleting and voiding transactions

▶ Memorizing transactions

● ●

*T*his is it. The big time. You're finally going to do those everyday Quicken things: entering checks, deposits, and transfers. Along the way, you'll also use some of the neat tools that Quicken provides for making these tasks easier, more precise, and faster.

Finding Your Checkbook

To enter checkbook transactions, use the register window (see Figure 4-1). If you can see a QuickTab that names the bank account you set up, you can click it to display the register window. (If you don't see the register window, click the Registr icon from the iconbar.)

If you've set up more than one account — say you've set up both a checking account and a savings account — you may need to tell Quicken which account you want to work with. Geez Louise, how can you tell if Quicken gets confused? Easy. The register heading shows the wrong account. To correct this problem, click the button naming the account near the bottom of the register; click Bob's to show Bob's checking account, Sue's to show Sue's checking account, and so on.

The starting balance you specified as part of setting up the account is the first amount listed. In Figure 4-1, for example, the starting balance is $4.16. Bummer.

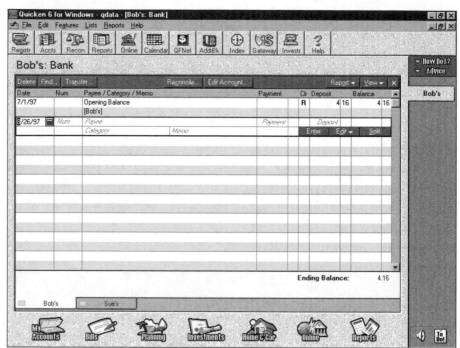

Figure 4-1:
The register
window.

The account name and type — Bob's:Bank — appears at the top of the register window.

As you move the selection cursor through the register window's fields, Quicken may display Qcards. Basically, these Qcards are little message boxes that tell you what goes where. These little reminders are helpful but can get a little tiresome in much the same way a backseat driver gets tiresome. I turned Qcards off because I reached my breaking point. When you reach your breaking point, you should turn them off, too. The easiest way to do this is to click the Qcards dialog box's Close box. This tells Quicken, "Geez, stop nagging me, will ya?" You can also choose the Help⇨Show Qcards command.

Recording Checks

First things first: You can enter checks using either the register window (see Figure 4-1) or the Write Checks window, described in Chapter 5.

You use the register window for the checks you don't want to print with Quicken; you use the Write Checks window to enter the checks you do want to print using Quicken. (This isn't an ironclad rule, but it does make things easier for you, so it's the rule we'll follow.)

Entering a check into the register

Okay, back to the chase. Entering a check in the register window is a simple matter of describing who you wrote the check to and how much you paid. Let's say, for the sake of illustration, that you paid $25.50 to the cable television company for your monthly cable service. Here's how you enter this check:

1. **Enter the check date.**

   Move the cursor to the Date field in the next empty row of the register (if it isn't already there) and type the date using the MM/DD format. July 6, 1997, for example, is entered as **7/6**. You usually won't have to type the year because Quicken retrieves the current year number from the little clock inside your computer.

   You can adjust the date in a Date field by using the + and - keys. The + key adds one day to the current date; the - key subtracts one day from the current date.

2. **Enter the check number.**

   Move the cursor (or tab) to the Num field and type the check number. Alternatively, move the cursor to the Num field and then when Quicken displays a list box of entries, such as ATM, Deposit, EFT, Next Check Number, Print Check, Send Online Payment, and Transfer Funds, select Next Check Number if you want. In this case, Quicken fills in the number with its guess as to the new check number — one more than the old check number. If this guess is right, of course, you can just leave it in place. If it isn't right, type over Quicken's guess with the correct number or use the + or - key to increase or decrease the check number.

3. **Enter the payee.**

   Move the cursor to the Payee field. Type the name of the person or business you're paying. If the cable company's name is Movies Galore, for example, type **Movies Galore**. (In the future, however, you probably will be able to select payee names from the list box.)

A neat little trick

The list box of Num entries that Quicken displays is expandable and editable. If you want to add some new Num entry to the drop-down list box, for example, click the Edit List button which appears at the bottom of the list. When Quicken displays the Edit Num List dialog box, click the New button and then complete the dialog box that Quicken displays. You can also edit any new Num entries you add by using the Edit Num List dialog box. I won't spend any more time describing here how this works; so if you want to figure out how it all works, just experiment. You can't hurt anything.

4. Enter the check amount.

Move the cursor to the Payment field and type the check amount — **25.50** in this example. You don't have to type the dollar sign, but you do have to type the period to indicate the decimal place and cents.

5. Enter the category.

Move the cursor to the Category field. Quicken displays a drop-down list box of category names from your Category & Transfer List. You can select one of these categories using the arrow keys or the mouse. Or if you're the independent type, just type the name yourself. A payment to your cable company may be categorized as "Utilities," for example.

If you go with the typing approach and you're not a super-fast typist, Quicken will probably be able to guess which category you're entering before you enter it. When you start typing **Ut**, for example, Quicken fills in the rest of the category name, "ilities," for you ("Ut" + "ilities" = "Utilities"). This is called *QuickFill,* and I'll talk about it later in the chapter in a bit more detail, in the section "A kooky (and clever) little thing named QuickFill."

6. Enter a memo description.

Move the cursor to the Memo field and describe the specific reason you're paying the check. You may identify the cable payment as the June payment, for example. If you are using Quicken for a business, you should use this field to identify the paid invoice — usually by entering the actual invoice number you are paying.

7. Click Enter.

Click the Enter button that appears in the transaction's row of the register. This option tells Quicken that you want to record the transaction into your register. Quicken beeps in acknowledgment, calculates the new account balance, and moves the cursor to the next slot, or row in the register.

Figure 4-2 shows the cable television check recorded into the register. You can't see it in the figure, but the amount in the Balance field after the $25.50 check shows in red. This *red ink* indicates that you've overdrawn your account. I don't need to tell you what that means. Overdraft charges.

Packing more checks into the register

Normally, Quicken displays several rows of information about each check you've entered. It also displays several rows of information about each of the other types of transactions you've entered, too. If you want to pack more checks into a visible portion of the register, click the View button (which appears in the top-right corner of the register window), and then choose the

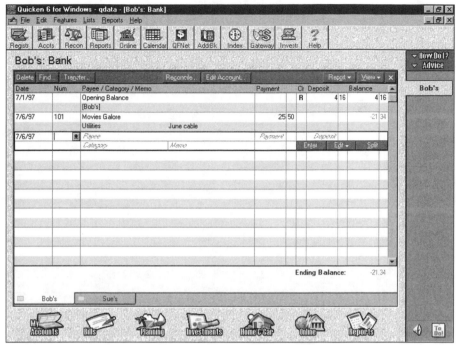

Figure 4-2:
The Quicken
register
after
recording
the check
to Movies
Galore.

One-Line Display command from the menu that Quicken displays. After you do
this, Quicken displays in a single-line format all the information in the register
except the Memo field (see Figure 4-3). To return to the double-line format, click
the View button and choose One-Line Display again.

What if you need to change a check after you've already entered it? Say you
make a terrible mistake, such as recording a $52.50 check as $25.20. Can you fix
it? Sure. Just use the arrow keys or click the mouse to highlight the check
transaction you want to change. Use the Tab and Shift+Tab keys to move the
cursor to the field you want to change. (You also can select the field by clicking
the mouse.) Then make your fix. Click the Enter button when you finish or press
Enter.

If you click the View button, you'll notice that it also displays a bunch of
commands that begin with the word *sort*. These commands all work the same
basic way. They let you reorganize the transactions shown in the register in
some new way: by date, amount, check number, and so forth.

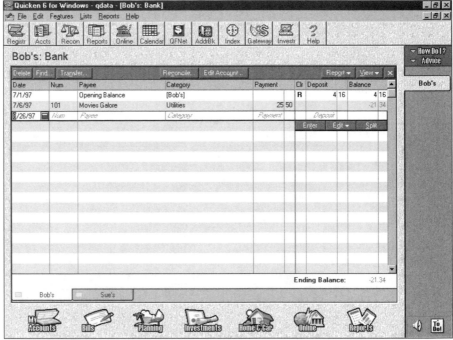

Figure 4-3:
How the
register
looks with
the One-Line
Display
format.

A kooky (and clever) little thing named QuickFill

Here's kind of a funny quirk about Quicken. If Quicken can guess what you're typing into a field, it will fill in the rest of the field for you. I already mentioned how this works when you type category names. But it gets even better than that.

The second time you use a payee name, for example, Quicken knows that it's the second time. Quicken also figures that, "Hey, there's probably stuff from the last Movies Galore transaction that'll be the same for this transaction." So guess what Quicken does if you press Tab to accept the payee name Quicken supplies after you've typed the first few letters of the name? It uses the last transaction's information to fill in all the current transaction's fields.

This isn't as dumb as it sounds. In fact, it's a real time-saver. Suppose that you did write a $25.50 check to Movies Galore for your June cable television bill. When you type **Movies Galore** to record the next month's cable television check, the amount will probably be the same. The complete payee name will certainly be the same, and the category will also be the same. So Quicken fills in all these fields, too.

Memorized transactions

Quicken provides another feature — memorized transactions — which is almost obsolete now that the QuickFill feature exists. Just because you may have heard about this tool, however, I'll quickly describe how it works.

A *memorized transaction* is simply one that you've stored on a special list. (To store the transaction, you select it in the register, click the Edit button, and then choose the Memorize Transaction command.)

To later use or abuse one of the memorized transactions, you display a list of the previously memorized transactions by choosing List➪Memorized Transaction. When Quicken displays the list, just select the one you want to reuse and click Use.

A memorized transactions list is a handy tool. But if you're feeling a little overwhelmed, don't spin your wheels trying to get up to speed on the feature. QuickFill almost always does the job for you because — get this — it automatically grabs memorized transactions from the list for you.

QuickFill doesn't do everything for you, however. You still need to make sure that the date and check number are correct. If Quicken "quickfills" a field with the wrong information, just replace the wrong information with what's right.

Recording Deposits

You know what? Recording a deposit works almost the exact same way as recording a check works. The only difference is that you enter the deposit amount in the Deposit field rather than enter the check amount in the Payment field.

Entering a deposit into the register

Suppose that you receive a $100 birthday gift from your elderly aunt, Enid. Here's how you would record this deposit into the register:

1. **Enter the deposit date.**

   Move the cursor to the Date field of the next empty row of the register (if it isn't already there) and type the date. Use the MM/DD format. July 10, 1997, for example, is entered as **7/10**. As with check dates, you have to enter the year only if the current year number, which Quicken retrieves from the little clock inside your computer, is wrong.

   You can adjust the date in a Date field in Quicken by using the + and – keys. The + key adds one day to the current date; the – key subtracts one day from the current date.

2. **Enter the code DEP into the Number field.**

Are you the meticulous type? Then go ahead and move the cursor to the Num field. In the drop-down list box that Quicken displays, select Deposit.

3. **Enter the name of the person from whom you received the deposit.**

In this case, move the cursor to the Payee field and enter **Aunt Enid**. (I don't mean to sound presumptuous, but, well, the next time Aunt Enid sends you birthday money, you'll be able to select her name from the Payee drop-down list box.)

4. **Enter the deposit amount.**

Move the cursor to the Deposit field and type **100**. Don't type the dollar sign — or any other punctuation. (If Aunt Enid sweats money and sometimes passes out $1,000 gifts, for example, you record the deposit as 1000 — not 1,000 or $1,000.)

5. **Enter the category.**

You know how this works by now. Move the cursor to the Category field and select the appropriate category. Alternatively, if you like living on the edge, try typing in the category name. Aunt Enid's check may be described as Gift Received. (This is an income category on the standard home category list.) A customer receipt may be described as Sales.

To add a category, move the cursor to the Category field and then click the Add Cat button to display the Set Up New Category dialog box. Refer to Chapter 2 if you have questions about how this works.

6. **(Optional) Enter a memo description.**

Move the cursor to the Memo field and describe something like the reason for the deposit. Aunt Enid's money may be described as Birthday Gift. If you're a business depositing a customer's check, though, use this entry to identify the invoice the customer is paying.

7. **Click Enter.**

This command tells Quicken that you want to record the transaction in your register. Quicken beeps in protest but then adds the transaction.

Figure 4-4 shows the check register after you've entered Aunt Enid's thoughtful gift. Your account's no longer overdrawn — so you've got that going for you. Maybe before you go any further, you should call Aunt Enid to thank her.

Changing a deposit you've already entered

Big surprise here, but changing a deposit works just like changing a check. First, use the arrow keys or click the mouse to select the deposit. Use the Tab and Shift+Tab keys to move the cursor to the field you want to change. Tab moves the cursor to the next field. Shift+Tab moves the cursor to the previous field. (You also can select the field by clicking the mouse.) Then make your fix and click Enter.

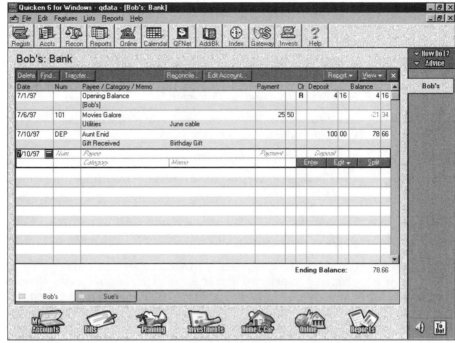

Figure 4-4:
A check
register
after you
record your
first deposit.

Recording Account Transfers

Account transfers occur when you move money from one account — such as your savings account — to another account — such as your checking account. But jeepers, why am I telling you this? If you've got one of those combined savings and checking accounts, you probably do this sort of thing all the time.

Oh, now I remember why I brought this up — Quicken makes quick work of account transfers as long as you already have *both* accounts set up.

If you don't have the second account set up, you'll need to do this first. If you don't know how, flip back to Chapter 2.

Entering an account transfer

Buckle up. I'll speed through the steps for recording an account transfer. For the most part, you record an account transfer the same way you record a check or deposit.

Suppose that you want to record the transfer of $50 from your checking account to your savings account. Maybe you want to set aside a little money — *little,* presumably, being a key adjective — to purchase a gift for generous Aunt Enid.

Here's what you need to do:

1. **Enter the transfer date.**

   Move the cursor to the Date field. Then type the date that you move the money from one account to another.

2. **Flag the transaction as a transfer.**

   Move the cursor to the Num field. When Quicken displays a drop-down list box, select the Transfer Funds entry.

3. **Enter a description of the transaction.**

   Use the Description field to describe the transfer — for example, For Aunt Enid's Next Gift. You know how this works by now, don't you? You just move the cursor to the field. Then you pound away at the keyboard. Bang. Bang. Bang.

4. **Enter the transfer amount.**

   Amounts transferred out of an account are entered in the Payment field. Amounts transferred into an account are entered in the Deposit field. So move the cursor to the right field (*right* as in *right and wrong* not *right and left*); then enter the transfer amount.

5. **Indicate the other account.**

   Move the cursor to the Category field and when Quicken drops down a list box of accounts, select the other account.

6. **(Optional) Enter a memo description.**

   Enter more information about the transaction (if it's needed) in the Memo field. Perhaps a gift idea for Aunt Enid?

7. **Click Enter.**

   This command tells Quicken that you want to record the transfer transaction into your register.

Figure 4-5 shows the check register after transferring money from your checking account to your savings account so that you'll have money to purchase something nice for Aunt Enid's next birthday. Maybe that new *Alice in Chains* compact disc.

Take a look at the Category field. Notice that Quicken uses brackets ([ ]) to identify the Category field entry as an account and not as an income or expense category.

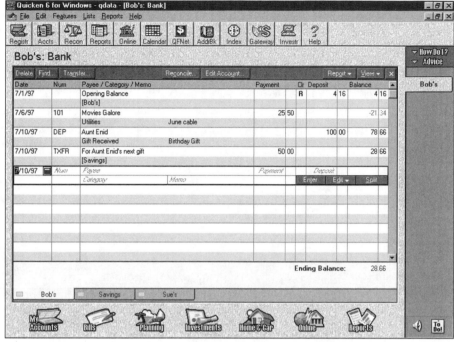

Figure 4-5:
The check register window after you enter the transfer transaction.

About the other half of the transfer

Here's the cool thing about transfer transactions. Quicken automatically records the other half of the transfer for you. Figure 4-5 shows the $50 reduction in the checking account because of the transfer. Quicken uses this information to record a $50 increase in the savings account. Automatically. Biddabam. Biddaboom.

To see the other half of a transfer transaction, select the transfer transaction using the arrow keys or the mouse. Then click the Edit button and choose Go To Transfer. Quicken displays the other account in a new register window (see Figure 4-6).

Changing a transfer you've already entered

Predictably, this works just like changing a check or a deposit. First, you select the transfer by using the arrow keys or by clicking the mouse. Then you use the Tab and Shift+Tab keys to move the cursor to the field that you want to change. Make your fix and then click Enter and go to lunch.

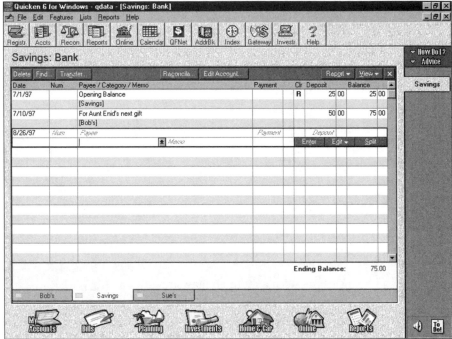

Figure 4-6:
The other
half of the
transfer
transaction.

Splitting Hairs

Here's a sort of Quicken riddle for you. Suppose that you've got a check that pays more than one kind of expense. You trot down to the grocery store, for example, and pick up $10 of junk food and junk beverages (which should be categorized as a Groceries expense) and $10 of 10W-40 motor oil (which should be categorized as an Auto expense). How do you categorize a transaction like this? Well, I'll tell you. You use a *split category*.

Here's how a split category works. When you're ready to categorize the check, you click the Split button, which appears in the Category drop-down list box for the selected transaction. When you click this button, Quicken displays the Split Transaction Window (see Figure 4-7).

Steps for splitting a check

If you're a clever sort, you probably already know how the Split Transaction Window works. Let's go through the steps anyway. Suppose that you want to categorize a $20 check that includes $10 for groceries and $10 for motor oil.

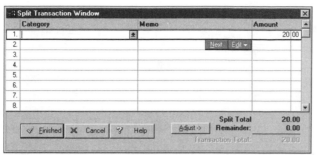

Figure 4-7:
The Split
Transaction
Window.

To categorize a check in the Split Transaction Window, do the following:

1. **Enter the first category name in the first category field.**

   Move the cursor to the category field (if it isn't already there). Activate the drop-down list box by pressing Alt+↓ or by clicking the down arrow, and then selecting the category name.

   (Despite what a dietitian may say, let's call the pork rinds, soda, and pretzels "Groceries.")

2. **Enter a memo description for the first categorized portion of the check.**

   Move the cursor to the first Memo field and then type whatever you want. (Maybe a description of the food you bought.)

3. **Enter the amount spent for the first category.**

   Move the cursor to the first Amount field and then type, well, the amount. If the first category is what we're calling Groceries and you spent $10 on this, you type **10**.

4. **Repeat Steps 1, 2, and 3 for each spending category.**

   If you spent another $10 on motor oil, for example, move the cursor to the second Category field and enter the category you use to summarize Auto expenses. Move the cursor to the second Memo field and enter a memo description of the expenditure, such as **motor oil**. Move the cursor to the second Amount field and enter the amount of the expenditure, such as **10**.

   Figure 4-8 shows a completed Split Transaction Window. You can have up to 30 pieces of a split transaction. Use the scrollbar and PgUp and PgDn keys to scroll through the list of split amounts.

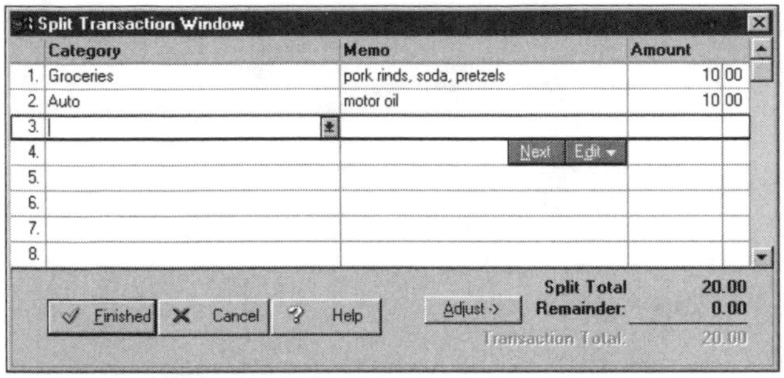

Figure 4-8:
The
completed
Split
Transaction
Window.

5. Verify that the Split Transaction Window shows no uncategorized spending.

If you find extra spending, either add the needed category or delete the split transaction line that's uncategorized. To delete a split transaction line, move the cursor to one of the fields in the line, scream "Hi-Ya" loudly, click the Edit button, and choose Delete. (I learned the "Hi-Ya" business in tae kwon do. The only other thing I learned, by the way, was that those chest protectors don't really protect middle-aged men during full-contact sparring. So I quit.)

If you want to insert a new line, move the selection cursor to the line above where you want to make your insertion, click the Edit button, and then choose Insert. If you're fed up and want to start over from scratch, click the Edit button and choose the Clear All command. (Quicken erases all the split transaction lines if you do this.)

6. Click Finished.

After you complete the Split Transaction Window — that is, you've completely and correctly categorized all the little pieces of the transaction — click Finished. Quicken closes the Split Transaction Window. If you didn't enter an amount in the Payment column of the register before opening the Split Transaction Window, Quicken will display a dialog box that asks whether the transaction is a payment or a deposit. You select an option button to make your choice known. To let you know that the transaction is one that you've split, however, the Category field shows the word --Split-- when you select the split transaction. Take a peek at Figure 4-9 to see this for yourself.

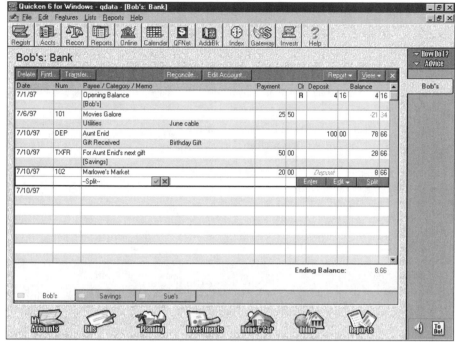

Figure 4-9:
The register
window.
Can you find
the word
Split?

Editing and deleting split categories

You can delete or change any individual line of a split category. To do this, you first display the Split Transaction Window by selecting the transaction and then clicking the check mark button, which appears in the register window's Category field after you record the transaction. After Quicken dutifully displays the Split Transaction Window, you can edit any of the fields by selecting them and then typing over their contents. You can delete any line of the split category by clicking the Edit button and choosing Delete. (If you want to delete all the lines of the split category so you can start over, choose Clear All instead.)

If you want to unsplit the transaction so you can assign it to a single category, you need to use a little trick. Click the X button that appears in the register window's Category field after you record the transaction.

Steps for splitting deposits and transfers

Wondering if you can split deposits and transfers? Well, you can. The steps for doing so work just like the steps for splitting categories for a check transaction. The basic trick — if you can call it a trick — is just to use the Split Transaction Window to list each of the category names and amounts.

Splitting hairs

Quicken assumes that any transaction amount you enter in the register window should agree with the total of the individual split transaction amounts entered in the Split Transaction Window.

If you're not sure what the split transaction amounts total is, your best bet is to NOT — I repeat, *NOT*— enter the amount on the register window. Instead, enter the individual split transaction amounts in the Split Transaction Window. When you leave the Split Transaction Window, Quicken totals your individual split amounts and then prompts you to see if the total is a payment or a deposit. Then it plugs this total into either the Payment or the Deposit field. If the total is a deposit, it plugs it into the Deposit field. If the total is a payment, it plugs it into the Payment field.

If you've already entered either a payment amount or a deposit amount but you're not sure that the split transaction amounts agree with what you entered, you can tell Quicken to adjust the Payment or Deposit amount on the register window to whatever the individual split transaction amounts total. To do this, click the Split Transaction Window Adjust button. In this case, Quicken adds up the split transaction lines and then plugs the total into the register. (This might best be called the "I don't care if it is a round hole, I want to pound this square peg into it" approach.)

By the way, Quicken shows any difference between the amount shown in the register window and the individual split transaction amounts. It shows this difference as the last split transaction line. So you'll be able to tell whether the individual splits agree with the payment or deposit amount shown in the register.

One other point I should make here is that you can mix and match categories and transfers in the Split Transaction Window. Some of the splits, for example, can be categories and some can be transfer accounts. It would be quite common to do this in a business setting (see Chapter 15 for more information).

Deleting and Voiding Transactions

You can delete and void register transactions using the Edit button's Delete Transaction and Void Transaction commands. If you've looked at the Edit button, of course, you've probably already guessed as much.

Using either command is a snap. Just highlight the transaction you want to delete or void by using the arrow keys or by clicking the mouse. Then choose the command. And that's that.

Use the Void Transaction command any time you void a check. Quicken leaves voided transactions in the register but marks them as void and erases the Payment or Deposit amount. So by using the Void Transaction command, you keep a record of voided, or canceled, transactions.

Use the Delete Transaction command if you want to remove the transaction from your register.

The Big Register Phenomenon

If you start entering a bunch of checks, deposits, and transfers into your registers, you'll shortly find yourself with registers that contain hundreds and even thousands of transactions. You can still work with one of these big registers using the tools and techniques I've talked about in the preceding paragraphs. Nevertheless, let me give you some more help for dealing with . . . (drumroll, please) . . . the big register phenomenon.

Moving through a big register

You can use the PgDn and PgUp keys to page up and down through your register, a screenful of transactions at a time. Some people call this *scrolling.* You can call it whatever you want.

You can use the Home key to move to the first transaction in a register. Just move the cursor to the first (or Date) field in the selected transaction and press Ctrl+Home.

You can use the End key to move to the last transaction in a register. Bet you can guess how this works. Move the cursor to the last (or Category) field in the selected transaction and press Ctrl+End.

Sort of a voiding bug . . .

When you mark a transaction as void, Quicken does three things. It sticks the word VOID at the very start of the Payee field, it marks the transaction as cleared, and it erases the amount in the Payment or Deposit field. So far, so good. But if you happen to later fill in the Payment or Deposit field, Quicken will use that payment or deposit amount to adjust the account balance — even though Quicken still shows the transaction as void. I keep thinking the folks at Intuit will fix this, but they haven't — at least not yet. The bottom line is that you need to make sure that you don't edit transactions after you've voided them. Otherwise, it's all too easy to foul up your account balance. I won't tell you about how I happened to learn this. . . .

Of course, you can use the vertical scrollbar along the right edge of the register window, too. Click the arrows at either end to select the next or previous transaction. Click either above or below the square scrollbar marker to page back and forth through the register. Or, if you've no qualms about dragging the mouse around, you can drag the scrollbar marker up and down the scrollbar.

Finding that darn transaction

Want to find that one check, deposit, or transfer? No problem. The Find command provides a handy way for doing just this. Here's what you do:

1. **Choose Edit↪Find & Replace↪Find from the menu bar or click the Find button in the register window.**

   Quicken, with restrained but obvious enthusiasm, displays the Quicken Find window (see Figure 4-10). You use this dialog box to describe the transaction you want to find in as much detail as possible. (Notice, by the way, that you don't click the Edit button to get to this command; you click the menu bar's Edit menu.)

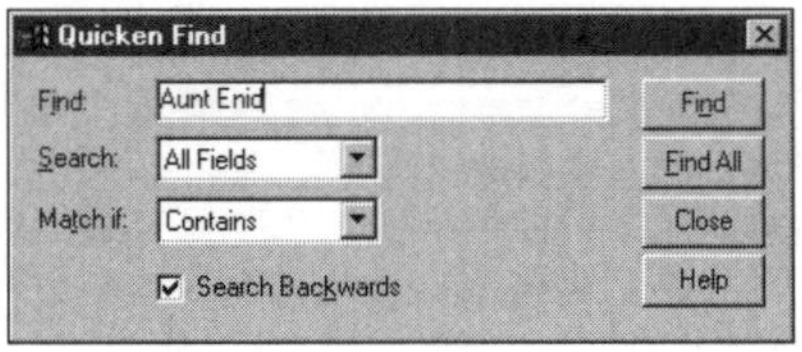

Figure 4-10:
The Quicken
Find
window.

2. **Enter the piece of text or number that identifies the transaction you want to locate.**

   Move the cursor to the Find text box. Then type the text or number. By the way, the case of the text doesn't matter. If you type **aunt**, for example, Quicken will find AUNT or Aunt.

3. **Specify which pieces, or fields, of the register transaction you want Quicken to look at.**

   Move the cursor to the Search drop-down list box arrow, drop down the list box, and then select the field Quicken should look at during the search: Amount, Cleared Status (the Clr field), Memo, Date, Category/Class (whatever is in the Category field), Check Number (what's in the Num field), or Payee. Or get truly crazy and pick the All Fields list entry so that Quicken looks both high and low.

4. **Tell Quicken whether you're using a shotgun or a rifle.**

You need to specify how closely what you stuck in the Find text box needs to match whatever you selected in the Search drop-down list box. To do so, open the Match If drop-down list box. Then select the appropriate matching rule:

- *Contains.* Select this rule if the field or fields you're searching just need to use a piece of text. If you enter **Aunt** into the Find text box and use this matching rule to search Payee fields, Quicken will find transactions that use the following payee names: Aunt Enid, Aunt Enid and Uncle Joob, Uncle Joob and Aunt Edna, and — well, you get the idea.

- *Exact.* Select this rule if the field you're searching needs to exactly match your Find text box entry. If you enter the Find text box entry as **Aunt**, for example, and you're searching Payee fields, Quicken looks for transactions where the Payee field shows Aunt — and nothing more or nothing less.

- *Starts With.* Select this rule if the field you're searching for just needs to start with what you entered in the Find text box. For example, you enter **Aunt** in the Find text box and you're searching the Payee fields. Quicken looks for transactions where the Payee field starts with the word Aunt — such as Aunt Enid or Aunt Enid and Uncle Ob. (Uncle Joob and Aunt Edna wouldn't cut the mustard in this case, though.)

- *Ends With.* Select this rule if the field you're searching for just needs to end with what you entered in the Find text box.

- *Greater.* Select this rule if the field you're searching for needs to hold a value that exceeds the number you entered in the Find text box. This makes sense, right?

- *Greater or Equal.* Select this rule if the field you're searching for needs to hold a value that either exceeds or equals the number you entered in the Find text box.

- *Less.* Select this rule if the field you're searching for needs to hold a value that is less than the number you entered in the Find text box.

- *Less or Equal.* Select this rule if the field you're searching for needs to hold a value that is less than or equal to the number you entered in the Find text box.

5. **Tell Quicken whether you want it to search forward or backward from the selected transaction.**

   Select the Search Backwards check box if you want to look backward starting from the selected transaction.

6. **Let the search begin.**

You click either the Fi_n_d or _F_ind All button to begin the search. If you click Fi_n_d, Quicken looks through the register and, if it can find one like you describe, it highlights the transaction. If you're thinking, "Well, that sounds straightforward enough," you're right. It is.

If you click _F_ind All, Quicken looks through the register and builds a list of all the transactions like the one you describe. Then it displays the list in an expanded version of the Find window (see Figure 4-11).

Quicken supplies another command that is similar to Find. The Edit menu's Find/Replace command lets you both locate and modify transactions that look like the one you describe. (To use the Find/Replace command, choose Edit⇨Find&Replace⇨Find/Replace.) For example, you might say you want to locate any transaction showing Aunt Enid as the payee so you can replace payee fields showing Aunt Enid with Great Aunt Enid. The Find/Replace command works in a fashion very similar to the Find command except that you need to describe what you want to modify in the found transactions. After you complete the initial dialog box that Quicken displays when you choose the command, Quicken displays a window listing the transactions it's found. (This window looks like the one shown in Figure 4-12.) You mark — by clicking — the transactions you want to modify and then click the Replace button.

Figure 4-11:
The Find window with a bunch of transactions that match the search criteria.

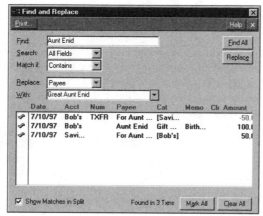

Figure 4-12:
The Find
and Replace
window.

You can't use the Find/Replace command to find and replace categories, by the way. But you can use another command, Recategorize. (To use the Recategorize command, choose the Edit⇨Find&Replace⇨Recategorize command.) For example, you might want to recategorize all your cable television payments as the Entertainment category (while earlier having categorized them as the Utilities category). When you choose the Recategorize command, Quicken displays the Recategorize window (shown in Figure 4-13). Enter the category you want to replace in the Search Category text box and the new replacement category in the Replace With text box. Next, click Find All to tell Quicken it should display a list of transactions that use the category you want to replace. Click the transactions you want to recategorize (to mark them) and then click the Replace button. I don't think you'll have any other questions about the Recategorize command or window, but if you do, click the window's Help button.

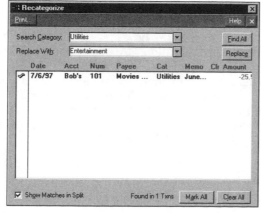

Figure 4-13:
The
Recategorize
window.

Pop-up Calendars and Calculators

Can I tell you just a couple more things? (If not, skip this section. If so, read on.) Quicken provides a pop-up calendar anytime you move the selection cursor to a Date field. To get to the calendar, you just click the button that appears at the right end of the Date field. Quicken displays a calendar for the current month (see Figure 4-14). All you have to do is select the day you want as the date. (If you want to see a calendar for a different month, click the << and >> buttons.)

Figure 4-14:
The pop-up
calendar.

Quicken also provides a pop-up calculator anytime you move the selection cursor to an Amount field. To get to the calculator, you just click the button that appears at the right end of the Amount field. Quicken displays a calculator like the one shown in Figure 4-15. This baby works like a regular, hand-held calculator. You just type the math you want to perform. Quicken displays the calculation result in the Amount field.

Figure 4-15:
The pop-up
calculator.

Do the calculator keys make sense? Here's how they work. Use the / (slash) key for division. Use the × for multiplication. Use the - (minus) and the + (plus) keys for subtraction and addition. Use the . (period) to indicate the decimal point. Use the % key to indicate that the number you just typed is a percentage and should be converted to a decimal value. Use the = (equal sign) to calculate the amount and remove the pop-up calculator. You can use the ← to remove, or clear, the last digit you entered. You can use the CE key to clear the last number entered into the calculator, and you can use the C key to clear the amount text box.

Chapter 5
Printing 101

I bet you can't guess what this chapter describes. Gee, you guessed it — how to print checks and reports.

Printing Checks

Printing checks in Quicken is, well, quick. All you need to do is collect the information you want printed on the check form, press a couple of keys, and enter the number you want Quicken to use to identify the check. Sounds simple enough, doesn't it? It is, as you'll read in the paragraphs that follow.

Collecting the check information

When you want to write a check, you collect the information needed to complete the actual check form and the information needed to record the printed check into your register. If you've worked with the Quicken register or read Chapter 4, you'll find this all rather familiar.

Make sure that the active account is the one on which you want to write checks. You can confirm this by looking at the register window's title bar. As Figure 5-1 shows, this title bar identifies both the name of the account that appears in the window (Bob's, for example) and the type of account (Bank, for example). If the account in the register window isn't the one you want, click the account's button at the bottom of the register window. Quicken then displays a register window for this account.

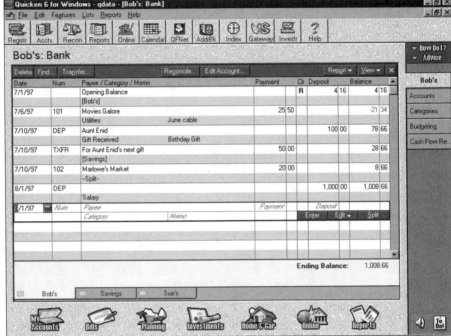

Figure 5-1:
The register
window
identifies
the account
name and
account
type.

To collect the information needed to print a check, take these steps:

1. **Display the Write Checks window.**

   Choose Features⇨Paying Bills⇨Write Checks. Figure 5-2 shows the Write Checks: Bob's window. Get ready for some excitement.

2. **Enter the check date.**

   First, use the mouse or Tab key to move the cursor to the Date field. Then type the date you'll print the check (probably today's date). Remember to type the date in a MM/DD/YY format — August 26, 1997, is entered as **8/26/97**. You don't need to enter the year if the year number that Quicken retrieves from your computer's internal system clock is correct. If you want, you can use your new friend, the pop-up calendar. You can also adjust the date by a day using + and −. You can also click the button at the end of the Date field to display a pop-up calendar. To select a date from this calendar, click one of its days.

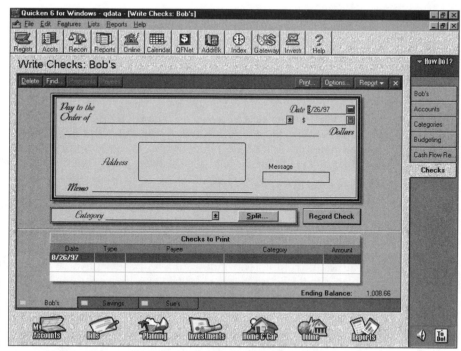

3. Enter the name of the person or business you're paying.

Move the cursor to the Pay to the Order of field and type away. For example, to write a check to me, type **Steve Nelson**. (Feel free to do this, by the way. If you send me a check, I'll even cash it as a sort of public service.) Or if you've written a check to the payee before, open the Pay to The Order of drop-down list box. When Quicken displays a list of the payees you've already used, just select one by using the mouse or the arrow keys.

4. Enter the amount of the check.

Move the cursor to the $ text box and type the amount. (If you are sending a check to me, be sure to make the amount nominal — for sure, not more than $10 or $20. . . .) When you move the cursor down to the next field, Quicken writes the amount in words on the line under the payee name and before the word Dollars.

5. Enter the payee's address.

If you plan to mail the check in a window envelope, move the cursor to the Address field. Then enter the name and address of the person or business you're paying.

Here's a little address-entry trick: You can copy the payee name from the Pay to the Order of text box to the first line of the Address field. Click the mouse or select the first line of the address field. Then press the ' (apostrophe) key.

6. (Optional) Enter a memo description of the check.

Move the cursor to the Memo field and enter a description (such as an account number or an invoice number) of why you are sending your money to this person or business. Or if you're sending someone a check because you didn't have time to go out and buy a real gift, type **Happy Birthday** in the Memo field. It's the little things that make a difference.

7. Enter the category.

Move the cursor to the Category field and type the category name for the expense you're paying with the check. If you don't remember the category name, activate the Category drop-down list box by pressing Alt+↓ or Ctrl+C. Then pick the category you want to use from the list. Figure 5-3 shows the completed window for a rent check payable to one of the nicer places in the fictional town of Pine Lake, the venerable Marlborough Apartments.

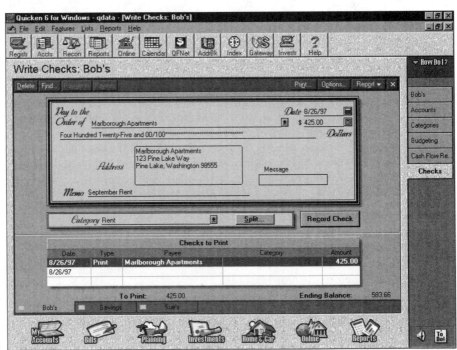

Figure 5-3:
A completed check.

Note: Pressing Alt+↓ displays just the Category drop-down list box, and pressing Ctrl+C opens the full-blown Category & Transfer List window.

You can assign a check to more than a single category by using the Split Transaction Windows dialog box. Using the Split Transaction Windows with the Write Checks window works the same way as using the Split Transaction Windows with the register window. (I described using the Split Transaction Windows with the register window in Chapter 4.) Okay. So why do I bring this up? You use the Splits Transaction Windows when a check pays more than one type of expense or is transferred to more than one account.

For example, if you're writing a check to pay your mortgage, with part of the check paying the actual mortgage and part of the check going into an escrow for property taxes, you can use the Splits Transaction Windows to describe the transaction's individual components. To split a check amount so that the amount is assigned to multiple spending categories, click the Splits button. Or press Ctrl+S. Either way, Quicken displays the Split Transaction Windows for you to indicate the categories and categorized amounts that make up the check total. If you have questions about how split transactions work, refer to Chapter 4.

8. Click Record Check.

Quicken records the check. It displays the current account balance, the ending account balance, and even adds a Checks to Print total at the bottom of the window. If you're working with a monitor that supports higher screen resolution, you'll also see a Checks to Print window that lists all the nitty-gritty about the checks you have to print (see Figure 5-3). Shoot, when you're finished with one check, Quicken even scrolls the completed check off the screen and replaces it with a new blank check that you can use to pay your next bill. It doesn't get much better than this, does it?

What if you make a mistake entering a check?

Don't worry; be happy. It's easy to fix mistakes you make if you haven't yet printed the check. If you press the PgUp and PgDn keys with the Write Checks window displayed, Quicken "pages" you through the check transactions. This way, you can display any check that you used the Write Check window to write (but have not yet printed).

When you find the incorrect check, you can fix the mistake in two ways. If you incorrectly entered some bit of check information, move the cursor to the field with the incorrect data and just type over the data.

Or if you're really mad or frustrated, you can delete the entire check by pressing Ctrl+D or by choosing Edit⇨Transaction⇨Delete. (I should fess up here and suggest that you delete the check if you accidentally entered a check to me, for example.)

Don't use this method to delete a check that you've already printed. To *void* a check that you've already printed, you must go into the register window. To display the register window, you can click the Registr icon from the iconbar. Then find the check in the register window, select the check, and void it by pressing Ctrl+V or choosing Edit⇨Transaction⇨Void. You should also write something such as **VOID** in large letters across the face of the printed check.

Printing a check you've entered

For some reason, when I get to this part of the discussion, my pulse quickens. I don't mean this as a pun. It just seems that there's something terribly serious about actually writing checks for real money. I get the same feeling whenever I mail someone cash — even if the amount is nominal.

I think the best way to lower my heart rate (and yours, if you're like me) is to just print the darn checks. To print the checks, do the following:

1. **Load the checks into your printer.**

   This process works the same way the process for loading any paper into your printer works. If you have questions about it, refer to your printer documentation. (Sorry I can't help more on this, but there are a million different printers, and I can't guess which one you have.)

2. **Choose Print Checks from the File menu (or press Ctrl+P).**

   As long as the Write Checks window is the active window, Quicken displays the Select Checks to Print dialog box, as shown in Figure 5-4. At the top of the dialog box, Quicken shows how many checks to print and the total dollar amount for those checks.

3. **Enter the first check number.**

   Move the cursor to the First Check Number box and enter the number printed on the first check form you'll print. Figure 5-4 shows 1777, for example, so the first check form is numbered 1777. To quickly increase or decrease the check numbers, use + or - from the numeric keypad.

Figure 5-4:
The Select
Checks to
Print dialog
box.

4. **Indicate which checks Quicken should print.**

   Select the All Checks option button under Print if you want Quicken to print all the checks you've entered by using the Write Checks window, which is the usual case. Select the Checks Dated Through option button under Print if you want to print all the checks through a certain date and then type that date in the text box. Or if you want to pick and choose which checks to print, select the Selected Checks option button.

5. **If you said you want to select which checks to print, click the Choose button.**

   Quicken, with some annoyance, displays the Select Checks to Print window, as shown in Figure 5-5. Initially, Quicken marks all the checks dated on or earlier than the current date by placing a check mark in the Print column. If you don't want to print a check, either leave the Print field for that check clear (unchecked) or click the field to remove the check mark. In Figure 5-5, only one check — the rent check — is marked print. When only the checks you want to print are marked to be printed, click the Done button to continue with this crazy little thing called check-printing. Quicken, happy with your progress, redisplays the Select Checks to Print dialog box (refer to Figure 5-4).

Print	Date	Payee	Category	Amount
	7/10/97	Marlowe's Market	Groceries	20.00
✓	8/26/97	Marlborough Apartments	Rent	425.00

Figure 5-5:
The Select
Checks to
Print
window.

6. **Indicate which Quicken check form you're using.**

Move the cursor to the Check Style drop-down list box, click the arrow so that the list drops down, and then select the check form you purchased: standard, voucher, or wallet checks.

7. **Tell Quicken if you're printing a partial page.**

If you're printing a partial page of forms on a laser printer, use the Checks on First Page option buttons to indicate the number of check forms on the partial page. Select the Three option button if there are three checks, the Two option button if there are two checks, or the One option button if there is one check.

8. **Indicate whether you want extra copies of the check form.**

To do so, enter the number of copies you want in the Additional Copies text box. (This text box appears only if you are set up for the voucher check style.)

If you use Quicken for business to keep accounts payable files, make copies of checks to attach to the invoices that the checks pay. Then if a vendor calls later, starts hassling you, and asks which check paid an invoice, you can easily check your accounts payable files to quickly answer that question and cover your derriere.

9. **Click OK and let the games begin.**

If you're using a partial starting page of forms, your printer may prompt you to manually feed the first page of forms. When it finishes, Quicken asks whether it printed your checks correctly (see Figure 5-6). If the check did print correctly, click OK. You're done. If the check didn't print correctly, enter the number of the first check that printed incorrectly and click OK; then repeat steps 3 through 8. Figure 5-7 shows a check made payable to Marlborough Apartments. At last, you get that landlord off your back.

Take a peek at the check shown in Figure 5-7. Basically, it's just like one you would fill out manually. The only difference is that your computer has written the check for you.

10. **Sign the printed checks.**

Then — and I guess you probably don't need my help here — put the checks in the mail.

Figure 5-6:
The Did
Check(s)
Print OK?
dialog box.

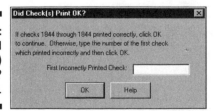

Did Check(s) Print OK?

If checks 1844 through 1844 printed correctly, click OK to continue. Otherwise, type the number of the first check which printed incorrectly and then click OK.

First Incorrectly Printed Check: [   ]

[OK]   [Help]

Oh where, oh where, do the unprinted checks go?

Unprinted checks — those you've entered using the Write Checks window but haven't yet printed — are stored in the register. To identify them as unprinted checks, Quicken sets their check numbers as Print. If you click the To Do icon at the bottom of the column of QuickTabs, Quicken displays the Quicken Reminders window, listing the things you have to do, such as checks you have to print. Just click the Print Checks button; Quicken displays the Select Checks to Print dialog box, and you're off and running. What's more, after you tell Quicken to print the unprinted checks, Quicken prints the checks in your register that have Print in the check-number field. All this is of little practical value in most instances, but it results in several interesting possibilities. For example, you can enter the checks you want to print directly into the register — all you need to do is enter the check number as Print. (Notice that you can't enter an address anywhere in the register, so this process isn't practical if you want addresses printed on your checks.) Another thing you can do is to cause a check you've printed once to print again by changing its check number from, say, 007 to Print. There aren't many good reasons you would want to change a check number. The only one I can think of is that you accidentally printed a check on plain paper and want to reprint it on a real check form.

A few words about check printing

Check printing is kind of complicated at first, isn't it?

For the record, I'm with you on this one. But you'll find that printing checks does get easier after the first few times.

Pretty soon, you'll be running instead of walking through the steps. Pretty soon, you'll just skate around things like check-form alignment problems. Pretty soon, in fact, you'll know all this stuff and never have to read "pretty soon" again.

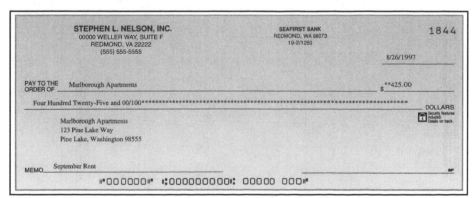

Figure 5-7:
A sample check.

What if I discover a mistake after I've printed the check?

This problem isn't as big as you might think.

If you've already mailed the check, you can't do a whole lot. You can try to get the check back (if the person you paid hasn't cashed it) and replace it with the correct check. (Good luck on this one.)

If the person has cashed the check, you can't get the check back. If you overpaid the person by writing the check for too much, you need to get the person to pay you the overpayment amount. If you underpaid the person, you need to write another check for the amount of the underpayment.

If you printed the check but haven't mailed it, void the printed check. This operation is in two parts. First, write the word **VOID** in large letters — in ink — across the face of the check form. (Use a ballpoint pen if you're using multipart forms so that the second and third parts also show as VOID.) Second, display the register window, highlight the check, and then choose Edit⇨Transaction⇨ Void from the menu bar, or press Ctrl+V. (This option marks the check as one that's been voided in the system, so Quicken does not use the voided check in calculating your account balance.)

Printing a Check Register

You can print a check register or a register for any other account, too. Click the Registr icon from the iconbar to display the register window. Then choose Print Register from the File menu.

Quicken then displays the Print Register dialog box, as shown in Figure 5-8. To print a register, you follow these magic steps:

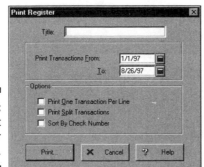

Figure 5-8:
The Print Register dialog box.

1. (Optional) Enter a register title.

If you're the sort who likes to add your own special titles to things, move the cursor to the Title text box. Then type the report title or description you want Quicken to print at the top of each and every page of the register.

2. (Optional) Limit the range of dates.

To print a register of something other than the current year-to-date transactions, use the Print Transactions From and To text boxes. This is pretty dang obvious, isn't it? You just move the cursor to the From and To text boxes and type the range of months the register should include.

3. (Optional) Tell Quicken to use a single line per transaction.

To print each check and deposit transaction on a single line, move the cursor to the Print One Transaction Per Line check box. Then press the spacebar or select the check box to mark it.

4. (Optional) Tell Quicken to print split transaction information.

To print the split transaction information — categories, memos, and amounts — move the cursor to the Print Split Transaction check box. Then press the spacebar or select the check box.

5. Tell Quicken to print transactions in check number order.

To print check and deposit transactions in check number order rather than transaction date order, move the cursor to the Sort By Check Number check box. Then press the spacebar or select the check box. (If you do print in check number order, your deposits will probably be listed before your checks because deposits usually don't have numbers.)

6. Click Print.

Quicken displays the Print dialog box (see Figure 5-9). You don't have to fool around with this dialog box. If you want to print a register pronto, just click OK. Then again, if you're the sort of person who likes to fool around with this kind of stuff, carry on with the rest of these steps.

Figure 5-9:
The Print
dialog box.

If you want to see the effect the different register-printing text boxes and check boxes have, just experiment. You can't hurt anything or anybody.

7. (Optional) Print the report to disk if you want.

To print the report to disk as a text file, select one of the following Print To option buttons:

ASCII Disk File if you want to create a text file, such as when you want to import the register into a word processing program

Tab-delimited Disk File, such as when you want to import the register into a database program (Oooh. . . . Fancy . . .)

123 (.PRN) Disk File, such as when you want to import the register into Lotus 1-2-3

If you do indicate that you want a disk file, after you click the Print button to start the ol' printing process, Quicken displays the Create Disk File dialog box as shown in Figure 5-10. This dialog box asks for the filename Quicken should create as part of printing the file to disk and the location where you want the file stored. Just enter the filename you want into — you guessed it — the File Name text box. (Use a valid DOS filename, of course.) Use the Directories and Drives list boxes to indicate where you want the file stored. Or don't do anything, and Quicken creates the file in the active Quicken directory — probably C:\QUICKENW. And what do you do with the disk file? You're on your own here. . . .

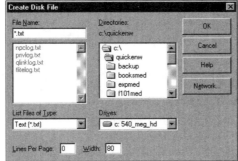

Figure 5-10:
The Create
Disk File
dialog box.

8. (Optional) Tell Quicken which pages to print.

Use the Print Range option buttons and text boxes to limit the pages Quicken prints. (See Figure 5-9.) How? Select the Pages option button, and then type the range of page numbers you want printed. That's simple enough, right?

9. (Optional) Color your world.

If you've got a color printer and want your register printed in color, select the Print in Color check box on the Print Report dialog box (see Figure 5-9). You can do this by selecting the check box.

10. (Optional) Trade speed for quality.

Or you can select the Print in Draft Mode check box to tell Quicken it should print faster and spend less time worrying about the quality of the printing job (see Figure 5-9). In other words, you can use this check box to trade print speed for print quality. Life is full of trade-offs, isn't it?

11. (Optional) Tell Quicken to scrunch the information so it fits across the page.

Use the Fit to One Page Wide check box to tell Quicken that you want its register information to fit across the width of the page (see Figure 5-9).

12. Click OK.

Now click OK one last time. Quicken finally prints the register. If you're still with me, take a look at Figure 5-11. It shows a printed register. (You get a printed register if you selected the Printer option button on the Print Report dialog box.)

Figure 5-11:
A printed
register.

		Check Register				
Bob's						Page 1
8/26/1997						
Date	Num	Transaction	Payment	C	Deposit	Balance
7/1/1997		Opening Balance cat: [Bob's]		R	4.16	4.16
7/6/1997	101	Movies Galore cat: Utilities memo: June cable	25.50			-21.34
7/10/1997	DEP	Aunt Enid cat: Gift Received memo: Birthday Gift			100.00	78.66
7/10/1997	TXFR	For Aunt Enid's next gift cat: [Savings]	50.00			28.66
7/10/1997	1845	Marlowe's Market cat: --SPLIT--	20.00			8.66
8/1/1997	DEP	 cat: Salary			1,000.00	1,008.66
8/26/1997	1844	Marlborough Apartments cat: Rent memo: September Rent	425.00			583.66

Chapter 6

Reports, Charts, and Other Cool Tools

● ●

In This Chapter

▶ Printing Quicken reports

▶ Using the Reports menu commands

▶ QuickZooming report totals

▶ Sharing information with a spreadsheet

▶ Editing and rearranging report information

▶ Creating a chart

▶ Using QuickReports and Snapshots

● ●

*Q*uicken enables you to summarize, slice, and dice register and account information in a variety of ways. This chapter describes how to use reports and produce graphs easily. This stuff is much easier to understand if you know how to print a register first. I describe this trick at the end of Chapter 5.

Creating and Printing Reports

After you know how to print checks and registers, all other printing in Quicken is easy, easy, easy.

Just the facts (of printing), ma'am

The transactions you enter in the register window and the checks you enter in the Write Checks window determine the information in a report. To print a report, just choose the Reports menu and tell Quicken which report you want to print (see Figure 6-1).

Figure 6-1:
The Reports
menu.

Quicken produces a bunch of different reports. To make sense of what might otherwise become mass confusion, Quicken arranges all its reports into four groups: Home reports, Business reports, Other reports, and Investment reports. (These sort of sound like PBS documentaries, don't they? "Tonight, Joob Taylor explores the secrets of baby-sitting in the *Home Report*.")

To see the reports in one of these groups, select the report group from the Reports menu. If you read the fast-paced and exciting Appendix A, "Quick and Dirty Windows 95," you know that those little triangles to the right of menu command names tell you that another menu follows.

Figure 6-2 shows the Home group of reports. Pretty exciting stuff so far, don't you think?

To print a Home report (or any other report, for that matter), choose the report from the appropriate menu. For example, to print the Home Cash Flow report, choose Reports⇨Home⇨Cash Flow.

Figure 6-2:
The Home
group of
reports.

Quicken displays the Create Report dialog box. This dialog box asks you to confirm your report selection and identify the range of dates the report should cover, as shown in Figure 6-3. You don't have to specify either piece of information. (Notice that the sample to the left of the report buttons shows roughly what the report you're creating looks like.)

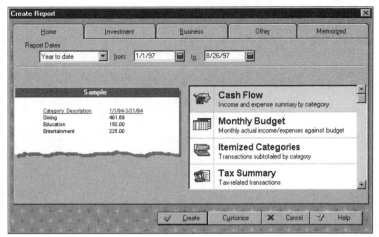

Figure 6-3:
The Create
Report
dialog box.

If you don't enter a new range of dates, Quicken assumes that you want to include transactions from the start of the current calendar year through the present date.

Notice that a report that shows account balances — such as the Home Net Worth report, the Business Balance sheet, or the Investment Portfolio report — doesn't need a range of dates because these reports show account balances as of a specific date. In these cases, if you don't enter a date, Quicken assumes that you want account balances for the current system date from your computer's internal clock.

If you select the wrong report, you can indicate that you want another report by selecting another report's button. The report buttons that appear on a tab of the Create Report dialog box match the commands of the same names listed on the Reports menu. For example, if you mark the Home tab of the Create Report dialog box, the list box shows the same reports as the Home Report submenu. Wild.

When you're ready to produce the report, click Create. Quicken then copies an on-screen version of the report to a new document window. Figure 6-4 shows an on-screen version of the Home Cash Flow report.

You can't see the entire on-screen version of a report unless your report is very small (or your screen is monstrously large). Use PgUp and PgDn to scroll up and down and use Tab and Shift+Tab to move left and right. Or if you're a mouse lover, you can click and drag various pieces of the scrollbars.

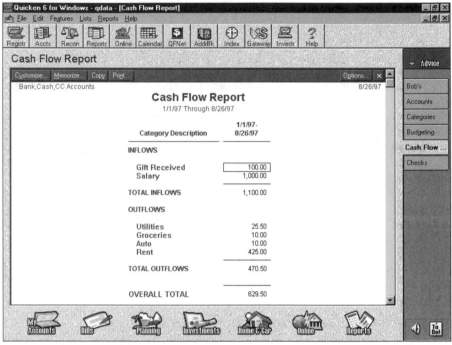

Figure 6-4:
Figure 6-4:
An on-
screen
version of
the Home
Cash Flow
report.

To print your report, click the Print button in the report window. Quicken displays the Print dialog box (see Figure 6-5).

Figure 6-5:
The Print
Report
dialog box.

To accept the given specifications — which will almost always be fine — just click OK. You'll never guess what happens next: Quicken prints the report!

When you're ready — but not before — remove the on-screen version of the report by closing the report document window. (You do so by clicking the Close button.)

Print dialog box settings

I almost forgot. The Print To option buttons let you tell Quicken where it should send the report it produces: to the printer or to a disk file. The check boxes let you control aspects of printing, and the Print Range option buttons and text boxes let you print a specific portion of the report.

I describe how these things work in Chapter 5, so I won't repeat the discussion. If you want the scoop, refer to the section about printing a check register.

Reviewing standard reports

Most of the time, you want to select one of the reports listed in the Home, Business, or Investment reports menu.

Tables 6-1, 6-2, and 6-3 describe Quicken's Home, Investment, and Business reports. (Some of these babies won't make sense unless you understand how to collect the information that goes into the report, as described in Chapters 12 and 13, and in Part IV.)

Table 6-1	Quicken's Home Reports
Report	*Description*
Cash Flow	Summarizes the money that flows into and out of an account by income and expense categories and by transfers. Cash is king, dude, so this report includes only transactions recorded in your bank, cash, and credit card accounts.
Monthly Budget	Summarizes income and expense categories and compares actual category totals to budgeted category amounts. This report includes only transactions recorded in your bank, cash, and credit card accounts. (For this report to make any sense, of course, you need to have a budget set up.)
Itemized Categories	Summarizes income and expense category totals. This report includes transactions from all your accounts.
Tax Summary	Summarizes income and expense category totals for those categories marked as tax-related. Like the Itemized Categories report, this report includes transactions from all your accounts.

(continued)

Table 6-1 *(continued)*

Report	Description
Net Worth	Lists all accounts, their balances, and the difference between the sum of the asset accounts and the sum of the liabilities accounts, which the report identifies as your net worth.
Tax Schedule	Summarizes income and expense category totals for those categories marked as tax-related and assigned to specific tax schedule lines. This report includes transactions from all accounts. (If you export Quicken information to a tax preparation package such as TurboTax, this report gets passed on to the package.)
Missing Checks	Lists all the checks you've written and flags any gaps in the check number sequence. (This report helps you identify missing checks.)
Comparison	Lets you compare category totals from two periods. You can use this report to compare January's activity with February's activity, for example. Remember: Because you are comparing two periods, you need to enter two transaction date ranges.

Table 6-2   Quicken's Investment Reports

Report	Description
Portfolio Value	Lists the current value of all securities in your investment accounts.
Investment Performance	A power-user report. This report calculates the internal rates of return delivered by each of the individual investments in your portfolio.
Capital Gains	Lists all the unrealized gains on individual investments you hold. (*Unrealized* means that the investment is worth more than what you paid for it, but because you still own the investment, your gain is unrealized. When you sell the investment, you realize the gain.)
Investment Income	Summarizes income and expense categories for transactions recorded in your investment accounts.
Investment Transactions	Lists transactions recorded for all your investment accounts.

Table 6-3	Quicken's Business Reports
Report	**Description**
P&L Statement	Summarizes income and expense category totals. This report includes transactions from all your accounts. It also helps you answer the business question, "Am I getting fairly compensated for the hassle and the risk?"
P&L Comparison	Lets you compare profit and loss by category for two periods. You can use this report to compare January's profit with February's profit.
Cash Flow	Summarizes the money received by and paid out of an account by income and expense categories and by transfers. This report includes only transactions recorded in your bank, cash, and credit card accounts.
A/P by Vendor	Summarizes unprinted checks by payee for all your bank accounts. (A/P stands for accounts *payable*.)
A/R by Customer	Summarizes uncleared transactions for all other asset accounts. (A/R stands for accounts *receivable*.)
Job/Project	Summarizes income and expense category totals with each class's information displayed in a separate column. You must be using an advanced Quicken feature called *classes* for this report to make any sense.
Payroll	Summarizes income and expense categories that begin with the word *payroll*. If you've done things right, you can use this report to prepare quarterly and annual payroll tax reports. (See Chapter 15 for the rest of the story.)
Balance Sheet	Lists all accounts, their balances, and the difference between the sum of your asset accounts and the sum of your liabilities accounts, which the report identifies as your equity. This report is almost identical to the Home Net Worth report.
Missing Checks	Lists all the checks you've written and flags any gaps in the check number sequence. This report helps you identify missing checks and is identical to the Home Missing Checks report.

(continued)

Table 6-3 (continued)

Report	Description
Comparison	Lets you compare category totals from two periods. You can use this report to compare January's activity with February's activity, for example. (Because you are comparing two periods, you must enter two transaction date ranges.) This report is identical to the Home Comparison report.

Finding the report you want

Okay, if you've just read or even skimmed the reports described in Tables 6-1, 6-2, and 6-3, you're probably a little overwhelmed. Quicken produces a bunch of different reports. How do you know which one provides the answers you want? What are you supposed to do? Sift your way through a couple dozen of these babies?

Thankfully, the answer is no. The newest version of Quicken provides something called EasyAnswers. In effect, EasyAnswers lets you identify the question that you want a report to answer. After you identify the question, Quicken produces the appropriate report. Here's how this all works:

1. Choose Reports➪EasyAnswer Reports.

Quicken displays the EasyAnswer Reports & Graphs dialog box (see Figure 6-6).

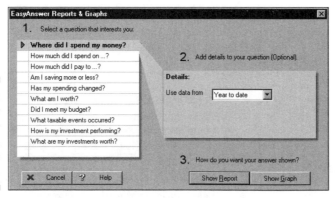

Figure 6-6:
The Easy Answer Reports & Graphs dialog box.

2. Indicate your question.

To tell Quicken what your question is, click one of the questions and then use the drop-down list boxes that accompany each question to further refine your question. For example, the "Where did I spend my money?" question lets you pick the period of time you're asking about: Last Year, Last Month, Current Year, Month To Date, and so forth.

3. Click Show Report.

Quicken produces a report that answers your questions. If you ask the question, "Where did I spend my money last year?" for example, Quicken produces a cash flow report that summarizes the previous year's income and expenses by category.

Those other reports

If you want to extract some financial tidbit, you can usually get what you want from one of the reports listed on the Home, Investment, or Business reports menus, especially if you use the EasyAnswers feature to find the right report!

However, I should tell you something else: Quicken is remarkably sophisticated in its reporting. It supplies several additional reports: Transaction, Summary, Comparison, Budget, and Account Balances.

To access these reports, choose Reports➪Other Report Family from the Create Report dialog box. Typically, you choose one of these report commands when you specify exactly what you want to appear in the report and how you want the report organized. You do so by using the Customize button.

I'm not going to describe how the Customize button works. I feel kind of bad about this because there are probably a few people out there who, late one night, will decide they want to know how to filter, sort, and customize. Of course, there are also people who will decide late some night that they want to know how to replace the transmission on a 1971 Triumph Spitfire. And I'm not describing that here, either.

If you still want to know how the Transaction, Summary, Comparison, Budget, and Account Balances reports work — or how the Customize button works — just noodle around. You can't hurt anything.

If you do play around with these items, you can save any custom report specifications that you create. To do so, click the Memorize button at the top of the report window. Quicken displays a dialog box that asks you to supply a name for your customized report. (You can also provide a default report date range.) After you name the customized report, Quicken lists it whenever you choose Reports➪Other➪Memorized Reports.

At the printing dog-and-pony show

You can do some neat things with the reports you've created. I won't spend a bunch of time talking about these things, but I do want to give you a quick rundown of some of the most valuable tricks.

Got a question about a number? Just zoom it

If you don't understand where a number in a report came from, point to it with the mouse. As you point to numbers, Quicken changes the mouse pointer to a magnifying glass marked with a *Z*. Double-click the mouse, and Quicken displays a list of all the transactions that make up that number.

This feature, called *QuickZoom,* is extremely handy for understanding the figures that appear on your reports. If you double-click the Gift Received number in the report (refer to Figure 6-4), for example, Quicken displays the QuickZoom Report shown in Figure 6-7.

Ah, yes. You remember Aunt Enid's thoughtful gift. You've got to send her that thank-you note.

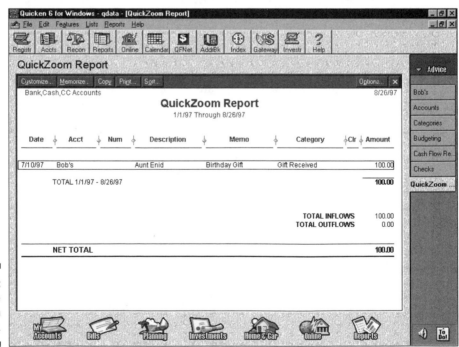

Figure 6-7:
The
QuickZoom
Report.

Sharing report data with spreadsheets

If you use a Windows spreadsheet such as Microsoft Excel, 1-2-3 for Windows, or Quattro Pro for Windows, you can copy the stuff that shows in a report window to the Clipboard. Select the information and then click the Copy button on the toolbar. Then you can start your spreadsheet program and choose Edit⇨Paste to paste the stuff from the Clipboard into your spreadsheet. This process really isn't very hard, so go ahead and try it. You might want to do this if you want to use a spreadsheet to analyze the report data.

Editing and rearranging reports

As you may have noticed, when Quicken displays the report window, it also displays a row of buttons, including (left to right) Customize, Memorize, Copy, Print, Sort, Options, and Close (refer to Figure 6-7). Earlier in the chapter, I talk about the Copy, Print, and Close buttons. So in the interest of fair play, I'll briefly discuss what the other buttons do. (Not all these buttons are available in every report document window. I don't know why, really. Maybe it's just to keep you guessing.)

You really don't need to worry about these other buttons. Read through the discussion that follows only if you're feeling comfortable, relaxed, and truly mellow. Okay?

Customizing

The Customize button works pretty much the same no matter which report shows in the document window.

When you click this button, Quicken displays a dialog box that lets you enter the report title and specify the range of dates the report should cover using text boxes. It also lets you choose from a variety of other options, too, such as which accounts to use, which transactions to use, and how the report's information should be arranged.

Memorizing

Let's say you get into this customization thing. If you do, you should know that you can save your customized reports by clicking the Memorize button. When you click Memorize, Quicken displays the Memorize Report dialog box shown in Figure 6-8. Mostly, Quicken displays this dialog box so you can give a name to your creation. If you want, you can also specify whether some special date range should always be used.

By the way, after you create a memorized report, you can reproduce it by choosing Reports⇨Other⇨Memorized Reports and then selecting the memorized report name.

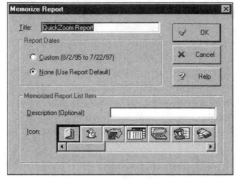

Figure 6-8:
The
Memorize
Report
dialog box.

Sorting

The Sort button displays a dialog box that looks suspiciously like the one shown in Figure 6-9. Using the Select Sort Criteria dialog box's list box, you can tell Quicken how the report's transactions should be sorted: by check number, by date, by payee, or by some other field.

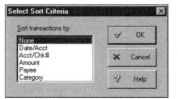

Figure 6-9:
The Select
Sort Criteria
dialog box.

What's the Options button for?

Most of the document windows that Quicken displays — the report window is just one example — also display an Options button. When you choose this button, Quicken displays a dialog box with a bunch of boxes and buttons that let you change the way the window looks or works.

If I were a really great writer — the John Grisham of computer books, for example — I might be able to whip up a riveting discussion of how the Report Options dialog box works. I'm going to do both you and my publisher a favor, however, by making a suggestion. Just play with these option settings if you're interested. You'll find it more fun and a better learning experience.

Charts Only Look Tricky

I love charts. I know that sounds goofy. But data graphics — as the snobs and academics call it — open up wonderful opportunities for communicating. And Quicken's charts are really easy to use.

To produce a Quicken chart, choose Reports⇨Graphs menu and select a graph.

After you select one of these graph commands, Quicken displays a dialog box in which you describe how you want the chart to look. If you choose the Income and Expense graphs command, for example, Quicken displays the Create Graph dialog box with the Income and Expenses button highlighted (see Figure 6-10).

Use the Graph Dates text boxes to tell Quicken which days or months of account information you want summarized in the graph.

Use the large option buttons to confirm the graph choice. These option buttons mirror the Graphs menu commands. As you probably guessed, Quicken highlights the option button for the graph you just selected from the Graphs menu, but now is your chance to change your mind.

Figure 6-10:
The Create
Graph
dialog box.

Finally, use the Customize button to display the Customize Graph dialog box. There you can pick and choose which accounts, categories, and classes you want included in the graph and tell Quicken whether you want it to show subcategories in the graph.

When you're ready to produce the graph, just command Quicken to do so. You can try saying, "Quicken, I command thee to produce a graph." Unfortunately, this command doesn't work. So your best bet is to click the Create button.

Figure 6-11 shows a picture of a bar graph of monthly income and expense figures and a pie chart that breaks down monthly spending. They're kind of cool, but you'll have much more fun looking at your own data in a picture. By the way, you can use QuickZoom on a chart to see a report that describes the data being plotted.

The other graph types work basically the same way. The Budget Variance Graph depicts your actual and planned spending and income in bar charts. The Net Worth Graph shows your total assets, total liabilities, and net worth by month in a bar graph. The Investment Graph displays a bar graph showing total portfolio and individual securities values by month. (If you're not working with Quicken's investments, of course, this last description sounds like gibberish. So you'll want to peruse Chapters 12 and 13 first.)

You can memorize customized graphs the same way you memorize customized reports. Just click the Memorize button at the top of the Graph window. Then, when Quicken prompts you, give the graph a name. To later reuse the graph, choose Reports⇨Graphs⇨Memorized Graphs, select the memorized graph from the list that Quicken displays, and click OK.

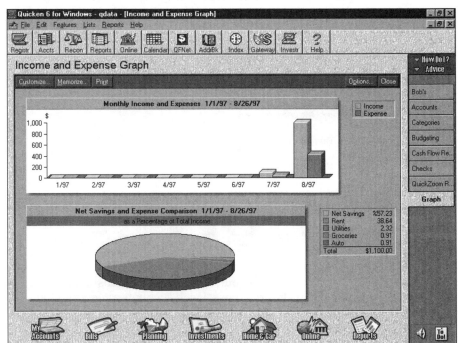

Figure 6-11:
The monthly Income and Expense Graph.

QuickReports and Snapshots: Last but Not Least

Before I forget, I need to tell you about two other variants of Quicken's reporting feature: QuickReports and Snapshots. Let's talk about QuickReports first. Quicken supplies a quick-and-dirty report called, cleverly enough, a QuickReport. If you're working with the register, you can produce a quick report that summarizes the things such as the checks written to a particular payee or the transactions assigned to a specific income or expense category. To produce a QuickReport, first move the cursor to the field you want to summarize in the report. Then click the Report button at the top of the register window. The report shown in Figure 6-12, for example, is a QuickReport summarizing all the transactions that use Aunt Enid as the payee. (Only one transaction is shown.)

Snapshots resemble QuickReports in that they're really easy to produce. All you do is choose Reports⇨Snapshots. Quicken displays a clever little report that summarizes some interesting financial tidbits — such as your most expensive spending categories or the categories that are most out-of-line considering your budget. The Snapshot reports are all really colorful because they use lots of graphics. So rather than showing you some bleak, black-and-white version of them here, how about if you just try Snapshots right now?

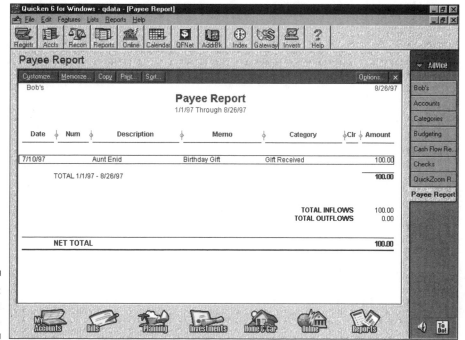

Figure 6-12:
Here's a
QuickReport.

Chapter 7
A Matter of Balance

. . . .

In This Chapter

▶ Selecting the account you want to balance

▶ Telling Quicken to balance an account

▶ Giving Quicken the bank statement balance

▶ Entering monthly service charges and interest income

▶ Marking account transactions as cleared or uncleared

▶ Verifying that the account difference is explained by uncleared transactions

▶ Ten things you should do if your account doesn't balance

. . . .

1 want to start this chapter with an important point: Balancing a bank account in Quicken is easy and quick.

I'm not just trying to get you pumped up about an otherwise painfully boring topic. I don't think balancing a bank account is any more exciting than you do. (At the Nelson house, we never answer the "What should we do tonight?" question by saying, "Hey, let's balance an account.")

My point is this: Because bank account balancing can be tedious and boring, use Quicken to speed up the drudgery.

Selecting the Account You Want to Balance

This step is easy. And you probably already know how to do it, too.

Click the Accts icon from the iconbar or choose Lists⇨Account. Quicken displays the Account List window (see Figure 7-1).

Next, select the account that you want to balance. Use the arrow keys to select the account and then press Enter. Or, if you have a mouse, double-click the account. Quicken displays the register window, which lists information about the account.

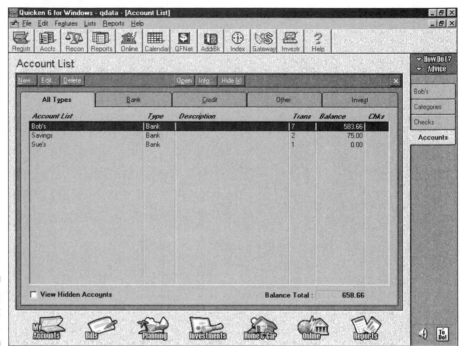

Figure 7-1:
The Account
List window.

Balancing a Bank Account

As I said, balancing a bank account is remarkably easy. In fact, I'll go so far as to say that if you have any problems, they'll stem from . . . well, sloppy record-keeping that preceded your use of Quicken.

Enough of this blather; let's get started.

Telling Quicken, "Hey, man, I want to balance this account"

To tell Quicken that you want to *balance,* or *reconcile,* your account records with the bank's records, click the Recon icon from the iconbar, choose Features⬄Banking⬄Reconcile, or click the Reconcile button. Quicken displays the Reconcile Bank Statement dialog box, as shown in Figure 7-2.

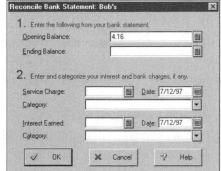

Figure 7-2:
The
Reconcile
Bank
Statement
dialog box.

Giving Quicken the bank's information

As you probably know, in a reconciliation you compare your records of a bank account with the bank's records of the same account. You should be able to explain any difference between the two accounts — usually by pointing to checks that you've written but that haven't cleared. (Sometimes deposits fall into the same category; you've recorded a deposit and mailed it, but the bank hasn't yet credited your account.)

The first step, then, is to supply Quicken with the bank's account information. You get this information from your monthly statement. Supply Quicken with the figures it needs as follows:

1. **Verify the Bank Statement Opening Balance.**

   Quicken displays a figure in the Bank Statement Opening Balance text box. If this figure isn't correct, replace it with the correct figure. To do so, move the cursor to the text box and type over the given figure. (If this is the first time you've reconciled, Quicken gets this opening balance figure from your starting account balance. If you've reconciled before, Quicken uses the Bank Statement Ending Balance that you specified the last time you reconciled as the Bank Statement Opening Balance.)

2. **Enter the Bank Statement Ending Balance.**

   Move the cursor to the Bank Statement Ending Balance text box and enter the ending, or closing, balance shown on your bank statement.

3. **Enter the bank's service charge.**

   If your bank statement shows a service charge and you haven't already entered it, move the cursor to the Service Charge text box and type the amount (for example, type $4.56 as **4.56**).

4. **Enter a transaction date for the service charge transaction.**

   Quicken supplies the current system date from your computer's internal clock as the default service charge date. If this date isn't correct, enter the correct one.

   Remember that you can adjust a date one day at a time by using either the + or – key.

5. **Assign the bank's service charge to a category.**

   Enter the expense category to which you assign bank service charges in the first Category text box — the one beneath the Service Charge text box. If you're using standard home categories, this category is Bank Charge. If you want to select a category from the Category & Transfer List window, open the drop-down list box by clicking the down arrow, then select the category by using the arrow keys, and press Enter.

6. **Enter the account's interest income.**

   If the account earned interest for the month and you haven't already entered this figure, type an amount in the Interest Earned text box (for example, type $.17 as **.17**).

7. **Enter a transaction date for the interest income transaction.**

   You already know how to enter dates. I won't bore you by explaining it again (but see Step 4 if you're having trouble).

8. **Assign the interest to a category.**

   Enter the category to which the account's interest should be assigned in the second Category text box. If you're using the standard home category list, this category is probably Interest Inc. To select a category from the Category & Transfer List window, open the drop-down list box by clicking the down arrow, then select the category, and press Enter.

9. **Tell Quicken that the reconciliation is complete.**

   To do so, just click OK.

Explaining the difference between your records and the banks

Next, Quicken compares your register's account balance with the bank statement's ending account balance. Then it builds a list of checks and deposits that your register shows but that haven't yet *cleared* (haven't been recorded by the bank). Figure 7-3 shows the window Quicken displays to provide you with this information.

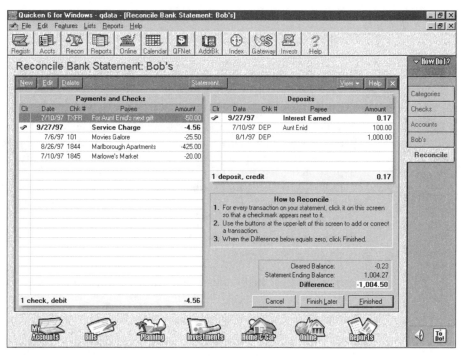

Figure 7-3:
The
Reconcile
Bank
Statement
window.

As Figure 7-3 shows, the Reconcile Bank Statement window is basically just two lists — one of account withdrawals and one of account deposits. The window also displays some extra information at the bottom of the screen: the Cleared Balance (which is your account balance including only those transactions that you or Quicken have marked as cleared), the Bank Ending Balance, the Difference between these two figures, and the number of checks and deposits that you or Quicken have marked as cleared.

If you don't like the order in which withdrawals and deposits are arranged, you can change it. Click the View button and choose Sort by Date, and Quicken reorders the transactions by date.

Marking cleared checks and deposits

You need to tell Quicken which deposits and checks have cleared at the bank. (Refer to your bank statement for this information.)

1. Identify the first deposit that has cleared.

You know how to do so, I'm sure. Just leaf through the bank statement and find the first deposit listed.

2. **Mark the first cleared deposit as cleared.**

    Scroll through the transactions listed in the Reconcile Bank Statement window, find the deposit, select it, and then mark it by clicking the Mark button or pressing the spacebar. Quicken places a check mark in front of the deposit to mark it as cleared and updates the cleared statement balance.

3. **Record any cleared but missing deposits.**

    If you can't find a deposit, you haven't entered it into the Quicken register yet. I can only guess why you haven't entered it. Maybe you just forgot, for example. In any event, return to the Quicken register and then enter the deposit in the register in the usual way — but enter a c (for "cleared") in the Clr column. This mark identifies the deposit as one that's already cleared at the bank. To return to the Reconcile Bank Statement window, click the Recon icon or click the Reconcile QuickTab.

4. **Repeat Steps 1, 2, and 3 for all deposits listed on the bank statement.**

5. **Identify the first check that has cleared.**

    No sweat, right? Just find the first check or withdrawal listed on the bank statement.

6. **Mark the first cleared check as cleared.**

    Scroll through the transactions listed in the Reconcile Bank Statement window, find the first check, select it, and then mark it by clicking the Mark button or pressing the spacebar. Quicken inserts a check mark to label this transaction as cleared and updates the cleared statement balance.

7. **Record any missing but cleared checks.**

    If you can't find a check or withdrawal — guess what? — you haven't entered it in the Quicken register yet. Display the Quicken register by clicking the Edit button. Then enter the check or withdrawal in the register. Be sure to enter a c (for "cleared") in the Clr column to identify this check or withdrawal as one that's already cleared at the bank. To return to the Reconcile Bank Account window, click the Close button. Or reactivate the Reconcile Bank Statement window by clicking its QuickTab.

8. **Repeat Steps 5, 6, and 7 for withdrawals listed on the bank statement.**

By the way, these steps don't take very long. It takes me about two minutes to reconcile my account each month. And I'm not joking or exaggerating. By two minutes, I really mean two minutes.

Does the difference equal zero?

After you mark all the cleared checks and deposits, the difference between the cleared balance for the account and the bank statement's ending balance should equal zero. Notice that I said, "should," not "will." Figure 7-4 shows a Reconcile Bank Statement window in which everything is hunky-dory and life is grand.

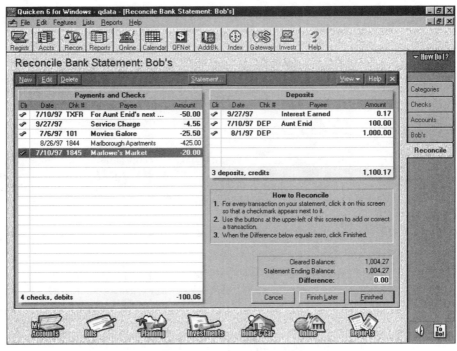

Figure 7-4:
The
Reconcile
Bank
Statement
window.

If the difference does equal zero, you're done. Just click the Finished button to tell Quicken that you're done. Quicken displays a congratulatory message telling you how proud it is of you, and then it asks whether you want to print a Reconciliation report.

As part of the finishing-up process, Quicken changes all the cs to Rs. There's no great magic in this transformation. Quicken makes the change to identify the transactions that have already been reconciled.

Can't decide whether to print the Reconciliation report? Unless you're a business bookkeeper or an accountant reconciling a bank account for someone else — your employer or a client, for example — you don't need to print the Reconciliation report. All printing does is prove that you reconciled the account. (Basically, this proof is the reason you should print the report if you *are* a bookkeeper or an accountant — the person for whom you're reconciling the account will know that you did your job and has a piece of paper to come back to later if there are questions.)

If the difference doesn't equal zero, you've got a problem. If you click Finished, Quicken provides some cursory explanations as to why your account doesn't balance (via a dialog box similar to that shown in Figure 7-5). This box tells you that you can force the two amounts to agree by clicking the Adjust button.

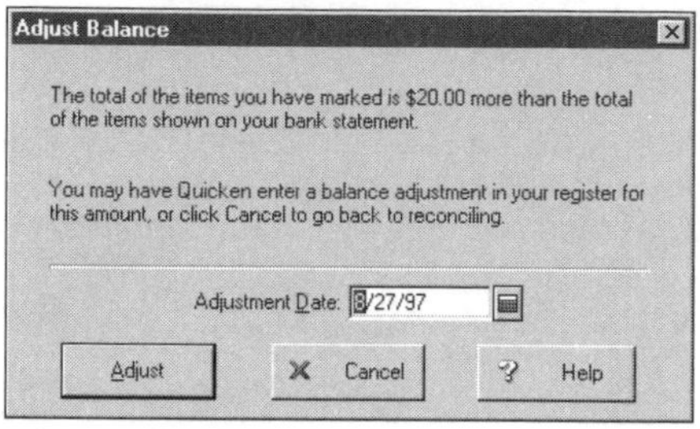

Figure 7-5:
The Adjust
Balance
dialog box.

Forcing the two amounts to agree isn't a very good idea. To do so, Quicken adds a cleared and reconciled transaction equal to the difference. (I talk about this transaction a little later in the chapter.)

If you want to reconcile later without saving your unfinished work, click Finish Later in the Reconcile Bank Statement window.

If you press Esc with the Reconcile Bank Statement window open, Quicken asks whether you want to save the work or quit without saving it.

If you tell Quicken you want to save your work, Quicken leaves your reconciliation work basically half done. The transactions that you marked as cleared still show a c in the Clr field. And you still have an explainable difference between the bank statement and your register. (You can also throw up your hands, give up, and tell Quicken you don't want to save your work. In this case, you need to start over next time.)

Either way, postponing a reconciliation and not choosing to adjust the bank account balance is usually the best approach. It enables you to locate and correct problems. (I give you some ideas about how to do so in the next section.) Then you can restart the reconciliation and finish your work. (You restart a reconciliation the same way that you originate one.)

Ten Things You Should Do If Your Account Doesn't Balance

Let me give you some suggestions for reconciling an account if you're having problems. If you're sitting in front of your computer wringing your hands, try the following tips.

Are you working with the right account?

Sounds dumb, doesn't it? If you have a bunch of different bank accounts, however, it's darn easy to end up in the wrong account. So go ahead and confirm, for example, that you're trying to reconcile your checking account at Mammoth International Bank using the Mammoth International checking account statement.

Look for transactions that the bank has recorded but you haven't

Go through your bank statement and make sure that you have recorded every transaction that your bank has recorded. Cash machine withdrawals, special fees or service charges (such as for checks or your safety deposit box), automatic withdrawals, direct deposits, and so on are easily overlooked.

If the difference is positive — that is, the bank thinks you have less money than you think you should — you may be missing a withdrawal transaction. If the difference is negative, you may be missing a deposit transaction.

Look for reversed transactions

Here's a tricky one. If you accidentally enter a transaction backwards — a deposit as a withdrawal or a withdrawal as a deposit — your account won't balance. And the error can be difficult to find. The Reconcile Bank Statement window shows all the correct transactions, but a transaction amount appears positive when it should be negative or negative when it should be positive. The check you wrote to Mrs. Travis for your son's piano lessons appears as a positive number instead of a negative number, for example.

Look for a transaction that's equal to half the difference

One handy way to find the transaction that you entered backwards — if there's only one — is to look for a transaction that's equal to half the irreconcilable difference. For example, if the difference is $200, you may have entered a $100 deposit as a withdrawal or a $100 withdrawal as a check.

I don't want to beat a dead horse, but the sign (that is, positive or negative) of the difference should help you find the problem. If the difference is positive — the bank thinks you have less money than your register indicates — you may have mistakenly entered a withdrawal as a deposit. If the difference is negative — the bank thinks you have more money than your register says — you may be missing a deposit transaction.

Look for a transaction that's equal to the difference

While I'm on the subject of explaining the difference by looking at individual transactions, let me make an obvious point. If the difference between the bank's records and yours equals one of the transactions listed in your register, you may have incorrectly marked the transaction as cleared or incorrectly left the transaction marked as uncleared.

I don't know. Maybe that was too obvious.

Check for transposed numbers

Transposed numbers occur when you flip-flop two digits in a number. For example, you enter $45.89 as $48.59.

These turkeys always cause accountants and bookkeepers headaches. If you look at the numbers, it's often difficult to detect an error because the digits are the same. For example, when comparing a check amount of $45.89 in your register with a check for $48.59 shown on your bank statement, both check amounts show the same digits: 4, 5, 8, and 9. They just show them in different orders.

Transposed numbers are tough to find, but here's a trick you can try. Divide the difference shown on the Reconcile Bank Statement window by nine. If the result is an even number of dollars or cents, there's a good chance that there's a transposed number somewhere.

Have someone else look over your work

This idea may seem pretty obvious, but it amazes me how often a second pair of eyes can find something that you've been overlooking.

If you're using Quicken at home, ask your spouse. If you're using Quicken at work, ask the owner or one of your coworkers (preferably that one person who always seems to have way too much free time).

Look out for multiple errors

By the way, if you find an error using this laundry list and there's still a difference, it's a good idea to start checking at the top of the list again. You may, for example, discover — after you find a transposed number — that you entered another transaction backwards or incorrectly cleared or uncleared a transaction.

Try again next month (and maybe the month after that)

If the difference isn't huge in relation to the size of your bank account, you may want to wait until next month and attempt to reconcile your account again.

Before my carefree attitude puts you in a panic, consider the following example. You reconcile your account in January, and the difference is $24.02. Then you reconcile the account in February, and the difference is $24.02. Then you reconcile the account in March, and, surprise, surprise, the difference is still $24.02.

What's going on here? Well, your starting account balance was probably off by $24.02. (The more months you try to reconcile your account and find that you're always mysteriously $24.02 off, the more likely it is that this type of error is to blame.)

After the second or third month, I think it's pretty reasonable to tell Quicken that it should enter an adjusting transaction for $24.02 so that your account balances. (In my opinion, this is the only circumstance that merits your adjusting an account to match the bank's figure.)

By the way, if you've successfully reconciled your account with Quicken before, your work may not be at fault. The mistake could be (drum roll, please) the bank's! And in this case, there's something else you should do. . . .

Get in your car, drive to the bank, and beg for help

As an alternative to the preceding idea — which supposes that the bank's statement is correct and that your records are incorrect — I propose this idea: Ask the bank to help you reconcile the account. Hint that you think the mistake is probably theirs. Smile a great deal. And one other thing — be sure to ask about whatever product they're currently advertising in the lobby. (This behavior will encourage them to think that you're interested in that 180-month certificate of deposit, and they'll be extra nice to you.)

In general, the bank's record-keeping is usually pretty darn good. I've never had a problem as a business banking client or as an individual. (I've also been lucky enough to deal with big, well-run banks.)

Nevertheless, it's quite possible that your bank has made a mistake, so ask them to help you. Be sure to have them explain any transactions that you've learned about only by seeing them on your bank statement.

Chapter 8

Housekeeping for Quicken

● ●

In This Chapter

▶ Formatting your floppy disks

▶ Backing up your Quicken data

▶ Knowing when and how often to back up your data

▶ Knowing what to do if you lose your Quicken data

▶ Creating and working with more than one set of Quicken data

▶ Setting up a new file password

▶ Changing a file password

● ●

*O*kay, chasing dust bunnies isn't something you need to worry about in Quicken, but you do have little housekeeping tasks to take care of. This chapter describes these chores and how to get them done right with minimal hassle.

Formatting Floppy Disks

You need someplace safe to store the financial information you collect with Quicken — someplace in addition to your computer's hard disk. No, I'm not talking about under your mattress nor of that secret place in the attic. I'm talking about floppy disks. So, you, my friend, need to know how to format a floppy disk.

A floppy disk needs to be formatted before you can store information on it. You can buy preformatted floppy disks. (The package says "Formatted Disks.") You also can buy unformatted floppy disks. The only trick is to make sure that you buy disks that match your drive in terms of density (low or high) and size (5 $\frac{1}{4}$ inches square or 3 $\frac{1}{2}$ inches square).

Size is easy to determine: Just get a ruler and measure one of the disks you're using. The disk is either 5 $\frac{1}{4}$ inches wide or 3 $\frac{1}{2}$ inches wide. Simple, huh?

Density is a little trickier because you can use both low- and high-density disks in a high-density drive. If you don't know the density of your drive, I suggest that you find the paperwork you got when you (or whoever) bought the computer. The paperwork should tell you whether the drive is high-density (by using the code HD or by giving you the amount of storage space that you have — 1.2MB on a 5^1/$_4$-inch floppy or 1.44MB on a 3 ^{1}/$_2$-inch floppy). You can also scrounge around to see whether you've been using low-density or high-density floppy disks. High-density floppy disks often have the HD secret code on them. Low-density disks, however, use the DS/DD secret code or give the amount of storage space — 360K on a 5 ^{1}/$_4$-inch floppy or 720K on a 3 ^{1}/$_2$-inch floppy.

Anyway, after you figure out the density and size thing, it's time to format the disk. Just follow these steps:

1. **Stuff a floppy disk of the right size and density into the correct floppy disk drive.**

   Start Windows Explorer and then right-click the floppy drive icon. To do this, click the Start button. Then choose Programs⇨Windows Explorer.

2. **Choose the For̲mat command from the menu that Windows 95 displays.**

   Windows Explorer displays the Format dialog box (as shown in Figure 8-1).

Figure 8-1:
The Format
dialog box.

3. **Use the Ca̲pacity drop-down list box to indicate the floppy disk density.**

4. **Click S̲tart.**

   Windows Explorer goes off and formats the disk. Next, you see a message that tells you the format is complete (see Figure 8-2).

5. **Click Close.**

6. **Remove the Format dialog box by clicking C̲lose.**

7. **Choose File̲⇨C̲lose to exit Windows Explorer.**

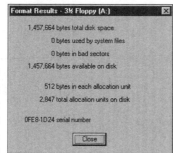

Figure 8-2:
The Format
Results
dialog box.

There's more to this formatting business than I've described here. If you want more information and you're adventurous, flip open the Windows user guide that came with your computer and look up the Format command in the index. If you're not adventurous, you should probably be buying preformatted floppy disks.

Note for Windows 3.1 Users: If you're using Windows 3.1, you won't have the Windows Explorer. And that means, of course, that you won't be able to use it to format your disks. So what do you do? The simplest thing for anybody to do, of course, is just buy preformatted disks. But you already know that, right? Right. Okay, the next simplest thing to do is use the File Manager. Start the File Manager by starting Windows 3.1 and then double-clicking on the Main program group. Then, when Program Manager displays the Main program group, double-click the File Manager program item. When File Manager appears, insert your floppy disk and then choose Disk➪Format Disk.

Backing Up Is Hard to Do

You should back up the files that Quicken uses to store your financial records. But you need to know how to back up before you can back up. Got it? So let's get to it. . . .

Backing up the quick and dirty way

You're busy. You don't have time to fool around. You just want to do a passable job backing up files. Sound like your situation? Then follow these steps:

1. Insert a blank, formatted floppy disk into your floppy drive.

If you have two floppy drives, the top one is the drive A and the bottom one is the drive B. I'm going out on a limb here and assuming you're using the ol' drive A.

2. **Verify that the file you want to back up is active.**

   Display the register window and make sure that it displays one of the accounts in the file you want to back up. You can do this by clicking the register's QuickTab. (If you don't remember setting up multiple files, don't worry. You probably have only one file — the usual case.)

3. **Start the backup operation.**

   Choose File⇨Backup from the menu bar. Quicken displays the Select Backup Drive dialog box, as shown in Figure 8-3.

Figure 8-3:
The Select
Backup
Drive dialog
box.

4. **Identify the backup floppy drive.**

   If necessary, open the Backup Drive drop-down list box and select the letter of the floppy drive you stuffed a disk into. If you've followed my sage advice, this is drive A.

5. **(Optional) Select the Select From List option button only if the file you're currently working on isn't the file you want to back up.**

   (If you want to back up the current file you're working on, you can skip to Step 7.)

   Okay, here's the deal. In Quicken, you can have more than one set of financial records, and each set of records gets stored in its own file. If you've been following along in this book, however, you probably have only one set of financial records so far. (In fact, I'd bet my neighbor's dog's life on it.) But if, by chance, you've used File⇨New to create an entirely new file, you need to indicate which file you want to back up.

6. **(Optional) Tell Quicken which file you want to back up — only if you have done Step 5.**

   After you select the Select From List option button and click OK, or press Enter, Quicken displays the Back Up Quicken File dialog box (shown in Figure 8-4) for you to select the file that should be backed up. Just select the file so that it appears in the File name text box. Figure 8-4 displays two files: QDATA.QDB, which you should have created, and BUSINESS.QDB, which I created to illustrate this step.

Figure 8-4:
The Back
Up Quicken
File dialog
box.

7. **Click OK.**

You see a message on-screen that says, "Aye, Cap'n, I'm working just as fast as I can" (or something to that effect). Then you see a message that says the backup is finished. Don't worry. You'll never see a message that says, "She's starting to break up, Cap'n. She can't take warp 9 much longer." You will see a warning message if the file you want to back up is too large. In this case, you'll need to shrink it. (Later in the chapter, I describe how you do this.)

So when should you back up?

Sure, I can give you some tricky, technical examples of fancy backup strategies, but they have no point here. You want to know the basics, right? So here's what I do to back up my files. I back up every month after I reconcile. Then I stick the floppy disk in my briefcase, so if something terrible happens at home, I don't lose both my computer and the backup disk with the data.

I admit that there are a few problems with my strategy, however. For example, because I'm backing up only once a month, I may have to reenter as much as a month's worth of data if the computer crashes toward the end of the month. In my case, I wouldn't lose all that much work. However, if you're someone with really heavy transaction volumes — if you write hundreds of checks a month, for example — you may want to back up more frequently than this, such as once a week.

A second problem with my strategy is only remotely possible but is still worth mentioning. If something bad does happen to the Quicken files stored on my computer's hard disk *and* the files stored on the backup floppy disk, I'll be up the proverbial creek without a paddle. I should also note that a floppy disk is far more likely to fail than a hard drive. If this worst-case scenario actually occurs, I'll need to start over from scratch from the beginning of the year. To prevent this scenario from happening, some people — who are religiously careful — make backups of their backups to reduce the chance of this mishap.

By the way, Quicken periodically prompts you to back up when you try to exit. (You'll see a message that basically says, "Friend, it would be a darn good idea for you to back up.") You can, of course, choose to ignore this message. Or you can take Quicken's advice and do the backup thing as described earlier.

You know what else? Here's a secret feature of Quicken: Quicken adds a subdirectory to the Quicken directory named Backup. And it'll stick a backup copy of your files in this directory every few days. (Sorry to be vague on this point, but it's hard to be specific and concrete when it comes to undocumented features.) More on this later, in the section entitled "Losing your Quicken data when you haven't backed up."

Losing your Quicken data after you have backed up

What happens if you lose all your Quicken data? First of all, I encourage you to feel smug. Get a cup of coffee. Lean back in your chair. Gloat for a couple of minutes. You, my friend, will have no problem. You have followed instructions.

After you've sufficiently gloated, carefully do the following to reinstate your Quicken data on the computer:

1. **Get your backup floppy disk.**

   Find the backup disk you created and carefully insert it into one of your disk drives. (If you can't find the backup disk, forget what I said about feeling smug — stop gloating and skip to the next section.)

2. **Start Quicken.**

   You already know how to do this, right? By the way, if the disaster that caused you to lose your data also trashed other parts of your computer, you may need to reinstall Quicken. Shoot. I suppose it's possible you may even need to reinstall Windows 95.

3. **Choose File⇨Restore from the menu.**

   Guess what? Quicken displays the Restore Quicken File dialog box. Figure 8-5 shows you what this box looks like.

   Quicken looks at the floppy disk in drive A and displays a list of the files stored on the floppy disk, as shown in Figure 8-5. (If you have only one Quicken file on the disk — the usual case — only one file is listed.) If your computer has another floppy disk in it and it's this other floppy disk that has the backup copy of the file, use the Look in drop-down list box to select the other floppy drive.

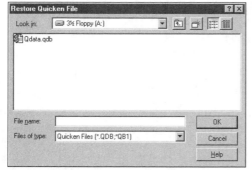

Figure 8-5:
The Restore
Quicken File
dialog box.

4. **Select the file you want to restore and click OK.**

   Use the arrow keys or the mouse to select the file you want to restore.

   If the file you select is the one Quicken used last, the program displays a message asking if it's okay to overwrite, or replace, the open file with the file stored on the floppy disk.

   When you restore a file, you replace the current, in-memory version of the file with the backup version stored on the floppy disk. Don't restore a file for fun. Don't restore a file for entertainment. Restore a file only if the current version is trashed and you want to start over by using the version stored on the backup floppy disk.

5. **Click OK.**

   Quicken replaces the file it's currently using with the one from the backup floppy disk. After it finishes, Quicken displays a message telling you that it has restored the file. You're almost done.

6. **Update the accounts' registers as necessary.**

   Using the register windows for each of the accounts in a file, reenter each of the transactions you recorded since you created the backup. Be sure that you update your accounts because you've almost certainly entered transactions since the last time you backed up.

   Just to be on the safe side, you should back up the file after you complete this process. It's probably a good idea to use a new floppy disk. I have heard that lightning never strikes the same place twice, but I'm not sure that the old saying is true. If you have hard disk problems or another recurring problem, whatever fouled up your file this time may rear its ugly head again — and soon.

Losing your Quicken data when you haven't backed up

What do you do if you haven't backed up your files in a while and you lose all the data in your Quicken files? Okay. Stay calm. It's just possible that all is not lost.

The first thing you can try is restoring from Quicken's backup directory. To do this, you follow the same file restoration steps I covered in the preceding section with one minor exception. When you get to the Restore Quicken File dialog box, you will use the Look in list box to indicate that you want to see the backup files in the BACKUP folder of the QUICKENW folder. As long as you followed Quicken's default installation suggestions, you can probably do this by selecting drive C from the Look in list box and then selecting the QUICKENW directory and then the BACKUP folder from the folder list box.

At this point, you'll probably see a list of files with names similar to the file you lost. If the file you lost had the name QDATA, for example, you may see two files named QDATA1 and QDATA2. Select the newest file, which will be the one with the "1" suffix, as in QDATA1; then click OK. Quicken will use the file to restore the current file. As alluded to earlier, this may just work. And if it does, you should feel very lucky. Very lucky indeed.

Okay. So let's say that you've tried the approach described in the preceding paragraph. Let's say it didn't work. What next?

All you have to do is reenter all the transactions for the entire year. Yeah. I know. It's a bummer. This method isn't quick, and it isn't pretty, but it works.

If you have copies of the registers, of course, you can use these as your information source to reenter the information in your files. If you don't have copies of the registers, you need to use your bank statements and any of the other paper financial records you have.

Files, Files, and More Files

As part of setting up Quicken, you create what Quicken calls a *file,* a place where all your accounts get stored (bank accounts, credit card accounts, investment accounts, and so on).

You can have more than one Quicken file at any time. In fact, it is wise to keep personal financial records separate from business financial records. You can use Quicken to create two files: a personal account and a business account.

In the old days, Quicken referred to personal account and business account files as *account groups.* I mention this fact for the benefit of those readers who are history buffs and, therefore, love to fill their heads with boring bits of technology trivia.

Using multiple files does have a little drawback, however. You can't easily record, in one fell swoop, account transfer transactions between accounts in different files. You need to record the transaction twice — once in the *source account,* the file where the transaction originates, and again in the *destination account,* the file where the transaction is being transferred to.

If the two accounts involved in a transfer are in the same file, all you have to do is enter the account name in the Category text box. Quicken then records the transfer in the other account for you.

Setting up a new file

To set up a new file so that you can create accounts in it, just follow these steps:

1. **Choose File⇨New from the menu bar.**

   Quicken displays the Creating new file: Are you sure? dialog box, as shown in Figure 8-6.

Figure 8-6:
The
Creating
new file: Are
you sure?
dialog box.

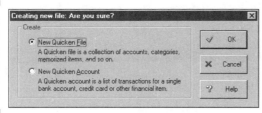

2. **Select the New Quicken File option button and then click OK or press Enter.**

   Quicken displays the Create Quicken File dialog box, as shown in Figure 8-7.

3. **Enter a name for the Quicken file.**

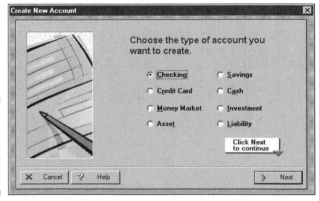

| Create Quicken File | ? ✕ |
| Save in: | 🖳 Quickenw ▼ 🗈 🗂 🏢 🏢 |

📁 Backup 📁 Inet 📁 Qw6beta
📁 Booksmed 📁 Mffdata 📁 Sample
📁 Expmed 📁 Netscape 📁 Sounds
📁 F101med 📁 Oli 📁 Toursbmp
📁 Guidemed 📁 Qfcbmp 📄 Qdata.qdb
📁 li 📁 Qw5files

Figure 8-7:
The Create
Quicken File
dialog box.

File name:	[ ]	OK
Save as type:	Quicken Files (*.QDB) ▼	Cancel
Categories...		Help

With the cursor positioned on the File name text box, type some meaning-ful combination of up to eight letters and numbers. You don't need to enter a file extension because Quicken supplies the correct file extension, QDB, for you.

Note: You can use the symbol characters on your keyboard, but this does get a little tricky. If you must use symbol characters in the filename, refer to the user documentation for Quicken.

4. Use the default file location.

Accept Quicken's suggestion to store the file in the directory called QUICKENW because there is no good reason to put it in some other file location.

5. Click OK.

Quicken displays the Create New Account dialog box, as shown in Figure 8-8.

6. Select one of the appropriate account option buttons.

| Create New Account | ✕ |

Choose the type of account you want to create.

⦿ Checking   ◯ Savings

◯ Credit Card   ◯ Cash

◯ Money Market   ◯ Investment

◯ Asset   ◯ Liability

Click Next to continue ⬇

Figure 8-8:
The Create
New
Account
dialog box.

✕ Cancel   ❓ Help   ▷ Next

You need to set up at least one account for the new file, so click the appropriate account button.

7. Describe the account.

When Quicken displays a Checking Account Setup dialog box such as the one in Figure 8-9, click the Summary tab. Fill out the text boxes to collect the starting account balance information for the new account. Because I have described how to fill out this dialog box in previous chapters, I won't go into detail here. If you need help in filling it out, refer to Chapter 2.

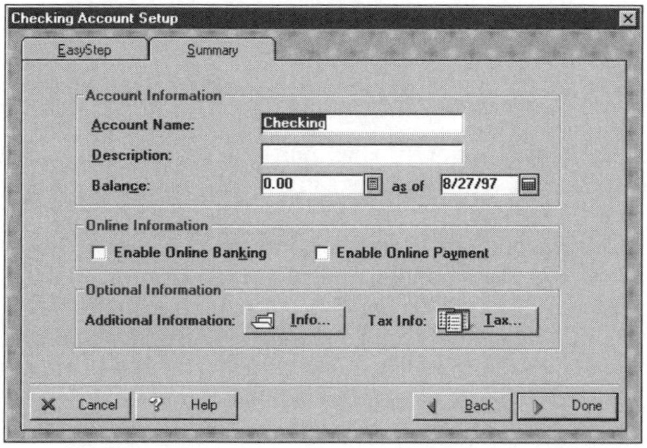

Figure 8-9:
The Checking Account Setup dialog box with the Summary tab showing.

For people who just have to be in the know ...

What Quicken refers to as a file is really a set of data and index files with the same filename, such as HOME, but different file extensions, such as QDB, ABD, QSD, QTX, and QMD. So when Quicken refers to the HOME file, it really is referring to the set of files that includes HOME.QDB, HOME.ABD, HOME.QSD, HOME.QTX, and HOME.QMD.

In most cases, you never need to know the distinction between the files in the set, but the knowledge may come in handy someday. For example, if you happen to stumble onto the Quicken directory, knowing about the set of HOME files keeps you from panicking when you see all the multiple copies of the HOME file. Or, on a more serious note, if you use a third-party backup utility, you need to know which of these files contain data that should be backed up.

Flip-flopping between files

You can work with only one file at a time. So, after you create a second file, you need to know how to flip-flop between your files. If you're recording business stuff, for example, you want to be using the business file. However, what if a transaction comes in that clearly is meant for your personal file and you want to enter it there immediately? Flip-flopping allows you to get from one file to another in no time.

Flip-flopping is easy: Just choose File⇨Open. Quicken displays the Open Quicken File dialog box. Pick the file you want from the File name text box and then click OK. Zap! You are in the new file.

When files get too big for their own good

You can enter a large number of transactions in a Quicken file; in fact, you can record tens of thousands of transactions in a single account or file. Wowsers!

In spite of these huge numbers, there are some good reasons to work with smaller files, if you can. For example, you can fit only about 2,500 transactions on a double-density, 5 ^{1}/$_4$-inch disk and 5,000 transactions on a double-density, 3 ^{1}/$_2$-inch disk. So working with files of a manageable size means you can more easily back them up on a floppy disk. Also, fewer transactions means Quicken runs faster because there's more memory available for Windows 95. (Windows 95 likes lots of memory — the same way some people like lots of ice cream.)

If your files have gotten too big for their own good, you can knock them down to size by creating a new file with just the current year's transactions in it. This means you have a copy of the big file you won't use anymore and a smaller, shrunken file with just the current year's transactions. This may sound like much ado about nothing, but it means you end up working with a smaller file. So, that probably means Quicken will run faster. (The memory thing comes into play again.) And smaller files should make backing up easier because you will probably be able to keep your files small enough to fit on a single double-density floppy disk.

Call me a Nervous Nellie — or a Nervous Nelson — but because shrinking a file involves wholesale change, I'd really feel more comfortable helping you through this process if you first back up the file you're about to shrink. I don't think that there's anything to get anxious about, but just in case something does go wrong during the shrinking process, I know that you would like to have a backup copy of the file to fall back on.

To shrink a Quicken file, follow these steps:

1. **Choose File➪File Operations➪Year-End Copy from the menu bar.**

   Quicken displays a portrait of Barry Nelson, the first actor to portray James Bond. No, not really — I just wanted to see if you were awake. Actually, Quicken displays the Year-End Copy dialog box, as shown in Figure 8-10.

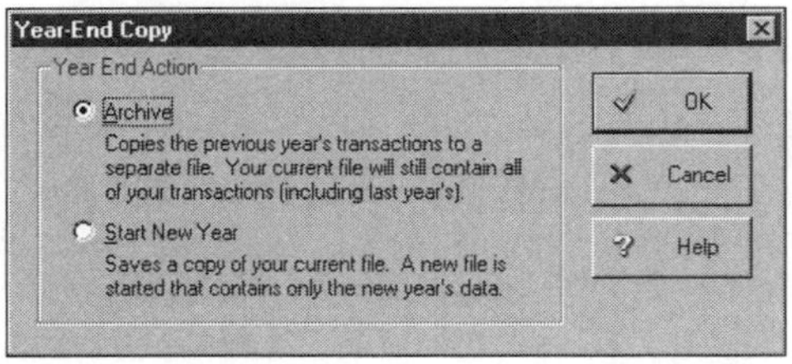

Figure 8-10:
The Year-End Copy dialog box.

2. **Select the Start New Year option button.**

   You know how this works — just click the mouse.

3. **Click OK.**

   Quicken displays the Start New Year dialog box, as shown in Figure 8-11.

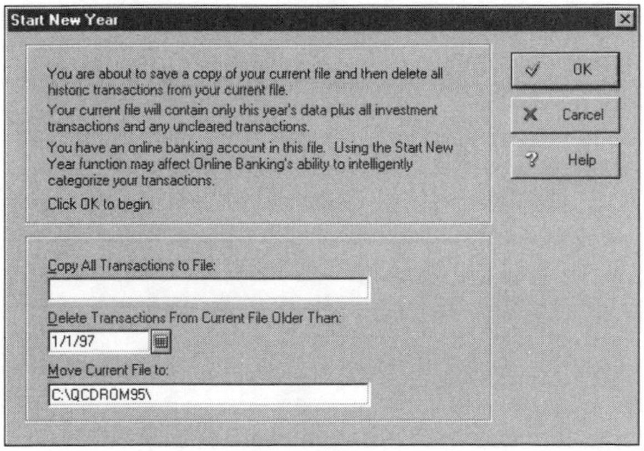

Figure 8-11:
The Start New Year dialog box.

4. **Enter a name in the Copy All Transactions to File text box.**

   Use a combination of up to eight letters and characters to name the "old transactions" file that Quicken creates. (It's in this file that Quicken will store all your old transactions.) At this point, the "old transactions" file you're creating actually mirrors the original file — in other words, it's an exact copy.

5. Specify a cutoff date.

Using the Delete Transactions From Current File Older Than text box, enter a cutoff date. All cleared transactions with a date that falls before this cutoff date will be deleted from the current Quicken file. (Remember, this is the file you work with and want to shrink.) I chose January 1, 1997, as the cutoff date in Figure 8-11 so that I could create a new file for all 1997 transactions. (Note that Quicken doesn't delete uncleared transactions, and it doesn't delete investment transactions.)

6. (Optional) Move the current file.

You do this step only if you want to change the location of the current file from the current Quicken directory to another directory. Type the path name of the new directory in the Move Current File to text box. If this optional step sounds confusing or complicated, don't worry about it because you have no good reason to change the directory right now anyway.

7. Click OK.

Quicken creates an "old transactions" file with the filename you gave it in the Start New Year dialog box. Quicken also deletes all the old transactions from the current file so that your current file contains only the transactions that are dated after the cutoff date.

Quicken then displays the message box shown in Figure 8-12 that tells you the file was successfully copied. Select the Old File option button if you want to use the "old transactions" file. Select the File for New Year option button if you want to use the current file you've just shrunk. Click OK after you have made your choice.

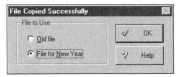

Figure 8-12: The File Copied Successfully dialog box.

If you want to see the old transactions file again, you can select it from the dialog box of the File➪Open command. You should *not* enter any new transactions in the old transactions file, however, because these new transactions will change the old file's ending account balance without changing the current file's beginning account balance.

Using and Abusing Passwords

I have mixed feelings about passwords. Theoretically, they let you lock up your Quicken data so that your rebellious teenagers (if you're using Quicken at home) or the night janitors (if you're using Quicken in a business) can't come in, print checks, process automatic payments, and just generally mess things up.

Using passwords sounds pretty good, of course. But before you set up a password and then start relying on it to protect your information, let me remind you that a Quicken password only prevents someone from accessing your data with Quicken. Using a password does not prevent someone from fooling around with your computer itself. If the night janitors — or, heaven forbid, your teenagers — are the nefarious types, they can erase your files with DOS or scramble them with another program, such as a spreadsheet or word processing program. And it's possible that they even can get in and manipulate the data with another checkbook or accounting program.

There's one other little annoying problem with passwords, too. Darn it, you have to remember them.

For these reasons, I think that passwords are best left to computer systems that use them on a global basis to control access to all programs and to computer systems that can track all users (you, your teenagers, the night janitors, and anyone else) by name. Your PC doesn't fall in this category.

Setting up a file password

You still want a password? Okay, with much trepidation, I give you the following steps for setting up a password for a Quicken file:

1. **Select the file you want to protect with a password.**

   If the file you want to password-protect is not the active file, choose File⇨Open from the menu and then either double-click the file you want or select it and click OK.

2. **Choose File⇨Passwords from the menu bar.**

   Quicken displays the — you guessed it — Passwords menu, which lists two commands: File and Transaction.

3. **Choose the File command.**

   Quicken displays the Set Up Password dialog box, as shown in Figure 8-13.

Figure 8-13:
The Set Up
Password
dialog box.

4. **Enter the password into the Password text box.**

   You can use up to 16 characters. Quicken doesn't differentiate between lowercase and uppercase characters, by the way, so Washington, wASHINGTON, and WASHINGTON are all the same from its point of view. Quicken doesn't display the actual characters you type; it displays asterisks instead. If you type **Dog**, for example, it displays ***. (Passwords require strict secrecy, you see.)

5. **Enter the password you want to use again — only this time into the Confirm Password text box — and click OK.**

   Congratulations! You're done.

Assigning a password to a file does not prevent you from doing anything with the file that you would normally do. However, the next time you try to use this file — after you start Quicken or when you try to select the file by using the File⇨Open command — Quicken will ask you for the file's password. You need to supply the password to gain access to the file.

Changing a file password

After you set up a file password, you're not stuck with it forever. You either can change the password or remove it by choosing File⇨Passwords.

If you've already set up a password, however, Quicken doesn't display the Set Up Password dialog box shown in Figure 8-13. Instead, Quicken displays a Change Password dialog box that asks for the password you're now using and the new password you want to use in the future (see Figure 8-14). Type the current password in the Old Password text box and the new password in the New Password and Confirm Password text boxes. Then press Enter. From now on, you need to use the new password to gain access to the file. If you don't want to use a password anymore, just leave the New Password and Confirm Password text boxes blank.

Figure 8-14:
The Change
Password
dialog box.

Change Password	☒
Old Password:	☑ OK
New Password:	✗ Cancel
Confirm Password:	？ Help

To remove the old password, leave the New & Confirm fields blank.

So what are transaction passwords?

After you choose File⇨Passwords from the menu bar, Quicken asks whether you want to create a file password or a transaction password. In general, you will be using a *file password* to protect the access into a Quicken file.

A *transaction password* works like a file password except that it requires the user to enter the transaction password if the date of the transaction the user is trying to enter is before a specified date. You specify the date, called the cutoff date, when you set up the transaction password.

Maybe it's just me, but transaction passwords don't make a lot of sense. I guess the logic is that you use a transaction password to prevent some idiot from fouling up last year's or last month's transactions. It seems to me, though, that there are a couple of easier approaches. One is that you can create and safely store backup copies of the Quicken file for last year or last month. Another is to not have idiots fooling around with your Quicken files. Jeepers, if somebody can't understand an instruction such as, "Use the current date," do you really want them mucking about in your books?

Chapter 9

Compound Interest Magic and Other Mysteries

. . . .

. . . .

*T*he folks at Intuit have added several nifty little calculators (most are dialog boxes called Planners) to recent versions of Quicken. I strongly encourage you to use these tools. At the very least, the calculators should make your work easier. And if you invest a little time, you should gain some enormously valuable perspectives on your financial affairs.

Noodling around with Your Investments

My favorite Quicken calculator is the Investment Savings Planner. I guess I just like to forecast portfolio future values and other similar stuff.

Using the Investment Savings Planner

Let's say that you want to know how much you'll accumulate if you save $2,000 a year for 35 years, using a stock mutual fund that you anticipate will earn 10 percent annually. Use the Investment Savings Planner to estimate how much you should ultimately accumulate.

1. **Choose Features⇨Planning⇨Financial Planners⇨Savings.**

   Quicken displays the Investment Savings Planner dialog box (see Figure 9-1).

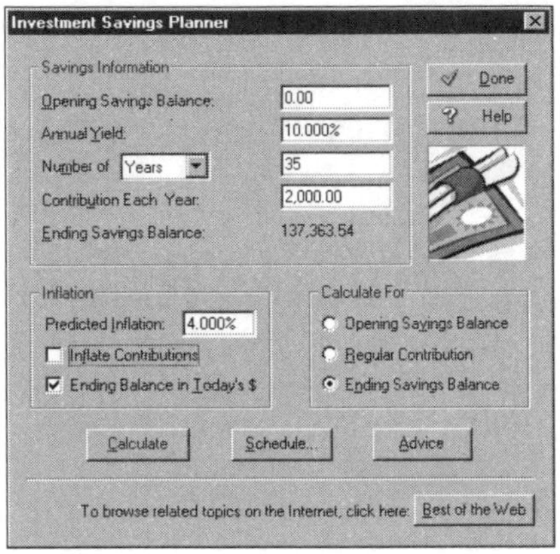

Figure 9-1:
The
Investment
Savings
Planner
dialog box.

2. **Enter what you've already accumulated as your Opening Savings Balance.**

   Move the cursor to the Opening Savings Balance text box and then type the amount of your current investments. If this amount is zero, for example, type **0**.

3. **Enter the Annual Yield that you expect your investments to earn.**

   Move the cursor to the Annual Yield text box and type the percent. If you plan to invest in the stock market and expect your savings to match the market's usual return of about 10 percent, for example, type **10** (don't type .10).

4. **Indicate how long you plan to let your investments earn income.**

   Move the cursor to the Number of drop-down list box and select the time period appropriate to your investments planning. (Usually, you will select years, as Figure 9-1 shows.) Then move the cursor to the Number of text box and indicate how long (enter the number of time periods) you want to maintain these investments.

5. **Enter the amount you plan to add to your investments every period.**

   Move cursor to the Contribution Each text box and enter the amount you plan to add. (Figure 9-1 shows how to plan a $2,000 annual contribution.)

6. **Enter the anticipated inflation rate.**

   Move the cursor to the Predicted Inflation text box and enter the inflation rate. By the way, from 1926 to 1992, the inflation rate has averaged just over 3 percent.

7. **Indicate whether you plan to increase your annual contribution as a result of inflation.**

   Select the Inflate Contributions check box if you plan to annually increase — by the annual inflation rate — the amount you add to your investment portfolio. Don't select the check box if you don't want to inflate the payments.

After you enter all the information, the Ending Savings Balance field shows how much you'll accumulate in present-day, uninflated dollars: $137,363.54. Hmmm. Nice.

If you want to know the amount you'll accumulate in future-day, inflated dollars, deselect the Ending Balance in Today's $ check box.

To get more information on the annual deposits, balances, and so on, click the Schedule button, which appears on the face of the Investment Savings Planner dialog box. Quicken whips up a quick little report showing the annual deposits and ending balance for each year you plan to add into the savings. Try it. You may like it.

How to become a millionaire

So you want to be a millionaire some day.

To learn how to realize this childhood dream, use the Calculate For option buttons, which appear on the Investment Savings Planner dialog box (on the Investment Savings Planner dialog box I just described). With these buttons, you click the financial variable (Opening Savings Balance, Regular Contribution, or Ending Savings Balance) you want to calculate. For example, to determine the annual amount you need to contribute to your investment so that your portfolio reaches $1,000,000, here's what you do:

1. **Select the Regular Contribution option button.**
2. **Select the Inflate Contributions check box.**
3. **Deselect the Ending Balance in Today's $ check box.**
4. **Enter all the other input variables.**

   Remember to set the Ending Savings Balance text box to **1000000** (the Ending Savings Balance field becomes a text box after you select the Ending Balance in Today's $ check box).

The Investment Savings Planner computes how much you need to save annually to hit your $1,000,000 target.

A timing assumption you should know

The Investment Savings Planner assumes that you will add to your portfolio at the end of the period — what financial planners call an *ordinary annuity*.

Starting from scratch, it'll take 35 years of roughly $2,500-a-year payments to reach $1,000,000.00 (see Figure 9-2). (All those zeros look rather nice, don't they?) Note that this calculation assumes a 10-percent annual yield.

"Jeepers, creepers," you say. "This seems too darn good to be true, Steve."

Figure 9-2:
The secret
to your
success:
$2,500 a
year for 35
years.

Well, unfortunately, the calculation is a little misleading. With 4-percent inflation, your million bucks will be worth *only* $253,415.48 in current-day dollars. (To confirm this present value calculation, select the Ending Savings Balance option button and the Ending Balance in Today's $ check box.)

The Often Unbearable Burden of Debt

To help you better manage your debts, Quicken provides a neat Loan Planner that computes loan payments and balances.

Using the Loan Planner to calculate payments

Let's say that one afternoon, you're wondering what the mortgage payment is on one of those monstrous houses: tens of thousands of square feet, acres of grounds, cottages for the domestic help, and so on. You get the picture — something that's a really vulgar display of wealth.

To learn what you would pay on a 30-year, $5,000,000 mortgage if the money costs 8.5 percent, use the Loan Planner:

1. **Choose Fe̲atures⇨P̲lanning⇨Financial P̲lanners⇨L̲oan.**

   Quicken displays the Loan Planner dialog box (see Figure 9-3 for a picture of this handy tool).

Figure 9-3:
The Loan
Planner
dialog box.

2. **Enter the loan amount.**

   Move the cursor to the Loan Amount text box and enter the amount of the loan. (If you're checking the lifestyle of the ostentatious and vulgar, type **5,000,000**.)

3. **Enter the annual interest rate.**

   Move the cursor to the Annual Interest Rate text box and enter the interest rate percent. If a loan charges 8.5 percent interest, for example, type **8.5**.

4. **Enter the number of years you want to take to repay the loan.**

   Move the cursor to the Number of Years text box and enter the number of years you'll make payments.

5. **Indicate how many loan payments you plan to make a year.**

   Move the cursor to the Periods Per Year text box and enter the number of loan payments you'll make in a year. If you want to make monthly payments, for example, type **12**.

Quicken calculates the loan payment and displays the amount in the Payment Per Period field. Yikes! $38,445.67 a month.

I guess if you have to ask how much the mortgage payment is, you really can't afford it.

To get more information on the loan payments, interest and principal portions of payments, and outstanding loan balances, click the Schedule button, which appears on the face of the Loan Planner dialog box. Quicken whips up a quick loan amortization schedule showing all this stuff.

Calculating loan balances

To calculate the loan principal amount, select the Loan Amount option button under Calculate For. Then enter all the other variables.

For example, those $38,446-a-month payments for the monster mansion seem a little ridiculous. So calculate how much you can borrow if you make $1,000-a-month payments over 30 years and the annual interest rate is 8.5 percent:

1. **Select the Loan Amount option button.**

2. **Type 8.5 in the Annual Interest Rate text box.**

3. **Type 30 in the Number of Years text box.**

4. **Type 12 in the Periods Per Year text box.**

5. **Type 1000 in the Payment Per Period text box.**

The Loan Planner computes a Loan Amount of $130,053.64.

The Refinance Planner

You won't read about the Refinance Planner here — but not because I'm lazy. (Believe it or not, I enjoy writing about things that help you make better financial decisions.) The Refinance Planner merely calculates the difference in mortgage payments if you make lower payments; then it tells you how long it would take with these lower payments to pay back the refinancing costs you incur.

For example, if you save $50 a month because you refinance and it costs $500 to refinance, the Refinance Planner tells you that it would take ten months of $50-a-month savings to recoup your $500.

You know what? Although you may want to know how long it would take to recoup the refinance costs, that information doesn't tell you whether it's a good idea to refinance.

Deciding whether to refinance is very, very complicated. You can't just look at your next few payments, like the Refinance Planner does. You also need to look at the total interest you would pay with the old mortgage and the new mortgage. And you need to factor in the time value of money.

I don't think there's any good reason to use the Refinance Planner; it just doesn't do what it purports to do.

So that I don't leave you hanging, however, let me give you two rules of thumb to help you make smarter refinancing decisions.

First, if you want to save interest costs, don't use refinancing as a way to stretch out your borrowing. That is, if you refinance, make sure that you make payments large enough to pay off the new mortgage by the same time you would have paid off the old mortgage. In other words, if you have 23 years left on your old mortgage, don't go out and get a 30-year mortgage. Find a lender who will let you pay off the new mortgage in 23 years.

Here's a second trick, if you can find a willing lender. Ask the lender to calculate the annual percentage rate (APR) on the new mortgage, assuming that you'll pay off the mortgage by the same time you would have paid off the old mortgage. (An APR includes all the loan's costs — interest, points, miscellaneous fees, and so on — and calculates an implicit interest rate.) If the APR on the new loan is lower than the current loan's interest rate, you would probably save money by refinancing.

Let me issue one caveat. When you base your refinancing decision on the comparison between the new loan's APR and the current loan's interest rate, you're saying that you'll live in your current house until the mortgage is paid.

I hope this information helps. As I said, mortgage refinancing decisions are tough if you truly want to save money.

The Retirement Planner

I think this is the book's most important section. No joke. Your financial future is much too consequential to go for easy laughs or cheap shots.

The dilemma in a nutshell

By the time the 30-something and 40-something crowd reaches retirement, Social Security coverage probably will be scaled back. As you may know, the current recipients are getting everything they paid in as well as most of what we pay in.

If you currently receive Social Security, please don't feel defensive or betrayed. I think your generation overcame challenges far more important (World War I, the Great Depression, World War II, the Cold War, the end of segregation, and so on) than the problem of inadequate Social Security funding we young ones face.

I know this sentiment sounds corny, but I think you've left the world a better place. I hope my generation does the same.

More about timing

The Retirement Planner assumes that you or your employer will add to your retirement savings at the end of the year — what financial planners call an *ordinary annuity*. If you or your employer adds to your retirement savings at the beginning of the year, you earn an extra year of interest. As a result, your after-tax income will be more than Quicken shows.

But the problem isn't just Social Security. More and more often, employer-provided pension plans are defined contribution plans, which add specific amounts to your pension (such as 2 percent of your salary), rather than defined benefit plans, which promise specific pension amounts (such as $1,000 a month). As a result, although you know that someone will throw a few grand into your account every so often, you don't know how much you'll have when you retire.

I urge you to think ahead about your financial requirements. Fortunately, Quicken's Retirement Planner can help you.

I'll get off my soapbox now. Thank you.

Making retirement planning calculations

Imagine that you've decided to jump into your employer's 401(k) thing (a type of profit-sharing plan), which will allow you to plop about $3,000 into a retirement account that you think will earn about 9 percent annually.

Fortunately, you don't need to be a rocket scientist to figure this stuff out. You can just use the Retirement Planner:

1. **Choose Features➪Planning➪Financial Planners➪Retirement.**

   Quicken displays the Retirement Planner dialog box, as shown in Figure 9-4.

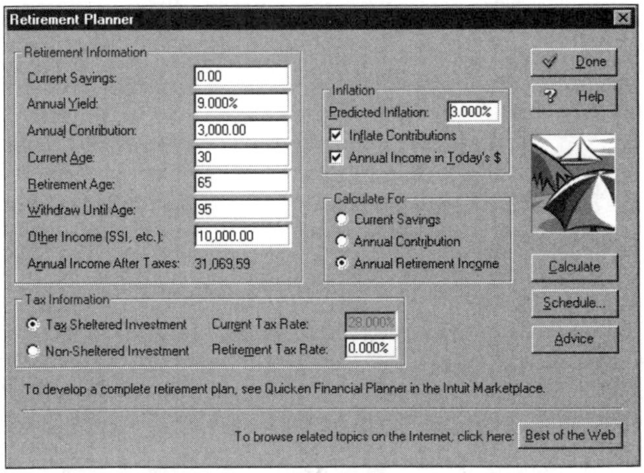

Figure 9-4:
The
Retirement
Planner
dialog box.

2. **Enter what you've already saved as your current savings.**

   Move the cursor to the Current Savings text box and type your current retirement savings (for example, if you have some individual retirement account money or you've accumulated a balance in an employer-sponsored 401(k) account). Don't worry if you don't have anything saved — most people don't.

3. Enter the annual yield that you expect your retirement savings to earn.

Move the cursor to the Annual Yield text box and type the percent. In the little example shown in Figure 9-4, I say the annual yield is 9 percent.

4. Enter the annual amount added to your retirement savings.

Move the cursor to the Annual Contribution text box and enter the amount that you or your employer will add to your retirement savings at the end of each year. In the example, I say that I plan to add $3,000 (refer to Figure 9-4).

5. Enter your current age.

Move the cursor to the Current Age text box and enter a number. You're on your own here, but let me suggest that this is a time to be honest.

6. Enter your retirement age.

Move the cursor to the Retirement Age text box and enter a number. Again, purely a personal matter. (Figure 9-4 shows this age as 65, but you should retire when you want.)

7. Enter the age to which you want to continue withdrawals.

Move the cursor to the Withdraw Until Age field and enter a number. Let's not beat around the bush here. This number is how old you think you'll be when you die. I don't like the idea any better than you do. Let me say, though, that ideally you want to run out of steam — there, that's a safe metaphor — before you run out of money. So go ahead and make this age something pretty old — like 95 (sorry, Grandma).

8. Enter any other income you'll receive — such as Social Security.

Move the cursor to the Other Income (SSI, etc.) text box and type a value (Figure 9-4 shows $10,000). Note that this income is in current-day, or uninflated, dollars.

9. Indicate whether you plan to save retirement money in a tax-sheltered investment.

Select the Tax Sheltered Investment option button if your retirement savings earns untaxed money. Select the Non-Sheltered Investment option button if the money is taxed. Tax-sheltered investments are things such as individual retirement accounts, annuities, and employer-sponsored 401(k)s and 403(b)s (a 403(b) is kind of a profit-sharing plan for a nonprofit agency). (As a practical matter, tax-sheltered investments are the only way to ride. By deferring income taxes on your earnings, you earn interest on the money you otherwise would have paid as income taxes.)

10. Enter your current marginal tax rate, if needed.

If you're investing in taxable stuff, move the cursor to the Current Tax Rate text box. Then enter the combined federal and state income tax rate that you pay on your last dollars of income.

11. **Enter your anticipated retirement tax rate.**

Move the cursor to the Retirement Tax Rate text box, then . . . hey, wait a minute. Who knows what the rates will be next year, let alone when you're retired? I think you should enter **0**, but remember that the Annual Income After Taxes is really your pretax income (just as your current salary is really your pretax income).

12. **Enter the anticipated inflation rate.**

Move the cursor to the Predicted Inflation text box and enter the inflation rate. By the way, from 1926 to 1992, the inflation rate has averaged just above 3 percent (see Figure 9-4).

13. **Indicate whether the annual additions will increase.**

Select the Inflate Contributions check box if the additions will increase annually by the inflation rate. (Because your salary and 401(k) contributions will presumably inflate if there's inflation, Figure 9-4 shows the Inflate Contributions check box selected.)

After you enter all the information, take a peek at the Annual Income After Taxes field (Figure 9-4, for example, shows $31,069.59). Not bad. Not bad at all. If you want to see the after-tax income in future-day, inflated dollars, deselect the Annual Income in Today's $ check box.

To get more information on the annual deposits, balances, income, and so on, select the Schedule button, which appears on the face of the Retirement Planner dialog box. Quicken whips up a quick, little report showing the annual deposits, income, and ending retirement account balances for each year you plan to add to and withdraw from your retirement savings.

If you're now bummed out about retirement

First, don't feel depressed. At least you know *now* if your golden years seem a little tarnished. After all, you acquired Quicken to help you sort out your finances. Now you can use Quicken and your newly gained knowledge to help improve your financial lot.

Basically, retirement planning depends on just three things:

- The number of years that the retirement savings will accrue interest
- The real yield (that is, adjusted for inflation) you earn — in other words, the annual yield minus the predicted inflation
- The yearly payments

Anything you do to increase one of these variables will increase your retirement income.

If you invest, for example, in something that delivers higher real yields, such as the stock market, you should see a big difference (of course, you usually bear more risk). Or if you wait an extra year or two to retire, you wind up making more annual payments and earning more interest. Finally, if you boost the yearly payments (for example, by participating in an employer-sponsored 401(k) or 403(b) plan, where your employer matches a portion of your contribution), you'll see a huge change.

Noodle around with the variables. See what happens. You may be surprised.

Playing retirement roulette

Use the Calculate option buttons to determine a retirement income variable. You can calculate current savings, annual contribution, or, as described earlier, the annual after-tax income.

To calculate the yearly payment required to produce a specific level of retirement income, for example, select the Annual Contribution option button. Then enter all the other variables — including the desired after-tax income. The Retirement Planner calculates how much you need to save to hit your target retirement income.

Cost of College

Ouch. I have a couple of daughters, so I know how you feel. Man, oh man, do I know how you feel.

The College Planner

Let's say that you have a child who may attend college in 16 years. And you haven't started to save yet. If the local university costs $9,500 a year and you can earn 9 percent annually, how much should you save?

The College Planner works like the Retirement Planner:

1. **Choose Features⇨Planning⇨Financial Planners⇨College.**

   Quicken displays the College Planner dialog box, as shown in Figure 9-5.

2. **Enter the annual college costs.**

   Move the cursor to the Annual College Costs text box. Then enter the current annual costs at a school Junior may attend. Figure 9-5 shows this amount as $10,000.

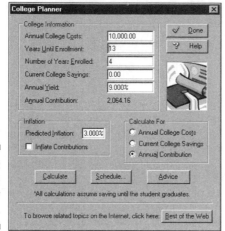

Figure 9-5:
The College
Planner
dialog box.

3. Enter the number of years until enrollment.

Move the cursor to the Years Until Enrollment text box and enter a number. For example, if Junior will start college in 13 years, type **13**.

4. Enter the number of years enrolled.

Move the cursor to the Number of Years Enrolled text box and enter a number. Assuming Junior doesn't fool around, type **4** or **5**.

5. Enter the amount of the current college savings.

Move the cursor to the Current College Savings field and enter an amount. Figure 9-5 shows this amount as $0.00.

6. Enter the annual yield that you expect the college savings to earn.

Move the cursor to the Annual Yield text box and type the percent. Figure 9-5 shows the yield as 9 percent.

7. Enter the inflation rate anticipated in college tuition.

Move the cursor to the Predicted Inflation text box and type the inflation rate percent. Figure 9-5 shows this rate as 3 percent.

8. Indicate whether you plan to increase your annual contribution as a result of inflation.

Select the Inflate Contributions check box if you plan to annually increase — by the annual inflation rate — the amount you save. Figure 9-5 shows this check box selected.

After you enter all the information, the Annual Contribution field shows how much you need to save each year until the child graduates from college.

Just to beat this thing to death, Figure 9-5 shows that the lucky student will attend four years at a college that currently costs $10,000 a year and that you expect to earn 9 percent annually and anticipate 3 percent annual inflation. Given these cold hard facts, you need to ante up $2,064.16 every year.

To get more information on the annual deposits, tuition, and balance, click the Schedule button, which appears on the face of the College Planner dialog box. Quicken whips up a quick little report showing the annual deposits, tuition, and ending college savings account balances for each year you'll add to, and Junior withdraws from, the college savings money.

If you're now bummed out about college costs

Look at the positive side: You now understand the size of the problem and the solution.

College planning depends on four things:

- College costs
- The number of years that the savings will earn interest
- The real yield (that is, adjusted for inflation) you earn — in other words, the annual yield minus the predicted inflation
- The yearly payments

I don't mean to sound like a simpleton, but there are three basic ways to successfully save for a college education:

- Reduce the costs (find a less-expensive school)
- Invest in things that deliver higher yields
- Boost the yearly payments

Use the Calculate option buttons to compute a specific financial variable. Select the variable you want to calculate and then input the other values. The College Planner computes the flagged variable.

Income tax expenses

The folks at Quicken added a very cool calculator to the last release of Quicken, a Tax Estimator. Okay — you two guys in the back row. Stop sniggering. I'm serious. I think it's really neat. Not because I like income tax planning and preparation. No, I think it's neat because this little tool makes it possible to estimate with a fair degree of accuracy one of the most complicated expenses of our little lives: federal income taxes.

Tax Planner calculator

The Tax Planner works pretty much like the other financial planning calculators. Here's the straight scoop:

1. **Choose Features⇨Taxes⇨Tax Planner.**

   Quicken displays the Tax Planner calculator, as shown in Figure 9-6.

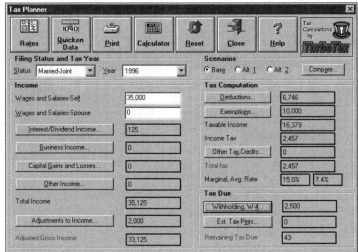

Figure 9-6:
The Tax
Planner
calculator.
Friends, it
doesn't get
any better
than this.

2. **Indicate your filing status.**

   Move the cursor to the Status field and click the down arrow. Then, when
   Quicken displays a list of possible filing statuses, pick the one you think
   you'll use this year: Single, Married filing separate, Married filing jointly,
   and so on.

3. **Indicate the tax year.**

   Move the cursor to the Year field and click the down arrow. After Quicken
   displays a pop-up box listing 1996 and 1997, select one of those years.

4. **Enter the wages and salaries you and your lovely or handsome spouse
   expect.**

   Move the cursor to the Wages And Salaries-Self field and type what you
   think you'll make this year. If your filing status isn't single, move the cursor
   to the Wages And Salaries-Spouse field and type what you think your
   spouse will make this year.

5. **Indicate approximately how much other taxable income you'll have.**

   Quick as you can, click the Interest/Dividend Income, Business Income,
   Capital Gains And Losses, and Other Income buttons and fill in the pop-up
   worksheets that Quicken displays. (In each case, Quicken's pop-up

worksheets prompt you for a handful of inputs.) If some income thingamajig doesn't apply, just leave it blank. Figure 9-7 shows the Interest/Dividend Income pop-up worksheet. This makes sense, right? You enter your taxable interest income into the first input field. You enter your taxable dividend income into the second field. When you're done, click OK. Quicken calculates the total and then plugs this value back into the Tax Planner calculator.

Figure 9-7:
The
Interest/
Dividend
Income
pop-up
worksheet.

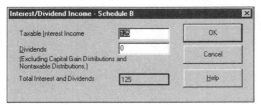

6. **Indicate whether you'll have any adjustments to your gross income.**

   This sounds too technical, I know. But there are really only a handful of these adjustments: IRA, SEP/IRA, and Keogh deductions; alimony; moving expenses; a couple of adjustments for self-employed types (half their self-employment tax and a chunk of their health insurance premiums); and any penalty on early withdrawals of savings. If you have one or more of these, click the Adjustments to Income button and fill in the appropriate blanks on the dialog box Quicken displays. When you're done, click OK.

7. **Estimate your itemized deductions.**

   Click the Deductions button and then describe any itemized deductions you have by filling in the blanks on the dialog box Quicken displays. You'll also need to answer a handful of questions including, "Is taxpayer a dependent?" and "Are you or your spouse blind or over age 65?" You answer these questions by selecting or deselecting check boxes. After you enter all this information, click OK. Quicken calculates your standard deduction and then uses whatever is larger for your return: your standard deduction or your total itemized deductions.

   For most people, only three itemized deductions — mortgage interest, property taxes, and charitable deductions — actually matter.

8. **Indicate the number of personal exemptions you'll claim.**

   You know the drill by now, right? Click the Exemptions button and then use the dialog box that Quicken displays to indicate the number of personal exemptions you get. When you're done, click OK. The basic rule is that you get one exemption for everybody in your family (you, your spouse if you're filing jointly, and your dependents) as long as they live at your house.

I should mention, however, that things get tricky if you've got shirt-tail relatives living at your house, if your kids live away from home or are married, or if some of the kids in the house have divorced parents. If you have questions because one of these situations sounds vaguely familiar, get the IRS return preparation instructions and read the part about who is and is not a dependent.

9. **Indicate whether you owe any other taxes or have tax credits you can use to reduce your taxes.**

   Click the Other Tax, Credits button and fill in the blanks on the dialog box that Quicken displays. When you're done, click OK. By the way, if you and your spouse get all your income from salaries and a handful of investments, you probably don't need to worry about this "other taxes and credits" business.

10. **Enter any estimated taxes or federal income withholding you've paid.**

    Click the Withholding, W-4 button and fill in the blanks on the dialog box that Quicken displays. When you're done, click OK. If you make estimated tax payments — and you'll know if you do — click the Est. Tax Pmts button and fill in the blanks on the dialog box that Quicken displays. All you are doing here is indicating how much you and your spouse have already had withheld and how much you'll have withheld from your future paychecks.

When you complete these ten steps, you'll be able to see not only what your total income taxes are, but also whether you'll need to increase your payments. (Look at the Remaining Tax Due field in the lower-right corner of the screen to see whether it looks like you're coming up short.)

If you want to print the tax planner information, click the Print button. If you want to erase all your inputs and start over, click the Reset button. After you're done using the calculator, click the Close button.

Some more Tax Planner tricks

You can try a couple of other Tax Planner tricks. First, rather than enter the data into text boxes (as I described here), you can tell the Tax Planner to grab taxable income and tax-deduction information from your registers. This is pretty straightforward as long as you're diligently using tax-related categories to track these income and expense amounts and — this is important — you've indicated the tax schedule line on which category totals should be reported.

You can update the tax rates and tax brackets by clicking the Rates button and then filling a worksheet that Quicken provides. (If you're still using Quicken 6 for Windows in 1998, for example, you'll either need to do this or get new tax rate information from Quicken to use the Tax Planner calculator.) This worksheet pretty much mirrors the tax schedules provided by the Internal Revenue Service, so if you're familiar with these, updating the tax rates should be a breeze.

Part III
Home Finances

The 5th Wave
By Rich Tennant

YUNT INSTITUTE OF COMPUTING

SUMMER PERFORMANCE

SIDESHOW MELODY

"ALL RIGHT, NOW, WE NEED SOMEONE TO PLAY THE PART OF THE GEEK."

In this part . . .

Are you going to be using Quicken for personal financial stuff? If so, you should know that there's more to the program than just the checkbook-on-a-computer business described in the preceding part. Quicken can help you manage and monitor things such as credit cards, home mortgages, and investments. If this stuff sounds interesting, keep reading.

Chapter 10

Credit Cards (And Debit Cards, Too)

*Y*ou can use Quicken to track your credit cards in much the same way you use Quicken to keep a checkbook. The process works very much the same, but with a few wrinkles.

First, I discuss whether you should even bother.

To Bother or Not to Bother . . .

I don't use Quicken to track my credit card purchases because I always pay my credit card balance in full every month. (Don't feel bad if you don't do this — it's like a natural law that CPAs like me must do this.) Therefore, I don't have an open credit card balance to track. What's more, when I pay the monthly credit card bill, I easily can use the Split Transaction Window to describe my spending categories: $3.53 on food for lunch, $52.64 for a car repair, and $217.54 for books (a personal weakness).

If you're in the same boat — meaning you use a credit card but you don't carry a balance — you don't need anything special to track your credit card purchases and, of course, you don't need to use Quicken to tell you your account balance because it's always zeroed out at the end of the month.

Of course, if you do carry a credit card balance — and most people do — you can set up a Quicken credit card account and use it for tracking credit card purchases. If you just need to keep track of how much you've charged during the month (even if you are going to pay the balance in full), you must also set up a credit card account and use it.

I should make one other point: In order to track not just what you charged by using spending categories, but also *where* you charged it by using the Payee field, you must set up a credit card account and use it.

My father-in-law uses a Quicken credit card account for this purpose. Although he doesn't carry a balance (or so he tells me), he does like to know how much he spends at International House of Pancakes, Kmart, and the truck stop. He could use the Split Transaction Window to record spending on things such as breakfast, clothing, and gasoline when he pays his credit card balance at the end of the month. But, the Split Transaction Window does not have a field to record where he said, "Charge it."

Setting Up a Credit Card Account

If you want to track credit card spending and balances with Quicken, you must set up a special credit card account. (In comparison, you use bank accounts to track things such as the money that flows into and out of a checking account.)

Adding a credit card account

To set up a credit card account, you follow roughly the same steps as you do to set up a bank account. Here's what you do:

1. **Click the Accts icon from the iconbar.**

   Quicken displays the Account List window, as shown in Figure 10-1.

2. **Click the New button on the Account List window.**

   Quicken displays the Create New Account dialog box shown in Figure 10-2.

3. **Select the Credit Card option button to display the Credit Card Account Setup dialog box (see Figure 10-3).**

4. **After Quicken displays the dialog box, click the Summary tab to move directly to the tab where all the action occurs.**

   (If you've been working with Quicken a bit, you don't need the extra hand-holding that Quicken provides when you click the Next button to move through the other tabs.)

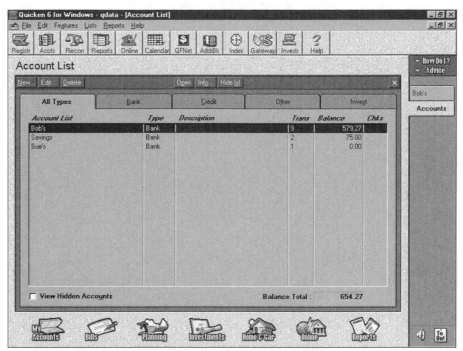

Figure 10-1:
The
Account List
window.

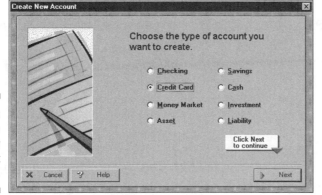

Figure 10-2:
The Create
New
Account
dialog box.

5. **Name the account.**

Why not do it, right? Move the cursor to the Account Name text box and type a name.

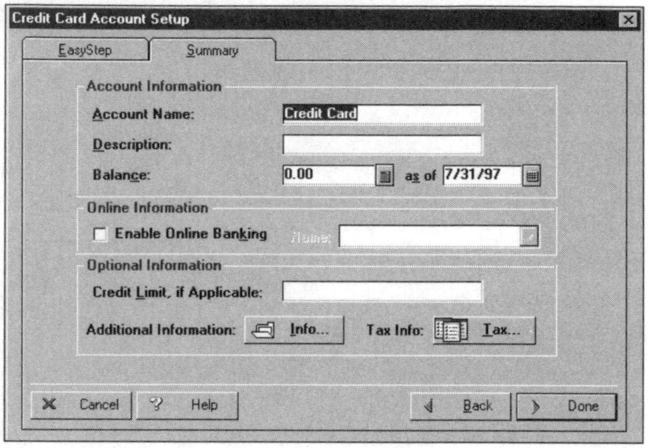

Figure 10-3:
The Credit
Card
Account
Setup dialog
box.

6. **Provide a description for the account (optional).**

Usually, it's enough to name an account. With a name, an account is easy enough to identify when you see it listed in places such as the Account List window. If a name isn't enough, however — usually because you've set up a bunch of different accounts — you can use the Description text box to further describe and identify the account. It is probably darn obvious to you how this works, but because I have a compulsive-obsessive personality, I need to say that you move the cursor to the Description text box and type something.

7. **Enter the balance you owed at the end of the last credit card billing period after making your payment.**

Move the cursor to the Balance text box and type the balance value using the number keys.

8. **Enter the date on which you will start keeping records for the credit card account.**

This should probably be the date you made your payment. Move the cursor to the as of text box and type a two-digit number for the month, a two-digit number for the day of the month, and a two-digit number for the year.

9. **Indicate whether you'll use Quicken's Bank Online feature.**

If you are using Quicken's Bank Online feature (which allows you to get a list of your credit card charges on disk or by modem), indicate this by selecting the Enable QuickBanking check box and by then selecting the bank that issued your credit card from the Name drop-down list box. (I ramble on about online banking later in the chapter.)

10. **Type in the amount of your credit limit (optional).**

    If you want, indicate the amount of your credit card limit by moving the cursor to the Credit Limit, if Applicable text box and then typing in whatever number the credit card company has arbitrarily decided is a reasonable balance for you to shoulder.

11. **Collect some additional information about the credit card (optional).**

    You can collect and store additional information about the credit card accounts you set up. To do this, click the Info button. Then, when Quicken displays the Additional Account Information dialog box, use its text boxes to store whatever information you want: the credit card company's name, your credit card account number (just in case you lose the credit card), and so forth.

    Ignore the Tax button. It doesn't apply to credit card accounts.

12. **Click Done.**

    Quicken redisplays the Account List window, as shown in Figure 10-1. But this time the window lists an additional account — the credit card account you just created.

Selecting a credit card account so that you can use it

To tell Quicken you want to work with an account, you use the Account List window — the same window you saw in Figure 10-1. Go figure.

Click the Accts icon from the iconbar to display the Account List window. After you display the window, select the account you want to use by double-clicking it. Quicken selects the account and displays the register window for that account so that you can begin recording transactions, as described in the next section.

Entering Credit Card Transactions

After you select a credit card account, Quicken displays a special version of the register window as shown in Figure 10-4.

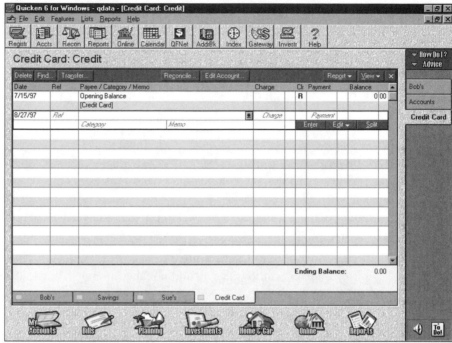

Figure 10-4:
The credit
card version
of the
Quicken
register.

A whirlwind tour of the Credit Card register

The Credit Card register works like the regular register window you use for a bank account. You enter transactions into the rows of the register. After you record a charge, Quicken updates the credit card balance and the remaining credit limit (if you entered the optional credit limit info when you set up the account).

You can use the same icons and commands as you do for your regular ol' bank account register. I talk about these in earlier chapters, so I won't regurgitate those discussions here. Old news is no news.

Recording a credit card charge

Recording a credit card charge is similar to recording a check or bank account withdrawal. For the sake of illustration, suppose that you charged $30.47 for dinner at your favorite Mexican restaurant. Here's how you record this charge:

1. Enter the charge date.

Move the cursor to the Date field (if it isn't already there) and type the date using the MM/DD format. For example, type July 15, 1997 as **7/15**. You usually don't have to type the year because Quicken retrieves the current year number from the little clock inside your computer. Or if you want, get crazy — click the down arrow at the end of the field and Quicken displays a pop-up calendar (described in Chapter 4) from which you can select the appropriate month and day.

Note: Don't bother with the Ref field. Quicken supplies it so you can record the credit card reference number — a bit of data that's usually about 20 characters long. You, my friend, have better things to do with your time, however. So just skip the field.

2. Record the name of the business you paid with a credit card.

Move the cursor to the Payee field and type the name of the person or business you paid. If the restaurant is Mommasita's Cantina, for example, type **Mommasita's Cantina** into the Payee field.

3. Enter the charge amount.

Move the cursor to the Charge field and type the total charge amount — **30.47** in this example. Don't type a dollar sign, but do type the period to indicate the decimal place and cents.

4. Enter the category.

Move the cursor to the Category field, open the drop-down list box, and select the appropriate category. A restaurant charge might be categorized as Entertainment, for example.

5. (Optional) Enter a memo description.

Move the cursor to the Memo field and type the specific reason you're charging the item, such as a special date with your spouse or an important business meeting.

6. Record the charge.

Click the Enter button or press the Enter key while the cursor is in the Category Memo field. Quicken beeps and then calculates both the new credit card balance and the remaining credit limit. Quicken then moves the cursor to the next slot in the register.

Figure 10-5 shows the charge at Mommasita's Cantina. Good food and reasonable prices — you can't ask for much more than that.

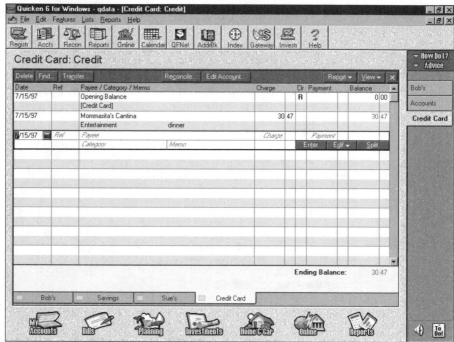

Figure 10-5:
The
charge at
Mommasita's
Cantina.

Changing charges you've already entered

Use the arrow keys or click the mouse to highlight the charge you want to change. Use the Tab and Shift+Tab keys or the mouse to move the cursor to the field that contains the misinformation you want to fix. You can then fix the entry and record the transaction. That's easy enough, isn't it?

Paying credit card bills

If you're tracking the credit card account balance with a credit card account like the one I'm describing here, Quicken provides two ways for you to pay a credit card bill.

Note, however, that if you're not using a credit card account, you record the check you send to pay a credit card bill in the same way you record any other check. And that means you don't have to read anything I'm about to say. Shoot. You shouldn't even be reading this chapter.

A most bodacious way to pay a credit card bill

This is pretty simple, so don't blink your eyes because you may miss the action.

Look at your credit card statement. Decide how much you want to pay. Select the bank account on which you'll write the check. Then write the check and record it in the bank account register — but as a transfer to the credit card account.

You're done. If you have questions, take a peek at the check transaction shown in Figure 10-6. It pays $100 of the credit card balance. The only trick — if you want to call it that — is that the credit card account is specified as the account to which the money is transferred. (You can see the other account by selecting the transfer transaction and pressing Ctrl+X.)

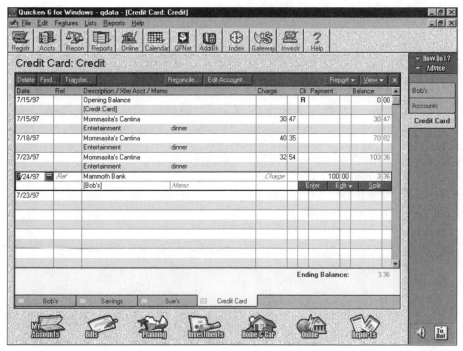

Figure 10-6:
A check transaction that pays a portion of a credit card balance.

If you look at the credit card account register now, you see that this check reduces the credit card balance by $100.

A less bodacious way to pay a credit card bill

You can also tell Quicken that you want to pay some portion of the credit card bill as part of reconciling the credit card's account balance.

I think this method is slightly more difficult. But if you want to reconcile your credit card account, think about using this second method. If you are reconciling a credit card statement and paying some portion of the credit balance at the same time, you may find this method more convenient. Who knows?

I describe how to reconcile a credit card account in the very next section.

That Crazy Reconciliation Trick

You know that trick where you compare your checking account records with your bank's records of your checking account? The one where you calculate the difference between what you think is your account balance and what the bank thinks is your balance? And this difference is supposed to equal the total of the transactions floating around out there in the system? You can do this same trick on your credit card account.

The actual reconciliation neat and straight-up

To reconcile a credit card account, first get your credit card statement. Next, display the credit card account in a register window.

What the nasty credit card company says

To tell Quicken what that nasty credit card company says, follow these steps, and put on some music if you can't seem to get the rhythm thing right.

1. **Click the Recon icon from the iconbar.**

   Quicken displays the Credit Card Statement Information dialog box, as shown in Figure 10-7.

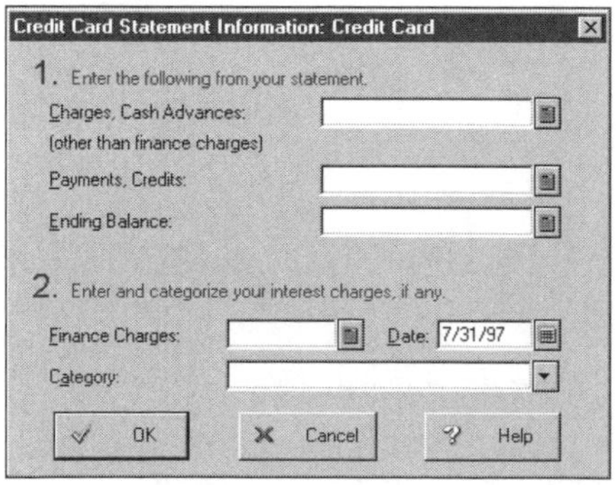

Figure 10-7: The Credit Card Statement Information dialog box.

2. **Enter the charges and cash advances that your statement shows.**

   Move the cursor to the Charges, Cash Advances text box and then type the number.

3. Enter the payment and credits that your statement shows.

You know the drill: Move the cursor to the Payments, Credits text box and type the number.

4. Enter the new balance shown on the credit card statement.

Now I bet this is a surprise. Go ahead and type the figure in the Ending Balance text box — even if you just can't believe you charged that much.

5. Enter the monthly interest charged by using the Finance Charges text box.

Pause for a moment of silence here if this is a sad, sad topic for you.

6. Assign the monthly interest to the appropriate spending category, such as Interest Exp.

Move the cursor to the Category text box and type the category name. (This is getting boring, isn't it? Move and type . . . Move and type . . . That's all I ever seem to say.) Remember that you can click the little down arrow at the end of the text box to see a list of categories to select from.

7. Click OK.

Quicken displays the Reconcile Credit Statement window (see Figure 10-8). You use it to tell Quicken which credit card charges and payments appear on your statement. (This step is akin to looking at a bank statement and noting which checks and deposits have cleared the bank.)

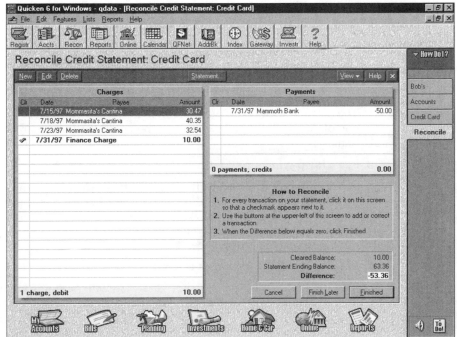

Figure 10-8:
The
Reconcile
Credit
Statement
window.

Ouch! Did I really spend that much?

After you give Quicken an overview of your credit card situation, you can note which charges have cleared and which charges haven't cleared.

If you're comfortable whipping through a bank reconciliation, you can probably do this with your eyes closed. If you need some help, leave your eyes open so you can read these steps:

1. **Find the first charge listed on the credit card statement.**

2. **Mark the charge as cleared.**

   Charges are listed in the left list box. Hmmm. It's not really any of my business, but maybe someone's eating at Mommasita's a bit too often?

   Scroll through the transactions listed in the Charges window until you find the charge and then click it. Or select the charge using the arrow keys and then press the spacebar. Quicken adds the check mark symbol in front of the list entry in the Clr column to mark this charge as cleared and then updates the cleared statement balance.

3. **Enter any missing charges.**

   If you can't find a charge, you probably did not enter it in the Quicken register yet. Open the credit card account register and then enter the charge into the register in the usual way — except enter a c (the letter *c*) into the Clr column by clicking the Clr field. By doing so, you identify the charge as one that's already cleared. After you finish, return to the Pay Credit Card Bill window.

   To quickly go to the Credit Card register, you can click its QuickTab.

4. **Repeat Steps 1, 2, and 3 for charges listed on the credit card statement.**

   Or until you're blue in the face.

5. **Find the first payment or credit listed on the credit card statement.**

   The payments and credits appear in the right list box. Figure 10-9 has only one of these. It's the $50 payment to the credit card company, Mammoth Bank.

6. **Mark the payment or credit as cleared.**

   Scroll through the transactions listed on the Payment window until you find the first payment or credit and then click it. Or select the credit and then press the spacebar. Quicken adds the check mark symbol in front of the list entry to mark the payment or credit as cleared and then updates the cleared statement balance.

7. **Enter any missing payments or credits.**

   If you can't find the payment or credit — and you probably know this — it means you haven't entered them into the Quicken register yet. Open the credit card account register and then enter the payment or credit into the register in the usual way, except put a c in the Clr column. Return to the Reconcile Credit Statement window when you finish.

8. **Repeat Steps 5, 6, and 7 for payments or credits listed on the credit card statement.**

If you record a transaction wrong, do this

As you're looking through the credit card statement, you may discover that you incorrectly recorded a transaction. If this happens, display the Credit Card register so that you can make the needed fixes.

Oh, that explains things

After you mark all the cleared charges and payments, the difference between the cleared balance for the credit card and the statement's ending balance should be zero.

Figure 10-9 shows how this looks. By the way, it's darned easy to reconcile with fictitious data.

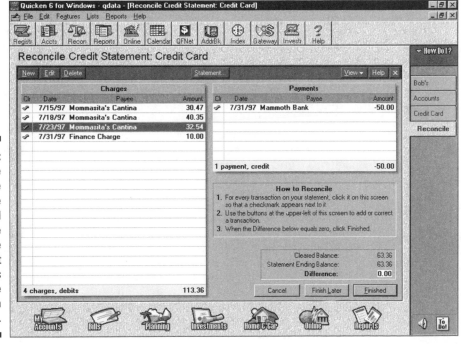

Figure 10-9:
When the difference between the cleared balance and the statement balance is zero, the reconciliation is complete.

Finishing the reconciliation

If the difference does equal zero, you're cool. You're golden. You're done. (This sort of makes you sound like chicken, doesn't it?)

All you need to do is click Finished to tell Quicken you're done. Quicken displays a congratulations message telling you how proud it is of you and then asks if you want to print a reconciliation report.

If you want to save a tree, skip the report. If you like paperwork, own stock in a paper company, or have a friend in the timber industry, print the report.

As you mark credit card transactions as cleared, Quicken puts a c in the Clr column of the credit card register. As part of finishing up, Quicken changes all these cs to Rs. There isn't any great magic in this. Quicken just does this to identify the transactions that have already been through the reconciliation process. (The c shows a transaction has been marked as cleared. The R shows a transaction has been reconciled.)

If the difference doesn't equal zero, you've got a problem. If you clicked Finished in spite of the problem, Quicken displays a message that has some cursory explanation as to why your account doesn't balance. This message also tells you that you can force the two amounts to agree by pressing Enter.

You know what, though? Forcing the two amounts to agree isn't a very good idea. To do this, Quicken adds a cleared transaction equal to the difference. (Quicken asks for a category if you choose the adjustment route.)

Despite the ease of making adjustments, a much better way is to fix the reason for the difference.

Chapter 7 provides some ideas for trying to figure out why a bank account that should balance won't. You can apply the same list of ten tips to credit card reconciliations if you're in a bad way.

Postponing the inevitable

You can postpone reconciling the account by clicking the Finish Later button. Doing so abandons your reconciliation work. Transactions that you marked as cleared still show the c in the Clr text box. You still have an inexplicable difference between the credit card statement and your register. Even so, postponing a reconciliation is usually better than forcing the cleared balance to equal the credit card statement balance. By postponing a reconciliation, you can hopefully find the problem or problems. You can fix them. Then you can restart the reconciliation and finish your work. (You restart a reconciliation the same way you originally start one.)

Paying the bill as part of the reconciliation

After you finish the reconciliation, Quicken politely asks if you want to pay the bill. Figure 10-10 shows the Make Credit Card Payment dialog box, which is the tool Quicken uses to collect the necessary data.

Figure 10-10:
The Make
Credit Card
Payment
dialog box.

You can probably figure out how to use this baby yourself, but hey, I'm on a roll. So here are the steps:

1. **Enter the bank account on which you'll write the check.**

   Open the Bank Account drop-down list box and select the account. Notice that the screen tells you what your register shows as the credit card balance, not what your credit card statement shows. I thought this was a nice touch.

2. **Indicate whether you'll print a check with Quicken or write one by hand.**

   Select the Printed Check option button if you want to print a check with Quicken. Select the Hand Written Check button if you'll write a check by hand.

3. **Click Yes.**

   If you told Quicken that you want to print a check, Quicken displays the Write Checks window so that you can tell Quicken to print a check. (See Chapter 5 for information on how to do this.) If you told Quicken that you want to write a check, Quicken displays the register window in which you can add the missing information to complete the transaction. (See Chapter 4 for information on this.) Quicken assumes that you want to pay the entire credit card balance.

Note: If you don't want to pay the entire credit card balance, you can edit the check amount that Quicken suggests after Quicken displays the Write Checks window or the register window.

4. **Enter the check into the Write Checks window or the register window.**

   Describe the check as one that you will either print with Quicken or write by hand.

As I said earlier in this chapter, this usually isn't the easiest way to pay a credit card bill. But, hey, you're an adult. You make your own choices.

So What about Debit Cards?

Debit cards, when you get right down to it, aren't really credit cards at all. They're more like bank accounts. Rather than withdrawing money by writing a check, you withdraw money by using a debit charge.

While a debit card looks (at least to your friends and the merchants you shop with) like a credit card, you should treat it like a bank account.

In a nutshell, here's what you need to do:

- ✔ Set up a checking account with the starting balance equal to the deposit you make with the debit card company.

- ✔ When you charge something using your debit card, record the transaction just as you would record a regular check.

- ✔ When you replenish the debit balance by sending more money to the debit card company, record the transaction just as you would record a regular deposit.

If all this sounds pretty simple, it is. In fact, I'd go so far as to say that if you've been plugging along, doing just fine with a checking account, you'll find keeping track of a debit card as easy as eating a bag of potato chips.

The Online Bank Hoopla

The newest release of Quicken provides an interesting new feature: online banking. What this means is that if you've got your credit card with a credit card company — probably a bank — that is set up to handle Quicken's online banking, you can grab your credit card statement directly from the credit card company.

The big hoopla concerning this feature — at least as it relates to credit cards — is that you don't have to enter the credit card transactions into a register. Rather, you retrieve them by using a modem.

Should you even bother?

Is the Bank Online/credit card thing a feature that you should look into? Does it really save you time? Is it a good deal? Inquiring minds want to know, so I'll tell you what I think. (I should point out that what I'm about to say next is just my humble opinion.)

I think it's well worth the fee you probably have to pay for the service when you consider the time savings. Shoot. If you're a heavy hitter running $20,000 or $30,000 a month in charges through your account, your time savings will be substantial. And you'll probably pay only a few dollars a month. (What you pay depends on the bank issuing the credit card.)

Something bothers me about the whole deal, however: You're really just receiving an electronic version of your statement. Which means — at least from my perspective — that it's more likely that you won't see erroneous transactions. And reconciling your bank statement against, well, your bank statement isn't going to make a whole heck of a lot of sense. (Golly gee, Batman, the charge to Mulva's Pet School appears on both statements, too!)

Another thing is that you do have some extra fiddling to do. Now there's nothing particularly complicated about grabbing credit card charges off another computer. Nor are there any special magic tricks you need to know to use a modem. (There is a secret handshake your computer and the bank's credit card computer do every time they want to talk, but you'll get the scoop on this once you join the club.) Nevertheless, the fiddling takes some time.

How to do it

Okay, so you've listened to my side of the story, but you still want to use Quicken's Bank Online feature with your credit card — and your bank is one that provides this service. "What next?" you're wondering.

Actually, the whole process is pretty simple. You need to contact your bank and tell it you want the service. You have to fill out some paperwork, and then, a few days later, you receive some information that you need as you set up the credit card. (If you've already set up the credit card account, you can add the information you need by displaying the Account List window, selecting the credit card account, and clicking the Edit button.) I talk about the Bank Online options earlier in the chapter, so I won't go into that again here.

After you have the account set up for online banking, you just choose Features⇨Online⇨Online Banking Investments. The first time you choose this command, Quicken has you sign up for something called an Intuit Online Services Membership. To sign up, you just fill in the blanks on a window that asks for your name and address. (This sign-up just lets Intuit and the bank know who you are.)

After Quicken displays the Bank Online window, identify your bank using the drop-down list box and then click the Get Online Data button. Quicken grabs your data from the bank. After it finishes, Quicken displays something called a Transmission Summary window (which does just what its title suggests). If you click OK, you can peruse the credit card transactions that Quicken downloaded. (*Downloading* just means your computer grabbed information from another computer. Because *grabbing* doesn't sound as cool, however, computer geeks long ago decided to call this process *downloading*.)

Note: For more information about Quicken's online banking feature, see Appendix B.

Chapter 11

Other People's Money

A popular financial self-help writer thinks that one of the secrets to financial success is using other people's money: the bank's, the mortgage company's, the credit people's, your brother-in-law's. . . . You get the idea.

Me? I'm not so sure that other people's money is the key to financial success. I do know that borrowing other people's money can turn into a nightmare.

Quicken can help you here. No, the folks at Intuit won't make your loan payments for you. But in a way, they do something even better. They provide you with a tool to monitor the money you owe other people and the costs of your debts.

Should You Bother to Track Your Debts?

I think it's a good idea to track your debts — car loans, mortgages, student loans, and so on — when lenders fail to tell you the amount you're paying in annual interest or the amount you owe after each and every payment.

If your lenders are doing a good job at keeping you informed, I don't think there's much sense in using Quicken for this purpose. Heck, it's their money. They can do the work, right?

Let me make one more observation. If lenders have half a clue, they send you a 1098 tax form at the end of every year. The number shown on that form equals your tax deduction if the interest stems from a mortgage, business, or investment loan. Note that personal interest expenses aren't deductible anymore, so there's little reason to track them unless you really want to be mean to yourself.

How Do I Get Started?

To track other people's money with Quicken, you must set up a *liability account*. *Liability* is a big word.

But it's easy to set up one of these babies. Just remember that you must set up a liability account for every loan or debt: your mortgage, your car loan, your student loan, and so on, ad nauseam.

Setting up a liability account for an amortized loan

An *amortized loan* is one on which you make regular, equal-sized payments. Over time, the principal portion of each payment pays off, or amortizes, the loan principal. If you borrowed money to purchase a house, a car, a Winnebago, or anything else that's really expensive and lasts for several years, chances are that your loan is of the amortizing variety.

Let me say just one more thing. Setting up a loan requires a couple of dozen steps. But none of the steps is difficult. And none takes that much time to complete. As long as you've got your loan information handy — the loan amount, interest rate, balance, and so on — you'll find it a snap to set up this type of account.

Here's the recipe for setting up a liability account:

1. **Click the Accts icon on the iconbar.**

   Quicken, now well accustomed to your sure-footed direction, displays the Account List window.

2. **Click the <u>N</u>ew button in the Account List window.**

   Quicken, with little or no complaint, displays the Create New Account dialog box that asks which type of account you want to create.

3. **Select the Liability option button, the Next button, and then the Summary button.**

   Quicken displays the Liability Account Setup dialog box, as shown in Figure 11-1.

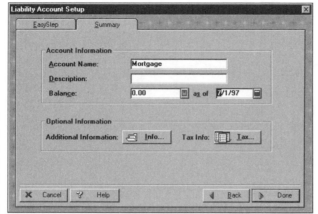

Figure 11-1:
The Liability
Account
Setup dialog
box.

4. **Name the liability.**

   Type something clever (and hopefully useful) in the Account Name text box.

5. **(Optional) Enter a description of the account.**

   If the account name isn't descriptive enough, you can enter the account number or the name of the lender, for example. And if that's not enough, you can click Info to collect additional information. Just fill out the dialog box Quicken displays.

6. **Enter the balance of your loan after your last payment.**

   (If you don't have this figure — and who does? — call your lender.) Move the cursor to the Balance text box and type the amount that you owe.

7. **Enter the date of your last payment in the as of text box.**

   This date is the date as of which you owe the balance you entered in Step 6. Type the date in MM/DD/YY fashion. (For example, type **7/1/97** for July 1, 1997.)

8. **Click Done.**

   Quicken displays a message box that asks if you'd like to set up an amortized loan for the new liability account.

9. If you want to set up an amortized loan, click Yes.

An amortized loan is just a loan with regular monthly payments that include both principal and interest. If you don't want to do this, click No. You're done. You can skip the rest of the steps. If you click Yes, Quicken displays the Loan Setup dialog box. Click the Summary tab to see the dialog box exactly as it's shown here (see Figure 11-2).

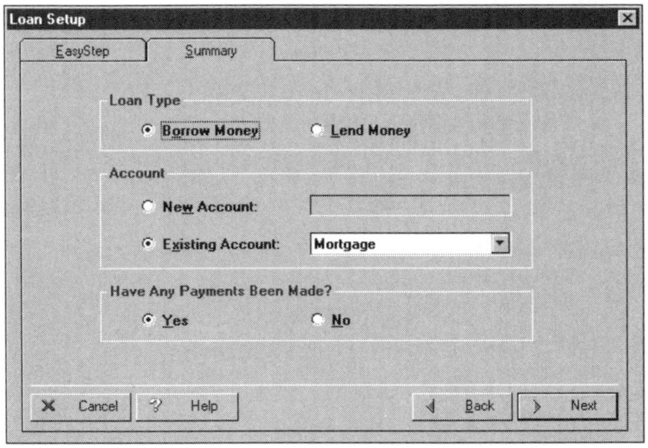

Figure 11-2:
The Loan Setup dialog box.

10. Provide some basic background information.

Use the Loan Type option buttons to specify whether you're borrowing money or lending money. And use the Have Any Payments Been Made option buttons to indicate, well, whether you've started making payments yet. (You shouldn't need to do another thing with the Account buttons and boxes.) Then click next. Quicken displays another set of boxes and buttons as shown in Figure 11.3.

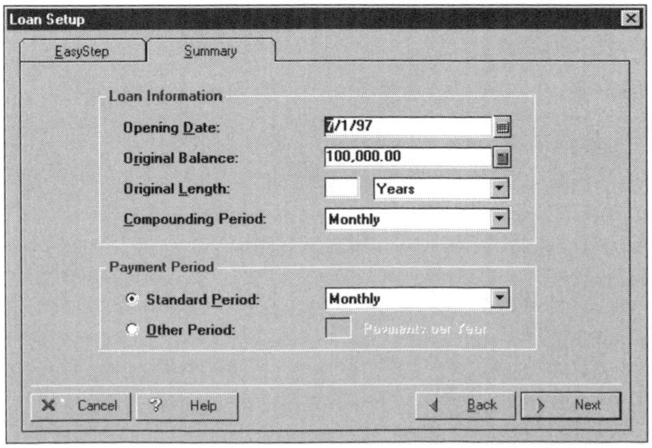

Figure 11-3:
Another Loan Setup dialog box.

11. Enter the date you borrowed the money in the Opening Date text box.

Quicken needs to know this date so that it can calculate the interest the loan started to accrue when you borrowed the money. The program suggests the as of date you supplied when you set up the liability account.

12. Enter the original loan balance.

Quicken plugs the number you set as the liability account starting balance into the Original Balance text box. If this amount isn't correct, no problem. Move the cursor to the Original Balance text box and then type the amount you originally borrowed.

13. Enter the loan term in years in the Original Length text box.

If you set up a 30-year mortgage, for example, type **30**. There's one tiny trick to entering this figure: If you set up a loan that includes a balloon payment, enter the number of years over which the loan will be fully paid. For example, loan payments might be calculated based on a 30-year term, but the loan might require a balloon payment at the end of seven years. In this case, type **7** in the Original Length text box.

14. Indicate how often the bank will calculate loan interest.

The interest compounding period usually equals the payment period.

15. Describe how often you'll make a loan payment by using the Payment Period options.

If you'll make regular monthly payments, for example, select the Standard Period option button and then open the Standard Period drop-down list box and select Monthly. If you can't find an entry in the Standard Period drop-down list box that describes how often you'll make payments, select the Other Period option button and then enter the number of payments you'll make each year in the Payments per Year text box.

16. Click Next.

Quicken displays another set of boxes and buttons in the Summary tab (see Figure 11-4).

17. Describe the balloon payment — if there is one.

The balloon payment option buttons and boxes let you alert Quicken to any balloon payment you're required to make in addition to the last regular loan payment. If the loan doesn't have a balloon payment, ignore this stuff. If the loan does have a balloon, select the Amortized Length option button; then use the Amortized Length text box and drop-down list box to specify the number of years or months (or whatever) the loan is amortized over. If you know that you have a loan payment (and know the loan payment amount) but don't know what or when it occurs, select the Calculate option button.

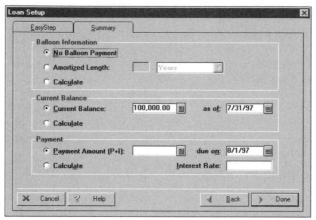

Figure 11-4:
Some more
buttons and
boxes you
can use to
describe the
amortized
loan.

18. Enter the current balance.

Specify how much you currently owe on the loan after making the last payment by using the Current Balance text box. You know the drill by now. Just move the cursor to the text box and pound a few number keys.

19. Enter the date as of which the current balance is, well, current.

Use the as of date field to indicate the date for which you've entered the current balance. By the way, all the standard date entry and date editing tricks apply to this text box. You can press the + and – keys, for example, to move the date ahead and back by one day. And you can click that icon at the right end of the date text box to display a pop-up calendar.

20. Specify the interest rate.

Enter the loan's interest rate into the Interest Rate text box. The loan interest rate, by the way, isn't the same thing as the APR, or annual percentage rate. You want to enter the actual interest rate used to calculate your payments. Enter the interest rate as a decimal amount. For example, don't type 7 5/8, type **7.625**. You should be able to get this amount from the lender or the prospective lender.

21. Describe the payment — if necessary.

If you've entered all the loan information that Quicken has requested in the preceding steps, you can just select the Calculate button and click Done. In this case, Quicken calculates the loan payment using the loan balance, term, balloon payment information, and interest rate you've already entered. If you haven't entered all this information — say you left out the balloon payment information because you don't know what it is — select the Payment Amount (P +I) button and then enter the loan principal and interest amount into the Payment Amount (P+I) text box. If necessary, edit the next payment date in the due on drop-down list box.

22. **Click Done.**

    Quicken displays the Set Up Loan Payment dialog box (see Figure 11-5.)

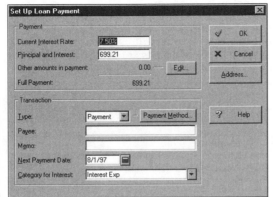

23. **Verify the principal and interest payment calculated by the program.**

    If it's wrong, you can keep going, but let me point out a minor but annoying problem. You probably entered one of the loan calculation inputs incorrectly, such as the loan balance, the loan term, or the interest rate. Fortunately, these errors are only a minor bummer. Later in the chapter (in the "Fixing loan stuff" section), I describe how to restart.

24. **(Optional) Indicate any amounts you pay besides principal and interest.**

    Click the E̲dit button. Quicken displays the Edit dialog box, which you can use to describe any additional amounts the lender requires you to pay. In the case of a mortgage, for example, you might be required to pay property taxes or private mortgage insurance. After you enter information and click OK, Quicken calculates the full payment and redisplays the Set Up Loan Payment dialog box.

25. **Indicate how you make payments.**

    Select one of the payment transaction types listed in the T̲ype drop-down list box. Payment means that you hand-write checks, Print Check means that you print checks by using Quicken, and Online Pmt means that you use Quicken's Online Banking to make electronic payments.

    If you print checks by using Quicken and want to put the payee's address on the check, click the A̲ddress button in the Set Up Loan Payment dialog box. Quicken displays a dialog box that you can use to input the payee's address.

26. Type the lender's name in the Payee text box.

The payee is just the name of the person or business who loaned you the money.

27. (Optional) Enter a memo description.

Does the lender always get mixed up when you send the check? Stick the loan account number in the check's Memo text box. I refrain from using this text box to comment on the fairness of the bank's interest rate, to mock the intelligence of the loan payment processors, or to perform other emotionally gratifying but generally unproductive acts.

28. Enter the date of your next loan payment in the Next Payment Date text box.

29. Enter the interest category.

Open the Category for Interest drop-down list box and select the appropriate category.

Quicken lets you schedule or memorize loan payments and electronic payments so that it can remind you of the payment or even make the payment automatically. I'm going to assume that you don't want to be doing this kind of stuff — at least not yet. If I'm assuming incorrectly, click the Payment Method button. Then fill out the dialog box that appears. It's not all that difficult.

If you're still confused, I talk about how you can use the Financial Calendar to schedule loan payments later in the chapter.

30. (Optional) Indicate that you want to make the loan payment immediately.

If you want to make the loan payment right this exact minute, click the Pay Now button. Quicken displays a message box that asks from which account the payment should be made. You select the account by using the message box's drop-down list box. Then click OK. Quicken enters the payment in the register and displays the View Loans dialog box. If you choose to make the payment immediately, this step is the last one you perform.

31. With the Set Up Loan Payment dialog box displayed, click OK.

Quicken removes the Set Up Loan Payment dialog box and displays the Account List.

32. Double-click the Liability accounts name to display its register (see Figure 11-6).

By the way, I want to apologize to you for describing a 32-step process. There's nothing I could do about it. But I feel bad anyway.

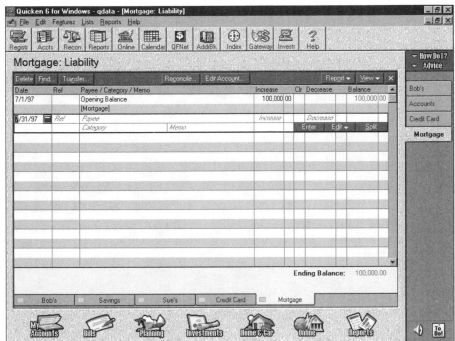

Figure 11-6:
The Liability
register.

Fixing loan stuff

Nobody's perfect, right? It's possible that you made a tiny little mistake in setting up either the loan or the loan payment. It doesn't need to be a major financial or personal crisis, however. Just use the View Loans window to identify the incorrectly described loan and then make your corrections (see Figure 11-7). If the View Loans window isn't displayed, choose Features⇨Paying Bills⇨Loans.

After you see the View Loans window, click the Choose Loan button and select the loan that you want to change. Quicken gives you all the dirt on the selected loan in the View Loans window's Loan Summary and Payment Graph tabs.

Changing loan or loan payment information

If you want to change something about the loan, click the Edit Loan button. Quicken displays the Edit Loan dialog box, which works exactly like the Loan Setup dialog box shown in Figures 11-2 and 11-3. Make your changes and click OK.

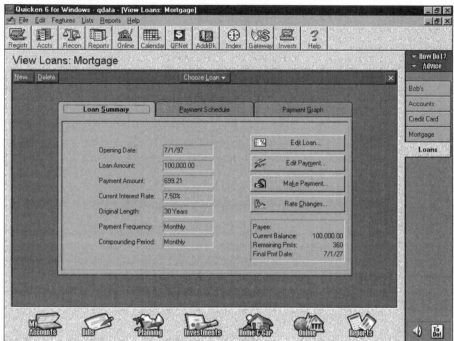

Figure 11-7:
The View
Loans
window.

To change something about the payment, click the Edit Payment button. Quicken displays the Edit Loan dialog box. Make your changes and click OK.

Working with adjustable rate loans

Before I wrap up this discussion, let me mention a couple other things. If you're working with a variable rate loan, you can click the Rate Changes button to display the Loan Rate Changes dialog box (see Figure 11-8). This dialog box has a very simple purpose in life: It lists the interest rates you entered for a loan and the dates these interest rates were used in loan calculations.

If you want to record new interest rates — because you have a variable rate loan and the interest rate changes, for example — click the New button in the Loan Rate Changes dialog box. Quicken displays the Insert an Interest Rate Change dialog box, as shown in Figure 11-9.

Use the Effective Date text box to indicate when the new interest rate becomes effective. You can either type in a date or open the drop-down list box and select a date from the calendar.

Enter the new interest rate in the Interest Rate text box. Quicken then recalculates the loan payment and sticks the new loan payment figure into the Regular Payment text box.

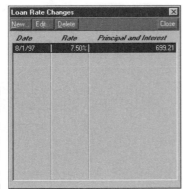

Figure 11-8:
The Loan
Rate
Changes
dialog box.

Figure 11-9:
The Edit
Interest
Rate
Change
dialog box.

Adding and removing loans

You can add and delete loans by using the View Loans window.

Delete a loan that you no longer need or shouldn't have added in the first place by selecting the loan from the Loan drop-down list box. Then click Delete.

You can add loans from the View Loans window, too (refer to Figure 11-7). To do so, click the View Loans window's New button. Quicken displays the Loan Setup dialog box and walks you through that sequence of steps to set up the loan that I describe earlier. For example, you fill out both the Loan Setup dialog box (refer to Figures 11-2 and 11-4) and the Set Up Loan Payment dialog box (refer to Figure 11-5).

Delivering a Pound of Flesh (aka Making a Payment)

After you set up a liability account, you're ready to give the lender his pound of flesh — that is, make a payment. Before you say that this phrase is just some sort of populist bull-dweeble, I want to remind you that this metaphor comes from Shakespeare — Shylock uses it in *The Merchant of Venice*.

Recording the payment

After you set up the loan and the loan payment, you're ready to record the payment in (drum roll, please) the register.

I'm trying to make the old Quicken register more exciting for you because you're probably becoming pretty darn familiar with it. And familiarity, as they say, breeds contempt.

Anyway, complete the following steps to record a payment:

1. **Display the View Loans window.**

   If the View Loans window isn't displayed, choose Fe̲atures⇨Paying Bi̲lls⇨L o̲ans.

2. **Display the Loan you want to pay.**

3. **Click the Make Payment button.**

   Quicken displays a message box that asks whether the payment you're making is a regular payment (one the lender expects) or an extra payment (perhaps to more quickly amortize the loan). After you select the payment type, Quicken displays the Make Regular Payment or Make Extra Payment dialog box. Figure 11-10 shows the Make Regular Payment dialog box, but the Make Extra Payment dialog box looks almost exactly the same.

Figure 11-10:
The Make
Regular
Payment
dialog box.

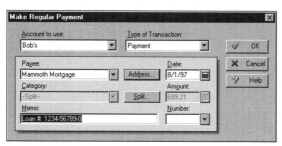

4. **Describe the loan payment.**

   I'm not going to give you the blow-by-blow account here. If you've gotten this far, you don't need my help. (Mostly, as you know, you just type stuff in boxes.)

5. **Click OK.**

   Quicken enters the loan payment in the Liability register and bank account register. You're done.

Handling mortgage escrow accounts

We should talk about one minor mortgage record-keeping annoyance — mortgage escrow accounts.

If you have a mortgage, you know the basic procedure. Although your mortgage payment may be $700 a month, your friendly mortgage company (while insisting that it trusts you completely) makes you pay an extra $150 a month for property taxes and other such things. In other words, even though you're paying only $700 a month in principal and interest, your monthly payment to the mortgage company is, according to this example, $850 ($700 + $150).

The mortgage company, as you probably know, saves this money for you in an *escrow account* or a set of escrow accounts. A couple of times a year the mortgage company pays your property taxes, and a time or two a year it pays your homeowner's insurance. If you have private mortgage insurance, it may pay this fee every month as well. And so it goes.

The question, then, is how to treat this stuff. As with most things, there's an easy way, which is rough, dirty, and unshaven, and there's a hard way, which is precise, sophisticated, and cumbersome.

You can choose whichever method you want. It's your life.

The rough, dirty, and unshaven method

Suppose that you do pay an extra $150 a month. You can treat this extra $150 as another expense category, such as Other Housing or Property Expenses. (I'm just making up these categories. If you can think of better ones, use your own.)

Nice. Easy. No fuss. These words and phrases pop into my head when I think about the rough, dirty, and unshaven method of mortgage escrow record-keeping. Figure 11-11 shows a sample Split Transaction Window filled out this way. (The payment isn't exactly $850 because the earlier example loan payment isn't exactly $700 — it's $699.21.)

Figure 11-11:
A mortgage payment with an escrow account treated as an expense.

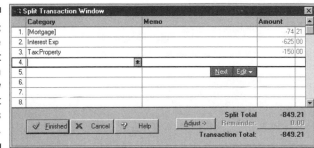

I use the rough, dirty, and unshaven method. Let me make a confession, though. This approach doesn't tell you how much moola you have stashed away in your escrow accounts. It also doesn't tell you how much you really spend in the way of homeowner's insurance, what you're entitled to claim as a property tax deduction, or how much they're bleeding you for private mortgage insurance.

To get these figures, you have to peruse the monthly and annual mortgage account statements — that is, if you get them. Or you have to call the mortgage lender and rattle a cage or two.

Still, with all of its shortcomings, I like the rough, dirty, unshaven method. It's easy to use.

The precise, sophisticated, and cumbersome approach

You say you can't live with the uncertainty, the stress, the not knowing? There's another approach just for you.

You can set up an *asset account* for each of the escrow accounts for which the mortgage company collects money.

You set up asset accounts as you set up other liability accounts. Because I already explained this process, I'll just refresh your memory quickly. You need to set up an asset account with its starting balance equal to the current escrow account balance. To do so, display the Account List window and click the New button to indicate that you want to create a new account. Identify the account as an asset account and give it a name. Then tell Quicken how much money is in the account as of a specific date.

If you've set up an account or two in your time, this process should take you about 40 seconds.

After you set up your asset account and record its current balance, you're ready to cruise. Record payments in the escrow as account transfers whenever you record the actual loan payment.

You need to do one other thing. When you set up an escrow account, you must record the payments that the bank makes from your escrow account to the county assessor (for property taxes) and to the insurance company (for things such as homeowner's and private mortgage insurance). You don't know when these payments are really made, so watch your monthly mortgage account statements.

When the mortgage company disburses money from the escrow account to pay your first property tax assessment, for example, you need to record a decrease equal to the payment for property taxes and then categorize the transaction as a property tax expense. This process isn't tricky in terms of mechanics. The account increases every loan payment. The account decreases when there's a disbursement.

Basically, the Asset Account register mirrors the checking account register. The only difference is that the Payment and Deposit fields in the latter are labeled Decrease and Increase in the former.

This second approach doesn't seem like all that much work, does it? And if you use this approach, you can track escrow balances and escrow spending precisely. You can, for example, pull your property tax deduction right from Quicken. Jeepers, maybe I should try the sophisticated approach next year.

Your Principal-Interest Breakdown Won't Be Right

I don't want to bum you out, but your principal interest breakdown will often be wrong. You might calculate interest expense as $712.48, for example, when your bank calculates it as $712.47. A few pennies here, a few pennies there, and pretty soon your account balance and interest expense tallies are, well, a few pennies off.

So you can't change the world

You can try calling the bank, telling whomever you talk to what a bozo he (or she) is, and then demanding that someone there correct your balance. (If this approach works for you, let me know.)

Or (and this method is really more practical) you can adjust your records to agree with the bank's. Here's how:

1. **Display the register for the liability.**

2. **Click the Reconcile button.**

   (Go ahead. Tap your keys very hard if you're angry that the bank won't adjust its records.) Quicken displays the Update Account Balance dialog box, as shown in Figure 11-12.

3. **Enter the correct (that is, the one the bank says is correct) account balance.**

   Type the correct figure in the Update Balance to text box. (The amount probably comes from the year-end or month-end loan statement.)

4. **Enter the last day of the month or year for which you're making the adjustment.**

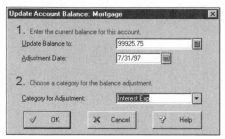

Figure 11-12:
The Update
Account
Balance
dialog box.

Enter a transaction date in the Adjustment Date text box. (The trick here is to use a transaction date that sticks the transaction that fixes the principal-interest split into the right month or year.)

5. Enter your interest expense category.

Type the correct category name in the Category for Adjustment text box. (To see a list of categories, open the drop-down list box.)

6. Record the adjustment.

When the Update Account Balance dialog box correctly describes the needed adjustment, click OK.

Do you think this adjustment business is kooky?

Does the whole adjustment transaction business make sense to you? At times, it can seem kind of backwards, so let me throw out a quick observation.

Remember that as you record loan payments, you split the loan payment between the interest expense category and a principal account transfer that reduces the liability. Here's the tricky part: When the liability gets reduced either too much or not enough, you need to fix both the liability balance *and* the principal-interest split.

Let me give you an example. Suppose that over the course of a year you record $.17 too little interest expense and therefore record $.17 too much principal reduction, despite your best efforts to be accurate. You need to increase the liability account balance by $.17 in this case, but you also need to increase the interest expense figure by $.17. By entering the interest expense category in the Category for Adjustment field, Quicken does these adjustments for you. Pretty cool, huh?

Automatic Loan Payments

Quicken has a couple of nifty features called Scheduled Transactions and the Financial Calendar that can help you with automatic loan payments.

The Financial Calendar and Scheduled Transactions features may be useful in other instances as well. For example, a business might use the Scheduled Transactions and the Financial Calendar to schedule and plan employee payroll checks, tax returns, and deposits.

Scheduling a Loan Payment

If a loan payment occurs regularly, you can set it up as a scheduled payment. When you do so, Quicken automatically records the payment for you based on a schedule.

Consider this example. Suppose that on the fifth day of every month your mortgage company taps your checking account for the full amount of your mortgage payment. (You, of course, have already authorized it to do so. The mortgage company can't take your money willy-nilly.) In this case, you can tell Quicken to record the mortgage payment on the fifth of each month. Kind of handy, right?

Follow these steps to set up such a scheduled transaction:

1. **Choose Features⇨Paying Bills⇨Financial Calendar or click the Calendar icon.**

   Quicken displays the Financial Calendar window, as shown in Figure 11-13. It shows a calendar for the current month and a list of transactions.

2. **Display the first month for which you want to schedule the transaction.**

   Using the Prev Month and Next Month buttons, select the starting month for the scheduled transaction.

3. **Identify the scheduled transaction and date.**

   Select the transaction for which you want to create a schedule. In Figure 11-13, for example, you may want to schedule the Mammoth Mortgage loan payment transaction to fall on the 5th. To do so, select the transaction by clicking it. Then drag the transaction to the 5th. When you release the mouse button, Quicken displays a dialog box that asks you to confirm the principal and interest breakdown. You won't know whether the breakdown is correct until you see the bank statement, so click OK. Quicken displays the New Transaction dialog box (see Figure 11-14).

Figure 11-13:
The
Financial
Calendar
window.

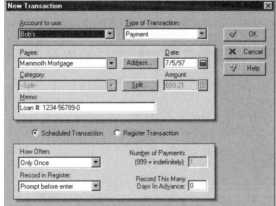

Figure 11-14:
The New
Transaction
dialog box.

4. Identify the account from which the payment should be made.

Open the Account to use drop-down list box and then select the appropriate account.

5. Verify that the transaction type is Payment.

Open the Type of Transaction drop-down list box and select Payment. (Of course, if you were setting up some other type of payment, you might choose something else.)

6. **Verify that the Payee, Date, and Memo fields are correct.**

They probably are. But I have kind of a compulsive personality. Because I've been telling you to check all this other stuff, I thought I'd also suggest you check these three fields.

7. **Use the Scheduled Transaction and the Register Transaction option buttons to indicate how often the scheduled transaction should occur.**

If you indicate a transaction is a scheduled transaction, use the How Often drop-down list box and the Number of Payments text box to indicate the payment frequency and the number of payments.

8. **Tell Quicken whether you want to double-check the scheduled transaction before it actually gets entered in the register.**

This is easy. Just open the Record in Register drop-down list box to select the Prompt before enter choice.

9. **Indicate the number of days in advance you want to be reminded of the scheduled payment.**

Move the cursor to the Record this many days in Advance text box and enter a number. This input actually determines how many days in advance Quicken displays a Reminder window to jog your memory about a scheduled transaction. (The Reminders window appears when you first start Quicken, as mentioned in Chapter 1. It also appears whenever you choose Features⇨Paying Bills⇨Reminders.)

10. **Click OK.**

Quicken adds the transaction to its scheduled transaction list.

Quicken takes the Paul Masson approach to finance — it will enter no transaction before its time. So when the time is right — meaning next month on the 5th for this example — Quicken enters the transaction automatically. Furthermore, Quicken enters the transaction automatically each month until you tell it to stop.

More stuff about scheduled transactions

You already know the most important thing about scheduled transactions: how to set one up. Here are some other nuggets of knowledge that you might find useful.

Quicken identifies a calendar day for scheduled transactions by marking the day with the color green. You can see which transactions are scheduled for a day by clicking that day.

Another thing: You don't have to use the Financial Calendar to set up scheduled transactions. You can choose Lists➪Scheduled Transactions instead. This command displays a window that lists all scheduled transactions and provides buttons that you can use to add, edit, or delete scheduled transactions. The functions of this window are pretty straightforward. To delete a scheduled transaction, for example, just select it from the list and click the Delete button.

More stuff about the Financial Calendar

The iconbar at the top of the Financial Calendar provides some other tools you may want to use. I'm not going to spend a lot of time on them; you'll have more fun trying them out yourself than you would reading about them. Nevertheless, let me give you a bird's-eye view:

- ✔ The Options button displays a dialog box you can use to select which accounts are listed on the Financial Calendar's list of transactions and how QuickFill works with the Financial Calendar.

- ✔ The Note button lets you post a note on a calendar day. You use this feature to create reminder notes. For example, you might want to post a note saying, "Remember Wedding Anniversary," on the big day. After you click this button, Quicken displays a dialog box in which you type the message. Then you click Save. Quicken's Billminder utility displays your calendar notes. The program also marks the calendar day with a little yellow square — a miniature Post-It Note. Click the square to read the message.

- ✔ The Close button removes the Financial Calendar from the Quicken desktop. But, shoot, you probably figured that out already, didn't you?

- ✔ The View button displays a menu of commands that let you specify which transactions should appear in the calendar, add an account balances graph to the calendar window and fiddle with the memorized transactions list. The transactions shown in that list box along the right edge of the Financial Calendar window, by the way, are memorized transactions.

Chapter 12

Mutual Funds

. . . .

In This Chapter

▶ Knowing when to use Quicken's investment record-keeping

▶ Setting up a mutual fund investment account

▶ Recording your initial mutual fund investment

▶ Buying mutual fund shares

▶ Recording mutual fund profits

▶ Selling mutual fund shares

▶ Adjusting your mutual fund shares

▶ Adjusting mutual fund price information

. . . .

I don't mean to scare you, but I think investment record-keeping is Quicken's most complicated feature. So it's time to get down to business. Time to stop pussyfooting around. Time to earn my pay.

To Bother or Not to Bother?

Quicken's investment record-keeping feature lets you do three important things:

✔ Track your interest and dividend income

✔ Track real and potential capital gains and losses

✔ Measure an investment's performance by calculating an internal rate of return

If you're a serious investor, these things probably sound worthwhile. But before you invest any time learning how Quicken's investment record-keeping works, be sure that you need all this power.

Are your investments tax-deferred?

If your investments are tax-deferred — if, for example, you're using individual retirement accounts (IRAs), 401(k)s, or Keoghs — you don't really need to track investment income and capital gains and losses. Tax-deferred investments have no effect on your personal income taxes. You get a tax deduction for the money you stick into IRAs, for example, and anything you take out is taxable.

With tax-deferred investments, you record all that you should need to know via your checking account. Checks earmarked for investment are categorized as "IRA Deductions," for example, while investment account withdrawals deposited into your checking account are categorized as "IRA Distributions." In other words, you don't need to set up special accounts for tracking your investments. Everything you need to keep track of gets tracked in your bank accounts.

Are you a mutual fund fanatic?

If you're a fan of mutual funds, you won't need Quicken to measure the fund's annual returns. The fund manager provides these figures for you in quarterly and annual reports.

Some investors don't need Quicken

Let me give you an example of someone who doesn't need to use Quicken's investments feature — me. Once upon a time, I bought and sold common stocks, fooled around with half a dozen mutual funds, and learned firsthand why junk bonds are called junk bonds. Over the last few years, though, I've simplified my financial affairs considerably.

I don't invest directly in stocks, bonds, or mutual funds these days; instead, I stick money into an IRA. My investments don't produce taxable dividends or interest income, nor do they produce taxable or tax-saving capital gains or losses. Money I put into the IRA is tax-deductible. And money I ultimately take out of the IRA will be taxable.

I'm also sticking with a handful of mutual funds, but I don't need to calculate the annual return — that's what mutual fund managers do. So I don't need to separately figure, for example, what my shares of Vanguard Index Trust delivered as an annual return when I include both the 3 percent dividend and the 10 percent price drop.

Because I don't need to track investment income, or track capital gains and losses, or calculate the progress of my investment portfolio, I don't need Quicken's investment record-keeping for my personal use.

Many investors do need Quicken

Of course, many people do benefit from Quicken's investment record-keeping. If you routinely buy stocks and bonds, you probably want to calculate your annual returns. What's more, if you try to monitor your capital gains and losses intelligently — and you should — you want to know both what you originally paid for securities and what they're worth currently.

The size of your investment portfolio isn't an issue. For example, I have two daughters who are saving money for college. (Actually, in a cruel twist of fate, *I* am saving; they're simply accumulating.) Although Beth and Britt haven't saved much money, and although they use mutual funds to keep things simple, they do three things that cause nightmarishly complex record-keeping for their poor, overworked, and grossly underpaid accountant — Dad: They reinvest their quarterly dividend income, pay annual maintenance fees, and coerce their parents into adding more and more money to their investment portfolios.

What's the big deal? All three things adjust the *basis* in the fund. And when Beth and Britt sell their mutual fund shares, their gain (or loss) will be determined by subtracting the basis from the sales proceeds.

The bottom line: Even though Beth and Britt don't have much money, I need to use Quicken to track their investments.

Tracking a Mutual Fund

If you still think that you need to track a mutual fund investment, you need to know how to set up a mutual fund account and then record your investment activities.

Even if you don't invest in mutual funds, you shouldn't skip this section. Understanding how mutual fund record-keeping works makes it much, much easier for you to track other, more complicated investments. Like stocks. Bonds. Krugerrands. Commodity options.

Setting up a mutual fund investment account

Setting up an investment account works the same way as setting up any other account:

1. **Click the Accts icon on the iconbar.**

   Quicken, ever the faithful companion, displays the Account List window.

2. **Click the New button on the Account List window.**

   Quicken dutifully displays the Create New dialog box you use to indicate you want to create a specific type of account. If you've seen one of these Account dialog boxes, you've seen them all — so I won't show them all as figures.

3. **Click the Investment button and click Next.**

   After Quicken displays the Investment Account Setup dialog box (see Figure 12-1), click the Summary tab.

Figure 12-1:
The Investment Account Setup dialog box.

4. **Name the investment.**

   Move the cursor to the Account Name text box and enter a name for the mutual fund. If you're investing in the Vanguard Index 500 Trust mutual fund, for example, you might type **Vanguard Index**.

5. **(Optional) Enter a description for the account.**

   Move the cursor to the Description text box and type a description.

6. **Select the Account Contains a Single Mutual Fund check box.**

   This tells Quicken, "Yeah, this is a mutual fund investment account."

7. **Indicate whether there's a cash account attached to this mutual fund.**

   There probably isn't, by the way. This "linked checking account" business typically applies to brokerage accounts. With a brokerage account, you need someplace to store the cash that you receive from selling securities and from receiving investment income. And you need someplace from which to get the cash you'll need when you purchase additional shares of some hot, new mutual fund. If you do indicate that there's a linked checking account, you'll need to describe or identify the account. If this is a new mutual fund investment and, therefore, a new linked checking account, click the New Account button and then use the Balance and as of boxes to give the opening balance and transaction date. If the linked checking account is an existing checking account, click the Existing Account button and then select the account from the Existing Account drop-down list box.

8. (Optional) Provide any additional account information.

You can click the Additional Information button to display the cleverly-named Additional Account Information dialog box. You can then use its text boxes to collect and store a bunch of additional information about the mutual fund account: the mutual fund management company, the account number, telephone number, and so forth.

9. Click the Tax button.

Quicken displays the Tax Schedule Information dialog box (see Figure 12-2).

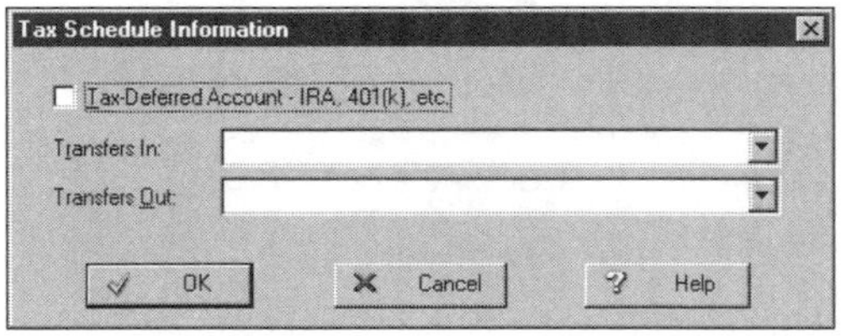

Figure 12-2:
The Tax Schedule Information dialog box.

10. Select the Tax-Deferred Account — IRA, 401(k), etc. check box if the investment is tax-deferred.

This tells Quicken that this information doesn't affect your taxes. As I mentioned earlier, I can't think of a good reason for tracking a tax-deferred mutual fund. But, hey, I just work here.

11. Indicate how transfers into this account and transfers from this account are reported on your tax return.

If this mutual fund is really an IRA, for example, and you've decided to track it with Quicken, activate the Transfers In drop-down list box and select the entry that describes the tax form and tax form line you'll use to report transfers into this account. (For example, in the case of an IRA, you might choose Form 1040: IRA Contribution Self.) Then activate the Transfers Out drop-down list box and select the entry that describes the tax form and tax form line you'll use to report transfers out of this account. You're doing this, by the way, so that Quicken's reports will show all your tax deductions and so that you can export data from Quicken to TurboTax. When you're finished, click OK to close the Tax Schedule Information dialog box.

12. Click Done.

Quicken displays the Set Up Mutual Fund Security dialog box, shown in Figure 12-3. The Name text box shows the name you entered in Step 4.

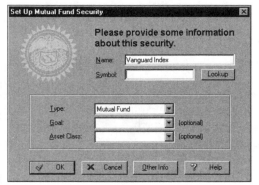

Figure 12-3:
The Set Up Mutual Fund Security dialog box.

13. (Optional) Enter the mutual fund symbol.

If you're going to download share price information via a modem — such as information from QuickenQuotes — move the cursor to the Symbol text box and enter the mutual fund's stock symbol.

14. Indicate the type of investment you're setting up.

Choose an investment type (Bond, CD, Mutual Fund, or Stock) from the Type drop-down list box.

15. Indicate why you're investing.

Choose your goal (College Fund, Growth, High Risk, Income, or Low Risk) from the Goal drop-down list box. This investment stereotyping seems sort of goofy, though. Are there really people who want high-risk investments? Reminds me of an old joke: How do you accumulate a million dollars in the stock market? Start with two million in the stock market.

16. (Optional) Describe the mutual fund's principal investment.

If you will track more than one investment with Quicken and want to monitor the amount you've invested in different asset classes, or investment categories — domestic bonds, domestic large cap, domestic small cap, global bonds, and so forth — activate the Asset Class drop-down list box. Then select the asset class that most closely matches the mutual fund's principal investment. (If this "asset class" business just seems confusing, don't worry about it.)

17. Click OK.

Quicken redisplays the Account List window — except now it lists the new investment account.

Recording your initial investment

After you set up a mutual fund investment account, you can record an initial purchase of fund shares.

Of course, you need to know the original price of those first shares. So dig through that kitchen drawer where you stuff bank statements, financial records, and those kooky birthday cards from Aunt Enid.

When you find the proper paperwork that shows the number of shares you purchased and the price per share, here's what you do:

1. **Open the investment account.**

    Display the Account List window; then select the investment account (with the arrow keys or by clicking the mouse). Click the Open button. Quicken displays the Create Opening Share Balance dialog box (shown in Figure 12-4), which asks for your starting account balance.

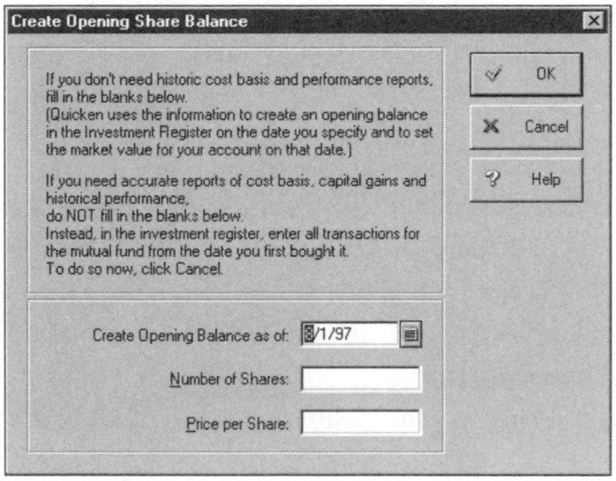

Figure 12-4:
The Create
Opening
Share
Balance
dialog box.

2. **Don't enter anything into the Number of Shares and Price per Share text boxes. Just click Cancel.**

    You don't — I repeat, don't — want to record your initial purchase with this dialog box.

    Quicken displays the investment account register (see Figure 12-5). You're in the big leagues now.

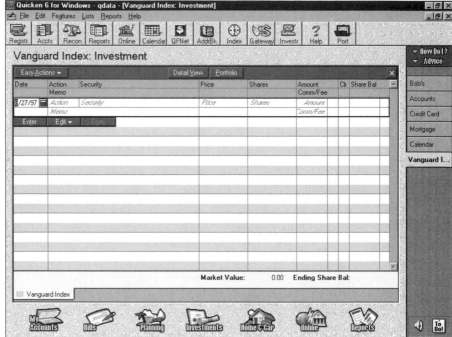

Figure 12-5:
The
investment
account
register
window.

3. Enter the date you first purchased fund shares into the first row's Date field.

Move the cursor to the Date field and type the date using the MM/DD/YY format. Type May 23, 1992, for example, as **5/23/92**. You also may select the date from the pop-up calendar.

4. Indicate that you're recording the prior purchase of shares.

When you move the cursor to the Action field, Quicken displays a down-arrow box, indicating a drop-down list box. From the drop-down list box, select ShrsIn. This tells Quicken, "Yeah, I've purchased some shares of this mutual fund, but I don't want you to adjust my checking account because I bought them a long, long time ago and I recorded the transaction then."

In some Quicken windows, drop-down list boxes don't appear until you move the cursor onto the field.

5. Accept the suggested security name.

The security name is the mutual fund account's name. Move the cursor past the Security field to the Avg. Cost field (Quicken changes the name of this field from Price to Avg. Cost when you select ShrsIn.

6. **Indicate what you paid per share.**

With the cursor on the Price field, enter the share price. You can type a fractional price — such as **10¹/₄** — but your mutual fund shares probably cost something in dollars and cents — such as 10.25.

7. **Indicate the size of your purchase.**

Tell Quicken the size of your initial investment — either total number of shares or total price.

- To enter the total number of shares, move the cursor to the Shares field (fractional shares are okay).

- To enter the total price, move the cursor to the Basis field.

Quicken calculates the piece of data you didn't enter. Suppose, for example, that you spent $500 to purchase 48.7805 shares of a mutual fund that cost $10.25 per share. If you enter the share price as $10.25 and the number of shares as 48.7805, Quicken calculates the total price. If you enter the share price as $10.25 and the total purchase as $500, Quicken calculates the number of shares purchased.

Life doesn't get much better than this, huh?

8. **(Optional) Enter a memo description.**

If you want to tie the purchase to a confirmation order number, for example, enter the data into the Memo field. I suppose that you could use this field to record anything: Kilroy was here. Save the Whales. Don't tread on me.

9. **Record the initial purchase of mutual fund shares.**

Click the Enter button.

Quicken beeps in agony and then records the transaction into the register. Figure 12-6, for example, shows a register that records a $500 purchase of shares in the Vanguard Index mutual fund.

Buying near

As you purchase shares — by sending a check to the mutual fund management company or by reinvesting dividends and capital gain distributions — you should record these transactions in the investment account register.

By writing a check

If you buy shares by writing a check, you have two ways to enter a description of the shares you've purchased.

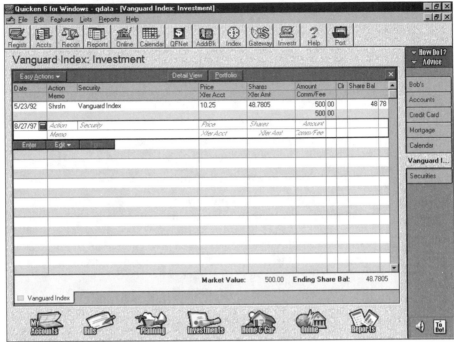

Figure 12-6:
The record
of an initial
purchase of
mutual fund
shares.

I think the easier way is to enter the transaction directly into the investment
account register, much as you enter checks and deposits into a bank account
register. (To display the investment account register, click its QuickTab.) To
record the purchase this way, follow these steps:

1. **Enter the purchase date into the first empty row's Date field.**

2. **Indicate that you're purchasing new shares by check.**

   Move the cursor to the Action field. From the Action drop-down list box,
   select the BuyX action. (You also can type the Action abbreviations
   directly into the field.)

3. **Accept the suggested security name.**

4. **Indicate what you paid per share.**

5. **Indicate the size of your purchase using either the shares or the Basis
   field.**

   Tell Quicken the size of your investment — either total number of shares
   or total price.

6. **(Optional) Enter a memo description.**

7. **Enter the bank account on which you'll write the check that pays for the shares.**

 From the Xfer Acct drop-down list box, select the account name.

8. **Enter the account transfer amount.**

 Move the cursor to the Xfer Amt field and enter the transfer amount.

9. **Enter the commission or fee that you paid.**

 Move the cursor to the Comm Fee field and enter the commission or fee you paid to purchase the shares. (This figure is included in the amount shown in the Amount field.)

10. **Record the purchase.**

 Click the Enter button. Quicken beeps with enthusiasm and then records your purchase of new shares. You are now, by definition, a capitalist. Congratulations.

Figure 12-7 shows a new shares purchase transaction recorded in the investment account register.

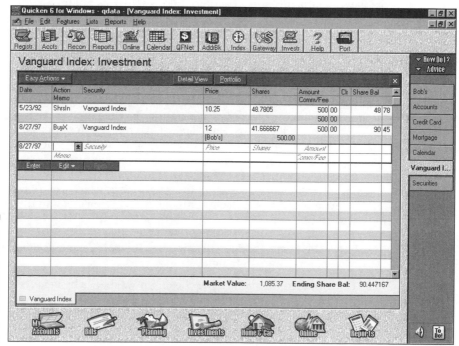

Figure 12-7: The record of a purchase of additional mutual fund shares.

Quicken offers another way to record a shares purchase: The Buy/Add Shares dialog box (see Figure 12-8) prompts you to enter the same information that you record when entering a mutual shares purchase transaction directly into the investment account register. Quicken then records the transaction into the register.

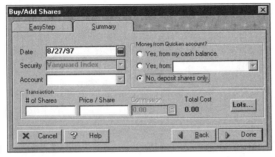

Figure 12-8:
The Buy/
Add Shares
dialog box.

To display the Buy/Add Shares dialog box, click the Easy Actions button, which appears at the top of the investment account register window. When Quicken displays a list of investment actions, choose the Buy Shares action and click the Summary tab. To record an investment purchase using the Buy/Add Shares dialog box, you just describe the purchase using the dialog box's buttons and boxes.

By reinvesting dividends, interest, or capital gains

When you reinvest your dividends, interest, or capital gains, you also have two methods available for recording the transaction: using the register or using the Reinvest Income dialog box. Here again, I like the register approach, so I'll describe it first. (Remember that you get to the investment account register by clicking its QuickTab.)

You can record your reinvestment transactions, in which you're buying new shares, by first displaying the investment account register and then by following these steps:

1. **Enter the purchase date (in this case, the reinvestment date) into the next empty row's Date field.**

2. **Tell Quicken that you're purchasing new shares by reinvesting.**

   Open the Action drop-down list box and select one of the following Reinvest actions:

- **ReinvDiv:** Reinvest dividends
- **ReinvInt:** Reinvest interest
- **ReinvLg:** Reinvest long-term capital gains
- **ReinvSh:** Reinvest short-term capital gains

Use the arrow keys or the mouse to select the appropriate reinvestment action and press Enter. Quicken enters the reinvestment abbreviation in the Action field. You also can type these abbreviations directly in the field after you've memorized them.

You don't need to determine whether the amounts you reinvest are dividends, interest, long-term capital gains, or short-term capital gains because the mutual fund statement tells you this. If you reinvest more than one type of gain, however, you need to record more than one transaction. For example, if the $50 you reinvest is part long-term capital gain and part dividend income, you need to record two transactions: one for the long-term capital gain reinvestment and one for the dividend income reinvestment.

3. **Accept the suggested security name, which Quicken places in the Security field.**

4. **Indicate the price per share that you paid using the Price field.**

5. **Indicate the size of your purchase.**

   You can give Quicken either the number of shares you're purchasing (using the Shares field) or the total dollar amount of the transaction (using the Basis field).

6. **(Optional) Type a brief explanation of the transaction into the Memo field.**

7. **Enter the commission or fee that you paid in the Comm Fee field.**

   The commission fee is included in the figure shown in the Amount field.

8. **Record the reinvestment transaction.**

   Click the Enter button.

Figure 12-9 shows $56.88 of dividends being reinvested in the mutual fund by buying shares that cost $13.65 a piece. Other reinvestments work basically the same way — except you use a different reinvestment action.

As mentioned earlier, the second way to record amounts you reinvest is to click the Easy Actions button and then select the Reinvest Income option. After you choose this command, Quicken displays the Reinvest Income dialog box (see Figure 12-10).

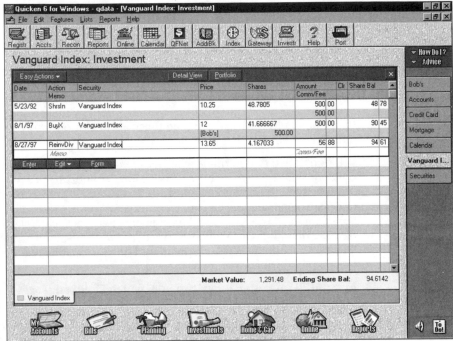

Figure 12-9:
How you
record the
reinvestment
of dividends.

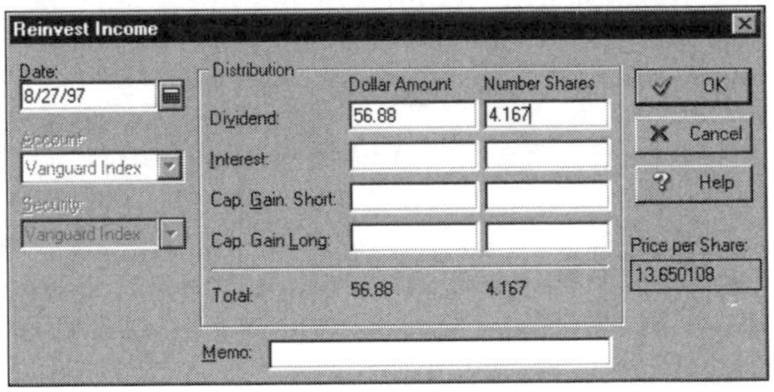

Figure 12-10:
The
Reinvest
Income
dialog box.

To describe an amount you're reinvesting, just fill in the text boxes, which are similar to the fields you fill in when you record the reinvestment directly into the register. After you click OK, Quicken takes the information you entered into the text boxes and records the reinvestment into the investment account register.

Although you can record reinvestment transactions either directly into the register, using the Reinvest Income dialog box does possess a noteworthy advantage. When you use the register approach, you need to record one transaction for each type of income reinvested. When you use the Reinvest Income dialog box, however, you can record the reinvestment of each type of income at the same time: dividends, interest, short-term capital gains, and long-term capital gains. All you need to do is fill out more than one set of Dollar Amount and Number Shares text boxes. Quicken then enters the separate transactions — one for each type of income — into the register.

Recording your profits

Every so often, you may receive distributions directly from the mutual fund company. Retirees, for example, often direct mutual fund managers to send dividend checks and capital gains directly to them rather than have the amounts reinvested.

To record these kinds of distributions, you go through a process very similar to those described earlier. For example, if you want to record an income transaction directly into the investment account register, you follow these steps:

1. **Enter the distribution date into the next empty row's Date field.**

2. **Tell Quicken that you're receiving a distribution from the mutual fund.**

   Open the Action drop-down list box and select the appropriate action to describe the distribution: DivX, to indicate that you're depositing dividends; CGLongX, to indicate that you're depositing long-term capital gains; or CGShortX, to indicate that you're depositing short-term capital gains. Again, when you've memorized these abbreviations — DivX, CGLongX, and CGShortX — you also can type them directly into the Action field.

   You don't need to determine for yourself whether a distribution is a dividend, a long-term capital gain, or a short-term capital gain because the mutual fund statement makes the distribution clear.

3. **Indicate the dividend or capital gains distribution amount.**

   Enter the amount in the Amount text box.

4. **(Optional) Type a brief description of the distribution in the Memo field.**

   Be creative — type your wedding anniversary, the name of your dog, or even a piece of data related to the dividend or distribution.

5. **Indicate into which bank account you'll deposit the dividend or distribution.**

   Open the Xfer Acct, or Transfer Account, drop-down list box and select the account into which you'll deposit the money.

6. Record the dividend or distribution transaction.

You can record the dividend in a bunch of ways, but why not just click the Enter button? Quicken records the reinvestment — bip, bap, boom. It's just that quick.

Figure 12-11 shows $50 of dividends being deposited into a checking account named Bob's.

If you don't want to enter the transaction directly into the investment account register, click the Easy Actions button and choose the Record an Income Event action. Quicken displays the Record Income dialog box (see Figure 12-12).

You record an income transaction in the Record Income dialog box in the same way that you record it directly in the register. You describe the income amount, the category, and the account into which the dividend, interest, or capital gains check is deposited.

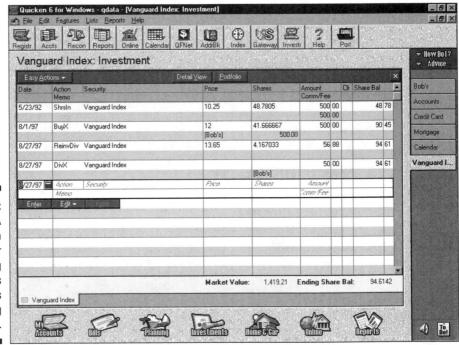

Figure 12-11: A transaction for depositing dividends into Bob's checking account.

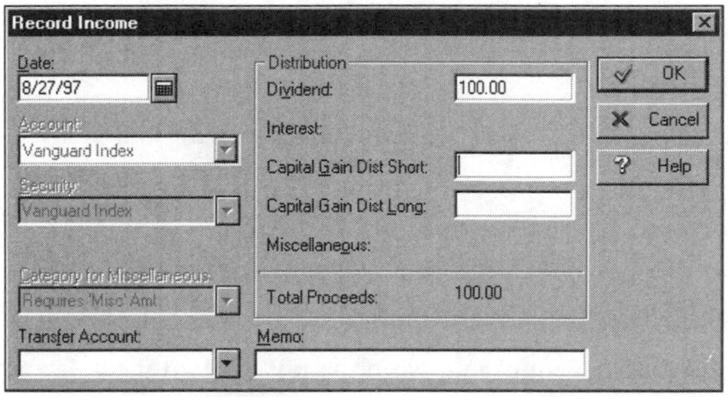

Figure 12-12:
The Record
Income
dialog box.

As with the Reinvest Income dialog box, an advantage of the Record Income dialog box is that you can record several types of income in one fell swoop. Quicken uses the information you type in the Record Income dialog box to enter up to four income transactions into the investment account register.

Selling dear

Selling mutual fund shares works basically the same way as buying them. You can record the sale of shares either directly into the register or by clicking the Easy Actions button and selecting the Sell action. (You get to the investment account register by clicking its QuickTab.) To record the sale of shares directly into the register, perform the following actions:

1. **Enter the sale's date into the next empty row's Date field.**
2. **Tell Quicken that you're selling shares.**

   Open the Action drop-down list box and select the SellX action. (Note that you also can type **SellX** directly into the field.)
3. **Accept the suggested security name, which Quicken places into the Security field.**
4. **Indicate the price per share that you received using the Price field.**

   With a little luck, your sale's price is more than you paid.

5. **Indicate the size of your sale by giving Quicken either the number of shares you sold or the total dollar amount of the sale.**

   Quicken calculates whatever you don't enter. For example, if you tell Quicken how many dollars you sell (using the Amount field), it calculates the number of shares you sell by dividing the total sales amount by the price per share. If you tell Quicken how many shares you sell (using the Shares field), it calculates the total sales amount by multiplying the number of shares by the price per share. I guess this is a handy feature.

6. **(Optional) Type a brief description of the sale in the Memo field.**

7. **Enter the bank account into which you'll deposit the sale's proceeds.**

   Open the Xfer Acct drop-down list box and select the appropriate account.

8. **Enter the account transfer amount.**

   Move the cursor to the Xfer Amt field and type the transfer amount. This amount is what you'll actually deposit into the transfer account. The transfer amount equals the total sales price less the commission you paid.

9. **Enter the commission or fee you paid to sell the shares in the Comm Fee field.**

   No wonder Bernie, your broker, does so well, huh? He makes money whether you do or not.

10. **Click the Enter button.**

    Quicken displays a message box that asks whether you want to specifically identify the shares you're selling. You get to answer Yes or No.

11. **(Optional) Indicate whether you want to use Specific Identification.**

    When Quicken displays the Yes or No message box that asks whether you want to identify specifically which lots you're selling.

    - Click No if you're selling all the shares because specific identification makes no difference in your case.

    - Click Yes if you aren't selling all your shares. Now you can pick and choose which shares to sell so that you can minimize the capital gains taxes you'll owe (good idea, huh?). Quicken displays the Specify Lots for Investment dialog box, shown in Figure 12-13.

12. **(Optional) Identify which lots you're selling.**

    What you do now is pick and choose which lots to sell to minimize the capital gains taxes you owe. A *lot* is simply a batch, or set, of shares that you purchased at one time. If you sell the most expensive lots, you reduce your capital gains and the taxes on those gains.

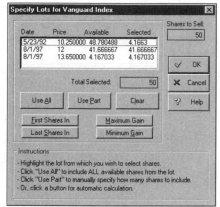

Figure 12-13:
The Specify
Lots for
Investment
dialog box.

To pick an entire lot, double-click it or select it with the mouse and click the Use All button.

To pick a portion of a lot, select it and click the Use Part button. Quicken displays the Specify Quantity dialog box that allows you to indicate how many shares of the lot you want to sell. To do this, just enter the number of shares into the Quantity text box. (I didn't provide a screen shot of this simple dialog box because all it has is one input field for Quantity.)

To clear your selections and start over, click the Clear button.

The Specify Lots for Investment dialog box also provides four nifty command buttons for automating the process of selecting lots. If you click the Maximum Gain or Minimum Gain button, Quicken picks lots for you in a way that produces the largest possible or smallest possible capital gain. Alternatively, you can click the First Shares In or Last Shares In button to sell either the oldest shares or newest shares first. This business about picking the lots you'll sell is rather arbitrary, of course. And by doing it, you can manipulate the capital gain you'll have and the capital gains taxes you'll pay. But it's all legal. And honorable. And it can save you money because you can time your capital gains so that they occur when they'll cost you least.

After the Specify Lots for Investment dialog box correctly shows all the shares you want to sell, click OK. Quicken records the sell transaction in the register.

Figure 12-14 shows shares being sold to pay for Beth's first-quarter community college tuition. Just a few pages ago, she was a little girl. And now she's leaving home. They grow up fast, don't they?

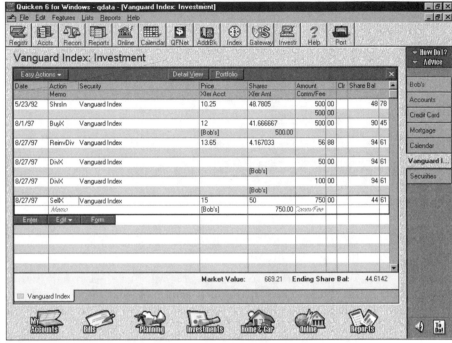

Figure 12-14:
The transaction for recording the sale of mutual fund shares.

If you don't want to record a sell transaction directly into the register, you can click the Easy Actions button and then click the Sell/Remove command. After you choose the command, Quicken displays the Sell/Remove Shares dialog box. Click the Summary tab, and you can enter the same information in the text boxes that you enter in the register's fields (see Figure 12-15). To identify shares specifically, click the Lots button.

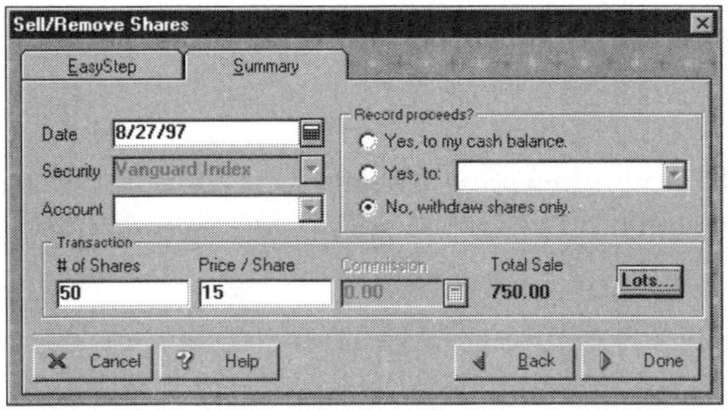

Figure 12-15:
The Sell/ Remove Shares dialog box.

What if you make a mistake?

If you make a mistake, don't worry — it's not a problem. You can edit an investment transaction in the investment account register the same way you edit check and deposit transactions in a bank account register. For example, you can click the fields with the incorrect entries, fix them, and then record the new, corrected transaction.

You also can select the transaction and click the Form button. Quicken then displays the investment dialog box that lets you change each of the pieces of the transaction. The dialog box that Quicken displays mirrors the investment dialog box you could have used originally to record the transaction. For example, the dialog box to edit a sell shares transaction looks much like the Summary tab of the Sell/Remove Shares dialog box shown in Figure 12-15.

Slightly tricky mutual fund transactions

I didn't describe every possible mutual fund transaction — although I have described every one I've encountered in the last 10 or 12 years. You should know, however, that Quicken does let you record three additional transactions by specifying several almost-magical actions: shares out, stock split, and reminder transactions.

How do I remove shares from an account?

You can tell Quicken to remove shares from an account without moving the money represented by the shares to some other account. Why would you want to remove a *shares-out* transaction? I can think of two situations:

✔ You erroneously added shares to the account with the shares in (ShrsIn) action and now you need to remove them or

✔ You are using an investment account to record old investment activity, such as activity from last year

The first instance is self-explanatory because you are simply correcting an error that you made. In the second case, however, you don't want to transfer the proceeds of a mutual fund sale to a checking account because the money from the sale is already recorded as a deposit at some point in the past.

You can record a shares-out transaction directly into the register by moving the cursor to the next empty row of the register and specifying the action as ShrsOut. Next, fill in the rest of the fields in the investment account register the same way you would for a regular ol' sell transaction. The only difference is that you won't give a Xfer Account.

You also can record a shares-out transaction with a dialog box. Click the Easy Actions button, choose the Sell/Remove Shares action, and fill in the Date and Transaction text boxes in the dialog box, leaving the Record Proceeds? Button set to "No".

The stock split and then doubled

Stock splits don't occur very often with mutual funds; however, when they do occur, the mutual fund manager, in effect, gives you a certain number of new shares (such as two) for each old share you own.

To record a stock split, you use the StkSplit action. Then you indicate the ratio of new shares to old shares. For a two-for-one split, for example, you indicate that you get two new split shares for each old unsplit share. The whole process is really pretty easy.

You can record a stock split by moving the cursor to the next empty row of the register and using the StkSplit action. You also can click the Easy Actions button, select the Stock Split action from the menu, and fill out the dialog box that asks about the split date, the new shares, the old shares, and, optionally, the share price after the split.

Quicken, will you remind me of something?

A reminder transaction is the electronic equivalent of a yellow sticky note. If you put a reminder transaction in the investment account register, Quicken's Billminder utility tells you there's a reminder message on the reminder date. You can't goof up anything by trying out reminders, so if you're curious, enter a reminder transaction for tomorrow and see what happens.

You can post a reminder note by moving the cursor to the next empty row of the register and using the Reminder action. Or you can click the Easy Actions button, select the Reminder Transaction action from the menu, and fill out the dialog box that asks you to fill out information about the reminder.

Reconciling an Account

You can reconcile a mutual fund investment account the same basic way you reconcile a bank account. The only real difference — and it doesn't affect reconciliation mechanics — is that you focus on mutual fund shares and not on account balance dollars. To begin reconciling a mutual fund investment account, click the My Accounts Activity Bar icon and choose the Reconcile an Account command. If you have questions about what to do next, refer to Chapter 7. It describes how you reconcile a bank account, but the same procedures apply to a mutal fund account.

Reports

I just want to say one thing about Quicken reports as they relate to your investments: *Remember that the reports are there.* (For more information, see Chapter 6.)

Menu commands and other stuff

For the most part, the commands and menus available for an investment account are the same as those available for all the other accounts Quicken supplies. I've written about the commands that I think are most helpful to new users in the preceding chapters of this book. If you have a question about how the Void Transaction command works, for example, refer to the Index, where you will be directed to a specific discussion of that command.

Updating Securities Prices

You can collect current market prices and store this information with your accounts. Just display the investment account that has the mutual fund shares. Then click the Port button or choose Features⇨Investments⇨Portfolio View. Either way, Quicken displays the Portfolio window (see Figure 12-16).

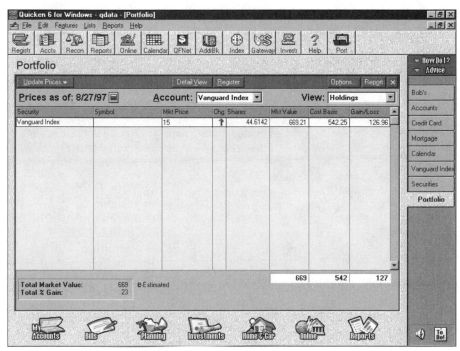

Figure 12-16: The Portfolio window.

To record the current market price for a security, use the arrow keys or click the mouse to select the security. Then move the cursor to the Mkt Price field and enter the current price. You also can use the + or - key to incrementally change the per share price by an eighth, or $.125.

Quicken updates the Total Market Value figure shown in the lower-left corner of the register window. After you update the market price, you can return to the register by clicking the Register button.

This chapter describes how you use the investments feature in Quicken for tracking your mutual funds. If you invest exclusively in mutual funds, the information you've now picked up should be all you need.

If you also invest directly in such things as stocks and bonds, you may want to turn to the next chapter. It describes how you use a Quicken investment account to track a brokerage account.

The Portfolio window

You can do more with the Portfolio window than just update share prices.

You can click the Report button to display an on-screen report of the securities you hold.

The Prices as of field lets you specify the date on which you want to see and set market prices and values. The Account drop-down list box lets you choose which account you want to see. And the View drop-down list box allows you to specify the information you see in the window. (Quicken provides different views of the information.)

The Options button displays a dialog box that lets you do a bunch of different stuff — including create customized views of the Portfolio window. (These different views show or emphasize different types of information.) The Update Prices button displays a menu of commands that let you download securities prices from the Internet and that let you see and modify a historical list of share prices. The Detail View button allows you to view detailed information about the selected security.

I'm not going to go into more detail here about what all these extra bells and whistles do. If you're a serious investor, however, take the time to explore these commands. You may gain some interesting insights into your investments.

Chapter 13
Stocks and Bonds

• •

In This Chapter

▶ Setting up a brokerage account

▶ Describing the securities in a brokerage account

▶ Transferring cash to and from a brokerage account

▶ Buying stocks and bonds from a brokerage account

▶ Recording dividends, capital gains, and other investment income from securities held in a brokerage account

▶ Recording margin interest, miscellaneous income and expenses, and return of capital

▶ Updating securities prices

▶ Adjusting your brokerage cash balance

▶ Adjusting your brokerage account shares

• •

*A*fter you understand how Quicken handles mutual fund investments, you'll find it a snap to work with a brokerage account. (Quicken calls this type of account a cash investment account.)

Setting Up a Brokerage Account

Setting up a brokerage account is similar to setting up a regular mutual fund account except for a couple of minor but predictable differences. Because you're still fairly new to this process, I'll go through it step by step:

1. **Click the Accts icon on the iconbar.**

   Quicken, the ever faithful companion, displays the Account List window.

2. **Click the New button in the Account List window.**

   Quicken displays the familiar but Create New Account dialog box that you use to specify what type of new account you want to create.

3. Click the Investment button.

When Quicken displays the Investment Account Setup dialog box, click the Summary tab. You don't need to step through the other tabs unless you're someone who loves excessive hand-holding.

Quicken displays the Investment Account Setup dialog box (see Figure 13-1).

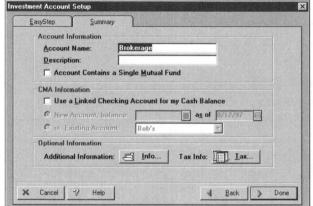

Figure 13-1:
The
Investment
Account
Setup dialog
box.

4. Name the investment.

Move the cursor to the Account Name text box and type the name of the broker. Or, if you don't have trouble remembering your broker's name, you can identify this account as the one you use to track your brokerage account with a name such as Brokerage. (I entered this name in Figure 13-1.)

5. (Optional) Enter a description of the account.

You can use the Description text box to store extra information about the account.

6. Leave the Account Contains a Single Mutual Fund check box unselected.

Leaving this check box unselected tells Quicken that the investment account is being used to track a brokerage account.

7. Indicate whether there's a cash management account (or some similarly titled cash account) attached to your brokerage account.

To do this, select the Use a Linked Checking Account for Cash Management check box. Most brokerage accounts — and maybe all brokerage accounts — have a linked cash account. You need someplace to store the cash you receive from selling securities and the cash you receive because you've earned dividend or interest income. The brokerage outfit you're with, of course, also wants someplace where it can quickly grab the cash whenever you buy anything.

8. **(Optional) Describe the linked checking account.**

   If you do indicate that there's a linked checking account, you'll need to describe or identify the account. If this is a new brokerage investment and, therefore, a new linked checking account, click the New Account button and then use the Balance and as of boxes to give the opening balance and transaction date. If the linked checking account is an existing checking account, click the Existing Account button and then select the account from the Existing Account drop-down list box.

9. **Click the Tax button.**

   Quicken displays the Tax Schedule Information dialog box (see Figure 13-2).

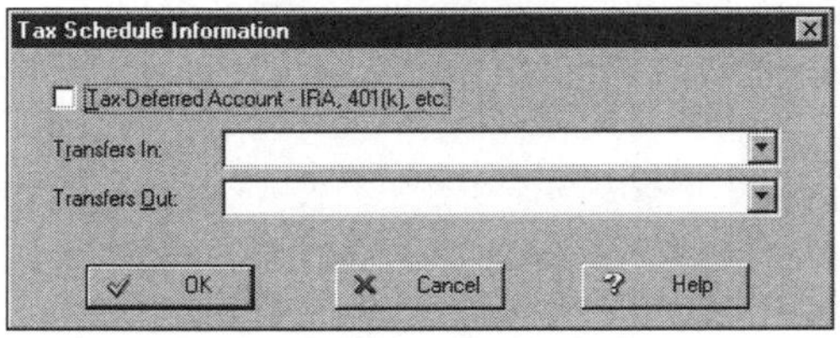

Figure 13-2:
The Tax
Schedule
Information
dialog box.

10. **Select or deselect the Tax-Deferred Account — IRA, 401(k), etc. check box as appropriate.**

    Basically, this check box tells Quicken whether the dividends, interest, and capital gains for this account affect your taxable income.

11. **Indicate where a tax-deferred account's transfers get reported for tax purposes.**

    Okay. This is kind of confusing. But here's the deal. If you've got your IRA money (or something like that) invested in a tax-deferred brokerage account, any time you add money to the account, that transfer may result in a tax deduction. And any time you take money out of the account, that transfer may result in taxable income.

    So, as you move money into and out of the brokerage account, you produce transactions that you need to report on your tax return at the end of the year. Quicken tracks these transactions for you, but you need to tell it where to stick the numbers it tallies. To do this, you first open the Transfers In drop-down list box and select the entry that describes the tax form and tax form line you use to report transfers into this account. (For example, in the case of an IRA, you may choose "Form 1040: IRA Contribution Self.") Then you open the Transfers Out drop-down list box and select the entry that describes the tax form and tax form line you'll use to report transfers out of this account. Whew.

12. **Click Done.**

    Quicken displays the Investment Setup dialog box which you can use to describe the individual investments you hold in your brokerage account.

There's an easier way to do all this, however, so click the Cancel button. Quicken redisplays the Account List window. If you want to begin entering investment transactions, select the account and then click the Open button. Quicken displays an investment account register window, as shown in Figure 13-3.

A change of course

In Chapter 12, I mentioned the Portfolio window in passing. My superficial coverage of the Portfolio Window stems largely from the fact that, for mutual funds, working from the register is easier. You already know how the register works, for example, if you've been tracking a bank account with Quicken. And for a single mutual fund, using the Portfolio window is overkill. Sort of like using industrial solvent to clean your kitchen floor.

When it comes to a brokerage account, however, using the Portfolio window makes more sense to use. Sure, it'll take you a few minutes to get used to the Portfolio window, but after you do, you'll find it much easier to work with.

To switch to the Portfolio window, by the way, display the investment account you want to work with. Then click the Port button or click the Port icon. Quicken displays the Portfolio window, as shown in Figure 13-4.

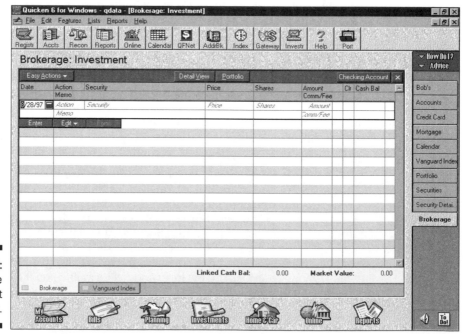

Figure 13-3:
The investment register.

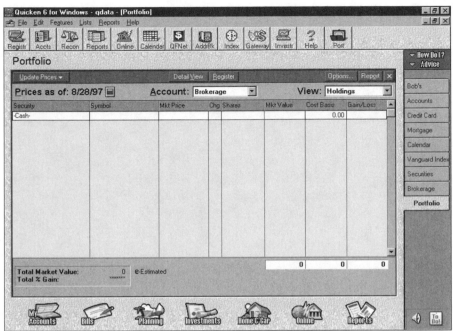

Figure 13-4:
The
Portfolio
window.

The really neat thing about a Portfolio window — at least as it applies to investment portfolios — is that it lets you look at your investment portfolio as a set of securities. In contrast, a register simply lists the investment transactions for an account.

Setting up security lists

Your account contains more than one type of *security*. You may have shares of Boeing, General Motors, or Chase Manhattan. You name it, and someone owns it.

You need to create a list of the securities — stocks, bonds, and so on — that your account holds.

To do so, complete the following steps after you set up the brokerage account:

1. **Choose Lists⇨Investment⇨Security.**

   Quicken displays the Security List window (see Figure 13-5). Note that any mutual funds you've already set up appear in the list as securities.

2. **Click the New button in the Security List window.**

   Quicken displays the Set Up Security dialog box, as shown in Figure 13-6.

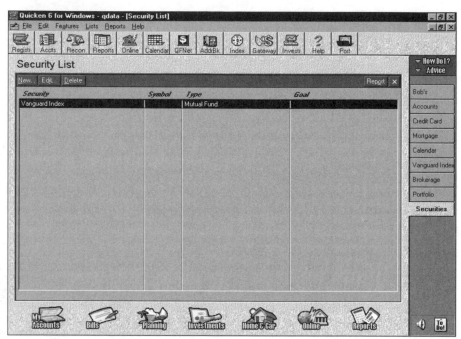

Figure 13-5:
The Security
List window.

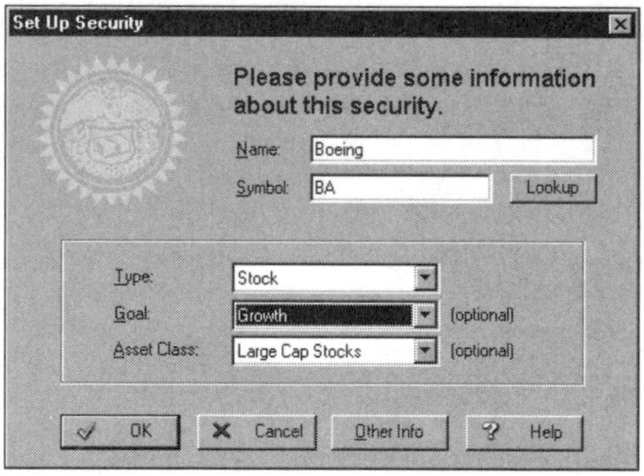

Figure 13-6:
The Set Up
Security
dialog box.

3. **Enter a name for the security in the Name text box.**

4. **(Optional and probably crazy) Enter the stock symbol for the security in the Symbol text box.**

   This step allows you to download share price information from a modem.

5. **(Optional) Indicate the type of security you're setting up by opening the Type drop-down list box and then selecting one of the types listed: Bond, CD, Mutual Fund, or Stock.**

6. (Optional) Indicate the purpose for which you're investing.

Open the Goal drop-down list box and then select one of the goals listed: College Fund, Growth, High Risk, Income, or Low Risk. If you're really into high-risk investments, by the way, please write me in care of the publisher. I've got an idea that I'm too conservative to test with my own money. What you do is take your money and go to Las Vegas. You place the minimum wager at a roulette wheel, betting on the color red. If you lose, you triple your wager and bet on red again. If you lose again, you triple your wager again and bet on red again. Assuming the table limit doesn't foul us up, you keep tripling your bets until you win. Then you start over again. I should tell you that I've created a computer model that simulates the aforementioned strategy. And it doesn't work. But it would sure be interesting to test the idea with real money. Yours.

You can choose either Lists⇨Investment⇨Security Type or Lists⇨ Investment⇨Investment Goal to display lists of the security types and investment goals. You can also use these commands to create new security types and investment goals — Sure-fire, Easy money, or Unconscionable profits, for example.

I don't think this option is all that important. If you want to use it, choose Lists⇨Investment⇨Security Type or Lists⇨Investment⇨Investment Goal and then click the New button in the dialog box that appears. Quicken displays another dialog box, in which you enter your new type or goal.

7. (Optional) Indicate the Asset class of your investment.

Open the Asset class drop-down list box and select one of the classes listed: Domestic Bonds, Large Cap Stocks, Small Cap Stocks, Global Bonds, International Stocks, Money Market, or Other.

8. Click OK.

Quicken redisplays the Security List window. It now lists the new stock, bond, or any other item you added.

9. Practice, practice, practice.

As necessary, repeat Steps 1 through 7 until you're sick to death of doing so or until you've described each of the securities in your brokerage account.

Treat mutual fund shares that you hold in a brokerage account the same way that you treat other stocks and bonds that you hold in the account. If you're confused, think of it this way: While many mutual funds are sold by brokers to their clients, some mutual funds are sold by the mutual fund manager directly to the public.

I don't want to get into the subject of load mutual funds versus no-load mutual funds — you pay a commission to buy load funds and you don't pay a commission to buy no-load funds — but if you're interested in how these two types of funds work, flip open *The Wall Street Journal* and look for advertisements from no-load fund managers such as Vanguard, Scudder, and T. Rowe Price. Give them a call, and they'll tell you why you think you should bypass the middleman — your broker. Next, talk to a broker, who will tell you why you *shouldn't* bypass the middleman. Then you make the decision.

What? You want *my* opinion? With much trepidation, I'll give it to you: I always use no-load mutual funds, because I'm a big fan of the do-it-yourself approach. However, I also think that a good broker — *good* is the operative word here — is well worth the commission fee if the broker helps you avoid expensive mistakes.

Working with cash

One of the differences between a brokerage account and a mutual fund account is that a cash management, or *money market,* account is attached to the brokerage account.

When you initially set up a brokerage account, your money goes into this account. (The broker buys you a doughnut and coffee in this meeting, remember?)

You purchase your first shares with the cash from this account. And when you sell shares, all cash proceeds go into this account.

Transferring cash to and from an account

Because you work with cash in a brokerage account, you need to know how to record the cash that flows in and out of the account. To do this, first display the Portfolio window and then click its Detail View button to display the Security Detail View window (see Figure 13-7).

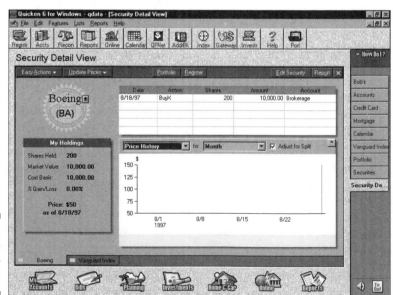

Figure 13-7:
The Security
Detail View
window.

To record the cash you transfer into a brokerage account, click the Easy Actions button in the Security Detail View window, and choose Transfer Cash into Account. Quicken displays the Transfer Cash In dialog box (see Figure 13-8). To record the amount of a cash transfer, confirm the transaction date, and then enter the dollar amount in the Amount field and specify the investment account receiving the cash in the Investment Account drop-down list box. Then click OK.

Figure 13-8:
The
Transfer
Cash In
dialog box.

To record the cash you transfer out of a brokerage account, click the Easy Actions button (which appears at the top of the Security Detail View window) and choose the Transfer Cash from Account command. Quicken displays the Transfer Cash Out dialog box (see Figure 13-9). To record the amount of a cash transfer, again confirm the transaction date and then enter the dollar amount in the Amount field and specify the investment account dispersing the cash in the Investment Account drop-down list box. Then click OK.

Figure 13-9:
The
Transfer
Cash Out
dialog box.

Sure, it's not all that complicated. But you'll impress your friends.

Buying near and selling dear

Buying and selling securities in a brokerage account closely resembles buying and selling shares of a mutual fund. You fill out almost the exact same fields.

To buy a security, for example, display the Security Detail View window and select the security using the unnamed drop-down list box. Then click Easy Actions, select the Buy/Add Shares action, and click the Summary tab. Quicken, ever responsive to your needs, displays the Buy/Add Shares dialog box (see Figure 13-10). When Quicken displays this dialog box, confirm that the Security drop-down list box identifies the stock, bond, or mutual fund you're purchasing. You use the Number of Shares, Price per Share, and Commission/Fee boxes to describe your purchase. (You can get this information from your order confirmation slip.) Use the Money from Quicken Account buttons to specify, "No, Quicken shouldn't adjust some bank account's cash balance for this transaction." Or to specify, "Yes, Quicken should adjust some bank account's cash balance." Then click Done when you're done. Pretty simple, right?

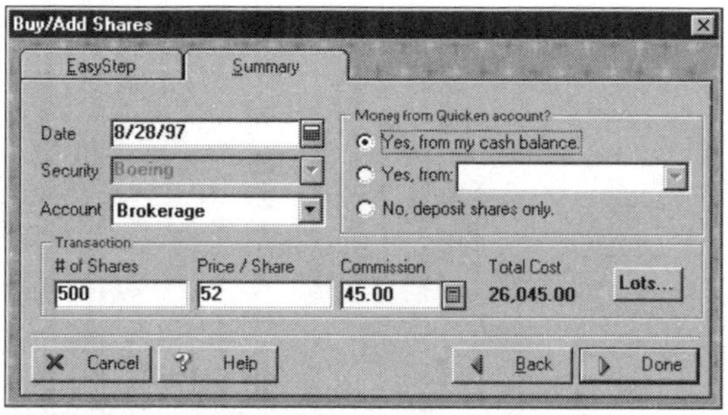

Figure 13-10:
The Buy/
Add Shares
dialog box.

Selling a security works in the same basic way. Display the Security Detail View window and select the security. Click the Easy Actions button, and select the Sell/Remove Shares command. When Quicken displays the Sell/Remove Shares dialog box (see Figure 13-11) click the Summary tab. The Security drop-down list box identifies the stock, bond, or mutual fund you're selling. You use the Number of Shares, Price per Share, and Commission/Fee boxes to describe your sale and the Record proceeds buttons and boxes to specify whether Quicken should adjust some bank account balance for this transaction. Then click Done.

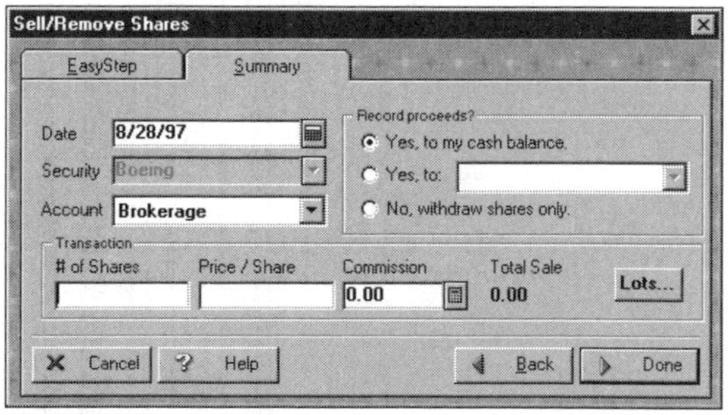

Figure 13-11:
The Sell/
Remove
Shares
dialog box.

If you want to control which *lots* are sold — a lot is just a chunk of securities you purchased together — you can click the Sell/Remove Shares dialog box's Lots button. Clicking this button tells Quicken to display a dialog box that lets you specify which lots you're selling. (I describe how to use this dialog box in Chapter 12, so I don't describe it again here.)

Dividends, capital gains, and other goodies

Taking care of this stuff is easy. Any time you receive investment income, click the Easy Actions button and choose the Record an Income Event command. When Quicken displays the Record Income dialog box, use the Security drop-down list box to identify the stock, bond, or mutual fund producing income and use the Distribution boxes to record the amount and type of income (see Figure 13-12).

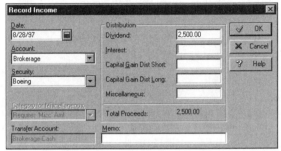

Figure 13-12: The Record Income dialog box.

Other not-so-tricky transactions

Quicken lets you record all sorts of transactions in a brokerage account. Not only can you do reminder and stock split actions (described for mutual fund accounts in Chapter 12), but you can also do a bunch of other things.

I'll briefly describe these other transactions and explain how to record them.

Bonds . . . James Bonds . . .

If you invest in bonds, you know that a bond's price is actually quoted as a percentage of its face value. A bond that sells for $950 with a face value of $1,000, for example, is quoted as 95 because the $950 price is 95 percent of the $1,000 face value. Quicken, however, doesn't let you describe a bond's price as a percent. So you enter the bond price as its price in dollars and cents.

Going for the gold

You can use Quicken to record precious metal investments. Let's say, for example, that you're hoarding Krugerrands. (*Krugerrands* are one-ounce gold coins minted in South Africa). For this investment, the price is the price per Krugerrand, and the shares figure is actually the number of ounces (equal to the number of Krugerrands). Because Quicken doesn't supply price-per-ounce and number-of-ounces fields, you insert the information into the Price and Shares fields. That makes sense, right?

Are you on the margin?

The Margin Interest Expense action records margin interest expense. To record it, click the Easy Actions button and then choose Advanced⇨Margin Interest Expense. When you do, Quicken displays the Margin Interest Expense dialog box, which you use to describe the cost of your financial adventure. Only the most sophisticated investors should be using margin anyway. So if you're one of these financial cowboys or cowgirls, I assume that you're smart enough to figure this stuff out on your own.

Paying miscellaneous expense

Sometimes you need to pay an expense. I've never seen one occur for a stock or bond — but my investing has been pretty conventional. Expenses sometimes do arise with brokerage accounts, real estate partnership interests (which can be treated like common stock shares), or precious metal investments (which can also be treated like common stock shares).

If you need to pay a fee for account handling or for storing those South African Krugerrands you've been hoarding, for example, you can record such an expense by clicking the Easy Actions button, choosing the Miscellaneous Expense action command, and then filling out the boxes on the Miscellaneous Expense dialog box that Quicken displays.

Recording a return of capital

One final thing: the old *return of capital* trick. Sometimes, the money you receive because you own a security isn't really income. Rather, it's a refund of part of the purchase price.

Consider this example. You buy a mortgage-backed security — such as a Ginnie Mae bond — for which the *mortgagee* (the person who borrowed the mortgage money) pays not only periodic interest but also a portion of the mortgage principal.

Obviously, you shouldn't record the principal portion of the payment you receive as income. You must record this payment as a mortgage principal reduction or — in the parlance of investment record-keeping — as a return of capital.

As another example, suppose that you invest in a limited partnership or real estate investment trust that begins liquidating. Some of the money the investors receive in this case is really a return of their original investment, or a return of capital.

To record a return of capital action, click the Easy Actions button and choose the Return of Capital action. When Quicken displays the Return of Capital dialog box, describe the security that's returning capital.

More Quick Stuff about Brokerage Accounts

Let me tell you a couple other quick things. You'll almost certainly find these tidbits helpful.

Monitoring and updating securities values

Regardless of whether you're working with a mutual fund account or with securities in a brokerage account, you can collect current market prices and store them with Quicken's account information.

To do so, display the investment account with the mutual fund shares or the securities you want to update using the Portfolio window.

To record the current market price for a security, use the up-arrow and down-arrow keys to select the security or click the security with the mouse. Next, move the cursor to the Mkt Price field and enter the current price. You can also adjust a price by eighths by using the – and + keys. The – key subtracts an eighth, or $.125, from the price shown. The + key adds an eighth, or $.125, to the price shown.

Adjusting errors

You can adjust the cash balance in a brokerage account and the shares balance in brokerage accounts if for some reason the figures are incorrect.

Oops, my brokerage cash balance is wrong

To adjust the cash balance in a brokerage account, choose Features⇨ Investments⇨Update Cash Balance.

Quicken next displays a dialog box that lets you specify the correct cash balance and the date as of which the figure you enter is correct. Fill in the text boxes and click OK. Quicken adjusts the cash balance.

Oops, my brokerage account shares balance is wrong

To adjust the shares balance for a security in a brokerage account, choose Features⇨Investments⇨Update Share Balance.

Quicken next displays a dialog box that lets you specify the security, the correct shares balance, and the date as of which the figure you enter is correct. Fill in the text boxes and click OK. Quicken adjusts the shares balance for the security you specified.

A few more words on the Portfolio view

Up to this point, I've mostly described how you get information into the Portfolio window. But before I stop talking about the Portfolio view, I want to give you a few tips on the ways you can use the Portfolio view to monitor your investments. I promise I'll only take a couple of minutes to do this.

About those hidden drop-down list boxes

Okay, the first thing to notice is that there are three drop-down list boxes near the top of the Portfolio window — just beneath the labeled command buttons. You see a date drop-down list box (which you open by clicking the Calendar button), an account drop-down list box (which lets you pick and choose the investment accounts you want included in your Portfolio View window), and the view of the portfolio. None of these drop-down list boxes are difficult to use. The tricky part is realizing that they're there. But now that I've alerted you to that fact, just experiment a bit. You'll see exactly how they work. And don't worry. You can't mess up any of your investment records by doing this.

A few final words about the register

Let me say one final thing about this investment record-keeping business. When you enter stuff into the Security Detail View window, Quicken takes your information and records transactions in the investment accounts register. You don't ever actually have to look at this investment account register. But I thought I'd at least alert you to its presence because you may stumble on it some day quite by accident. If that happens, don't muck about with it. Just close the window and pretend you didn't see anything.

Maybe I should tell you one other thing, too. You can use the investment register by entering transactions directly into it. However, it's really easier if you use the Security Detail View window.

Chapter 14

Petty Cash and Mad Money

● ●

In This Chapter

▶ Setting up a cash account

▶ Entering cash transactions

▶ Handling checks you cash

▶ Updating your petty cash or mad money balance

● ●

*Y*ou can track petty cash in your business as well as the petty cash in your wallet by using a special Quicken cash account. To track the cash, you must set up a cash account and then enter the increases and decreases into the cash account's register. Sure, this isn't exactly rocket science, but shoot, I thought I'd just quickly go over this stuff to show you how easy it really is. Okay?

Adding a Cash Account

To set up a cash account, you follow roughly the same steps as you do for setting up a bank account. Because you've probably already set up a bank account, you can move quickly through the following steps for setting up a cash account:

1. **Click the Accts icon on the iconbar.**

   Quicken displays the Account List window. You remember this puppy, the one you've seen a thousand times already.

2. **Click the New button on the Account List window to set up a new account.**

   Quicken, of course, is no dummy, so it displays the Create New Account dialog box shown in Figure 14-1.

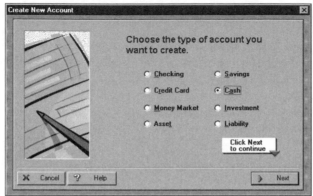

Figure 14-1:
The Create
New
Account
dialog box.

3. Select cash account.

You know how to do this, don't you? You just click the Cash button and then click the Next button. Quicken, ever mindful of your purpose, displays the Cash Account Setup dialog box.

4. Click the Summary tab.

Quicken moves you to the dialog box tab in which you'll describe the cash account as shown in Figure 14-2.

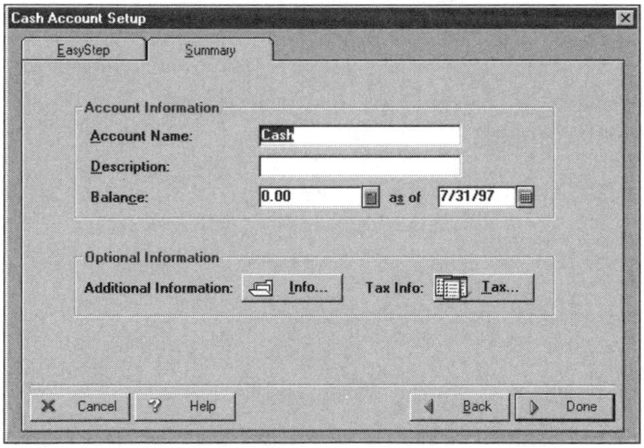

Figure 14-2:
The
Summary
tab of the
Cash
Account
Setup dialog
box.

5. Name the account.

Move the cursor to the Account Name text box and type a name.

6. **(Optional) Enter a description for the account using the Description text box.**

   You can type whatever you want as a description — petty cash, mad money, slush fund, and so on — to help you more easily identify this particular account when you've got a bunch of different accounts set up.

7. **Enter the cash balance you're holding.**

   Move the cursor to the Balance text box and type the balance value by using the number keys.

8. **Enter the account balance date.**

   Move the cursor to the as of (or date) text box and type the two-digit month number, the two-digit date number, and the two-digit year number (probably the current date).

9. **(Optional) Collect some additional information about the cash account.**

   I don't know why you'd want to do this, but you could. To collect this extra data, click the Info button. Then, when Quicken displays the Additional Account Information dialog box, type some additional account information there.

10. **(Optional) Ignore the Tax Information button.**

    If you have read much of this book, you are probably well aware of what the Tax Information button does. It displays a dialog box that lets you indicate whether the account you're setting up is tax-deferred. This same dialog box also lets you indicate that transfers into and out of this account impact your taxable income in some way. I cannot conceive, however, of a reason why you would want to use this button or its dialog box for a cash account. No way.

11. **Click Done.**

    Quicken redisplays the Account List window. Well, golly, it shows the new cash account.

Tracking Cash Inflows and Outflows

After you set up a cash account, you can use it to track the cash you receive and spend in the same way that you track the deposits and checks for a bank account.

To record your cash inflows and outflows, use the register window. To display the register window for the cash account you just set up, for example, open the Account List window by clicking the Accts icon on the iconbar and then double-clicking the cash account in the list in the window. Figure 14-3 shows the cash account version of the register window. I entered a few transactions — just to give you an idea of the sorts of transactions you might record if you lived the way that I do.

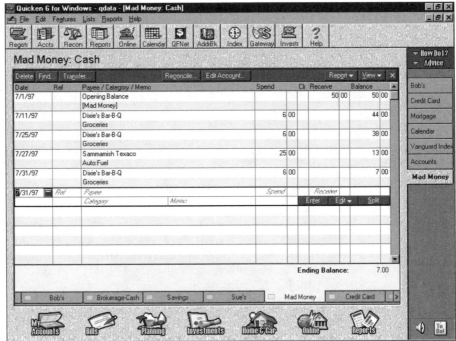

Figure 14-3:
The cash account version of the register window.

To record the amount of money you spend, fill in the Date, Payee, and Spend fields. To record the amount of money you receive, fill in the Date, Payee, and Receive fields. To track the reasons you're receiving and spending the cash, use the Memo and Category fields.

About Checks You Cash instead of Deposit

By the way, you don't necessarily need to set up a cash account if you like to spend cash (rather than, say, write checks or charge on a credit card). If you just cash a check and you do have a bank account set up, there's another way that may be simpler: Just use the Split Transaction Window to show both the income category (Salary, for example, for an individual) and the way you're going to use the money.

For example, if you cash a $1,000 check and you plan to use the $1,000 for spending money, you may show a positive $1,000 in the Salary category and a minus $1,000 in the Entertainment spending category. Figure 14-4 shows this trick.

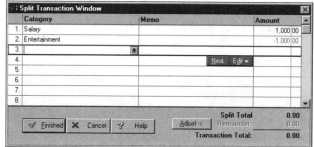

Figure 14-4:
A zero-
amount
transaction
is one handy
trick.

Note that the transaction shown in Figure 14-4 produces a transaction that equals zero. This is correct. Cashing the check that you never deposited doesn't affect your checking account balance. But by filling out the Split Transaction Window as shown in Figure 14-4, you do end up recording both the $1,000 of income and the $1,000 of expense.

Don't worry. I won't ask why you're carrying around $1,000 in cash.

Updating Cash Balances

You can update a register's cash balance to reflect what you actually have in petty cash, your wallet, under the mattress, in the cookie jar, or wherever else you keep your cash by doing the following steps:

1. **Display the cash account register.**

2. **Click the My Accounts Activity Bar icon and choose the Reconcile an Account command.**

   Quicken displays the Update Account Balance dialog box, as shown in Figure 14-5.

3. **Enter the actual cash balance in the Update Balance to text box.**

4. **Enter a date in the Adjustment Date text box.**

5. **Choose the category that you want to update in the Category for Adjustment drop-down list box.**

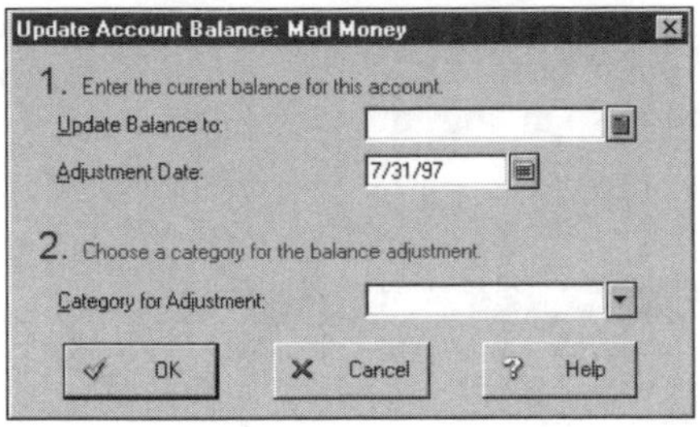

Figure 14-5:
The Update
Account
Balance
dialog box.

After you click the arrow to the right of the drop-down list box, you get a list of all the categories that you have set up.

6. After you finish, click OK.

Quicken updates the cash account's balance.

Part IV
Serious Business

The 5th Wave   By Rich Tennant

I __WILL__ REMEMBER MY PASSWORD TO THE PAYCHECK FILE.
I __WILL__ REMEMBER MY PASSWORD TO THE PAYCHECK FILE.
I __WILL__ REMEMBER MY PASSWORD TO THE PAYCHECK FILE.

In this part . . .

1 f you use Quicken in a business, you'll find it helpful to get some information about how to use it for payroll, customer receivables, and vendor payables. Sure, you could learn these things by sitting down with your certified public accountant, having a cup of coffee, and paying about $100 an hour.

Or you can read on, pretend that we're chitchatting over coffee, and save the $100.

Chapter 15

Payroll

- -

In This Chapter

▶ Creating categories and accounts necessary to prepare payroll

▶ Getting an employer ID number

▶ Where to get Social Security, Medicare, and federal income tax withholding information

▶ Calculating an employee's gross wages, payroll deductions, and net wages

▶ Recording a payroll check in Quicken

▶ Making federal tax deposits

▶ Filing quarterly and annual payroll tax returns

▶ Producing annual wage statements such as W-2s

▶ Handling state payroll taxes

- -

*M*any people use Quicken in a business. Many businesses have employees. Many employees want to be paid on a regular basis. Methinks, therefore, that many people will find information on preparing the payroll helpful. I should warn you, however, what we're about to discuss gets a bit ugly. Payroll with Quicken is, well, terrible. If you're planning to use it for doing payroll, do yourself a favor and buy Quickbooks Pro (another Intuit product). But if you're determined to use Quicken 6 for payroll, I'll explain how you do it.

Getting Ready for Payroll

To prepare payroll checks and summarize the payroll information that you need to prepare quarterly and annual returns, you need to set up some special accounts and categories. You also need to do some paperwork stuff. I describe how to do both things in this section.

Getting Quicken ready

To do payroll in Quicken, you'll need to set up several liability accounts, a payroll expense category, and several payroll expense subcategories. Fortunately, none of this is particularly difficult.

I'm going to describe how you do this for purposes of United States federal income and payroll taxes. If you employ people in one of the states that has a state income tax — California, say — you may also have state payroll taxes to deal with. But you can track and process these the same way you process the federal taxes.

I should say that the same thing is probable if you employ people outside the United States. But, hey, there are a couple hundred countries in the world. So check with someone from the country of employment for specific advice.

Setting up liability accounts

You need to set up three liability accounts to deal with federal payroll and income taxes: one named *Payroll-SS* to track Social Security, one named *Payroll-MCARE* to track Medicare, and one named *Payroll-FWH* to track federal income taxes owed. (I should confess that these aren't my names. They're the names Quicken expects you to use.)

To set up a liability account for any of these payroll tax liabilities, follow these steps:

1. **Click the Accts icon on the iconbar.**

   Quicken displays the Account List window. You've probably seen this window about a hundred times before. If you want to see the window right now, though, click the Accts icon and look at your screen.

2. **Click the New button in the Account List window.**

   Quicken displays the Create New Account dialog box. If you've been reading this book cover-to-cover, you've seen this baby a bunch of times before. If you want or need to see it now, though, you can just follow along on-screen.

3. **Click the Liability button and then click the Next button.**

   This tells Quicken you're going to set up a Liability account. Quicken displays the Liability Account Setup dialog box.

4. **Click the Summary tab.**

   Quicken displays the Summary tab of the Liability Account Setup dialog box, as shown in Figure 15-1.

5. **Enter the appropriate account name: Payroll-SS, Payroll-MCARE, or Payroll-FWH.**

   Move the cursor to the Account Name text box and type in the right name.

6. **Optionally, enter a description, if you want, in the Description text box.**

   I think the standard payroll tax liability names are pretty obvious, so I just go with them alone.

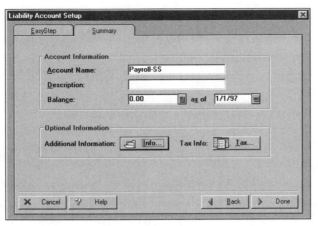

Figure 15-1:
The
Summary
tab of the
Liability
Account
Setup dialog
box.

7. Enter the current amount you owe for the payroll tax liability.

Move the cursor to the Balance text box and enter whatever you already owe. Or if you're just starting and you owe nothing, type **0**. (If you do owe something but you don't have a clue in the world as to how much, the easiest thing to do is to figure out what you owe now, before going any further. Sorry.)

8. Enter the as of date.

Move the cursor to the as of (or date) text box. Type the date on which you owe the balance you entered in the Balance text box. This is probably the current date.

9. Click Done.

Quicken adds the new liability account and displays a message box that asks whether you want to set up an amortized loan for this liability.

10. Click No.

This choice tells Quicken that you don't want to set up an amortized loan for the liability account. Quicken, only slightly bent out of shape, redisplays the Account List window.

11. Repeat Steps 2 through 10 for each of the other payroll tax liability accounts you want to add.

Remember that you need at least three payroll tax liability accounts — Payroll-SS, Payroll-MCARE, and Payroll-FWH — for the people you employ in the United States. And if you live in a state with income taxes, you either need to move or set up a fourth account: Payroll-SWH.

The only trick to naming other payroll tax liability accounts is that you need to start each liability account name with the word *Payroll*. No, this isn't some rule I made up arbitrarily. There really is a reason for this. The Quicken Payroll report prints information on all the accounts and categories that start with the word *Payroll*.

Setting up a payroll expense category

You'll also need to set up a payroll expense category, which isn't tough. Here's all you have to do:

1. **Choose Lists⇨Category/Transfer.**

   Quicken, with no hesitation, displays the Category & Transfer List window. Figure 15-2 shows this puppy.

2. **Click New.**

   Quicken displays the Set Up Category dialog box (see Figure 15-3).

3. **Enter Payroll as the category name.**

   Move the cursor to the Name text box and type **Payroll**, as shown in Figure 15-3.

4. **Optionally, enter a description of the category.**

   If you want, you can type a description in the Description text box. Figure 15-3 doesn't show any description; I figured that with a name like "Payroll," I wouldn't get too confused.

5. **In the Type section, select the Expense option button.**

   This choice tells Quicken that you're setting up an expense category. But you probably know this, right?

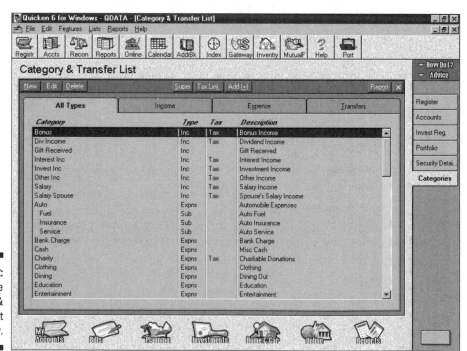

Figure 15-2:
The Category & Transfer List window.

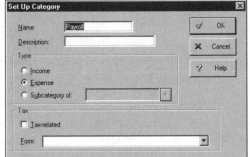

Figure 15-3:
The Set Up
Category
dialog box.

6. **Indicate whether the payroll tax is tax-deductible.**

   If you're preparing payroll for a business, select the Tax-related check box. If you're preparing payroll for a household employee — like a nanny, say — don't select the Tax-related check box. This little check box merely tells Quicken that this category should be included on the Tax Summary report. Household employee payroll expenses aren't tax-deductible — as you probably know.

7. **Click OK.**

   Quicken adds the category to the category list and redisplays the Category & Transfer List window. You've almost completed this part of the mission, Commander Bond.

Setting up the payroll subcategories

There's one other thing you need to do to get Quicken ready for payroll. You need to set up subcategory expenses for employee gross wages, the company's share of the Social Security taxes, and the company's share of the Medicare taxes. Quicken expects you to use *Gross, Comp SS,* and *Comp MCARE* as subcategory names. So that's what you'll do, okay?

1. **Display the Category & Transfer window if it isn't already displayed.**

   Choose Lists⇨Category/Transfer. If you can't remember what this window looks like, refer to Figure 15-2.

2. **Click New.**

   Quicken displays the Set Up Category dialog box (refer to Figure 15-3).

3. **Enter the appropriate payroll expense subcategory name: Gross, Comp SS, or Comp MCARE.**

   For example, move the cursor to the Name field and type **Gross** or **Comp SS** or **Comp MCARE**.

4. **Enter a description of the subcategory in the <u>D</u>escription text box.**

   Because the subcategory names are a little more cryptic, you may want to use the <u>D</u>escription text box to document things such as what Comp SS means. (I used Social Security-Emplyr).

5. **In the Type section, select the S<u>u</u>bcategory of option button.**

   This option tells Quicken you're setting up a subcategory.

6. **Indicate that the subcategory falls into the Payroll expense category by moving the cursor to the S<u>u</u>bcategory of text box and type Payroll.**

   Or because this is a drop-down list box, you can open the list box and select the payroll expense category from it.

7. **Click OK.**

   Quicken adds the subcategory to the category list and redisplays the Category & Transfer List window.

8. **Repeat Steps 2 through 7 for each of the remaining payroll expense subcategories you need.**

Remember that for employees working in the United States, you need at least three subcategories: Gross (for tracking gross wages), Comp SS (for tracking Company Social Security taxes), and Comp MCARE (for tracking employer Medicare taxes).

Congratulations, James. You saved the world again. You created the liability accounts and categories that you need to track the amounts you pay employees and the payroll taxes you withhold and owe.

Getting the taxes stuff right

There are also a couple of other things you need if you want to do payroll the right way.

Requesting (or demanding) an employer ID number

First, you need to file the SS-4, or Request for Employer Identification Number form, with the Internal Revenue Service (IRS) so you can get an employer identification number. You can get this form by calling the IRS and asking for one. Or if you have a friend who's an accountant, he or she may have one of these forms. (See, there is a reason to invite people like me to your dinner parties.)

In one of its cooler moves, the IRS changed its ways and now lets you apply for and receive an employer identification number over the telephone. You still need to fill out the SS-4 form, however, so you can answer questions the IRS asks during the short telephone-application process. (You also need to mail or fax the form to the Service after you have your little telephone conversation.)

QuickPay

I'm assuming that you aren't using QuickPay here. But you should know that QuickPay is a software program provided by Intuit. QuickPay works with Quicken to calculate things like gross wages, federal and state income taxes, and Social Security and Medicare taxes. In my humble opinion, QuickPay isn't necessary if you have only one or two employees and your employees are always paid the same amount. For example, if your only employee is a nanny or a secretary and the person is paid a straight salary, I don't think you save time by using QuickPay.

If you have a few employees, though, or they're paid an hourly rate and work different numbers of hours every week, get smart. Simplify your financial life and your payroll bookkeeping by buying QuickPay. In your situation, you'll find QuickPay invaluable and well-worth the $50 or so Intuit charges. And, no, I don't earn a sales commission by getting you to buy more software from Intuit. (I just use QuickPay for my business and know how much time it saves me.)

So what about Social Security, Medicare, and withholding taxes?

You need to do two things before you can know how to handle all those taxes. First, you need your employees to fill out a W-4 form to let you know what filing status they will use and how many personal exemptions they will claim. Guess where you get blank W-4 forms? That's right … from your friendly IRS agent.

The second thing you need to do is get a Circular E Employer's Tax Guide publication. The Circular E publication is the pamphlet that tells you how much you should withhold in federal income taxes, Social Security, and Medicare from a person's salary. You can get this form and the additional federal and state forms that you must fill out to satisfy the government requirements for hiring employees, too, just by calling those friendly people at the Internal Revenue Service.

Paying Someone for a Job Well Done

After you tell Quicken to get ready to do payroll and you collect the needed tax information, you're ready to pay someone.

Figuring out the gross wages figure

This should be pretty easy. Does Raoul make $15 an hour? Did he work 40 hours? Then you owe him $600 because $15 times 40 equals $600. Is Betty's salary $400 a week? Then you owe her $400 for the week.

All that deductions stuff

Your next step — after you know how much you're supposed to pay Raoul or Betty — is to figure out what big brother says you must withhold.

To figure this out, you need both Raoul's and Betty's W-4s to find out their filing status and personal exemptions. Then just flip to the page in the Circular E that describes withholding for a person claiming that filing status and paid by the week.

If Raoul is single and claims just one personal exemption, for example, you would flip to the page like the one shown in Figure 15-4. Remember that Raoul is paid weekly. I circled the number in the table in Figure 15-4 that shows what Raoul is supposed to pay in federal income taxes, Social Security, and Medicare.

SINGLE Persons—WEEKLY Payroll Period
(For Wages Paid in 1996)

If the wages are—		And the number of withholding allowances claimed is—										
At least	But less than	0	1	2	3	4	5	6	7	8	9	10
		The amount of income tax to be withheld is—										
$600	$610	98	84	71	61	54	46	39	32	24	17	10
610	620	101	87	74	63	55	48	41	33	26	18	11
620	630	104	90	76	64	57	49	42	35	27	20	13
630	640	107	93	79	66	58	51	44	36	29	21	14
640	650	109	96	82	68	60	52	45	38	30	23	16
650	660	112	98	85	71	61	54	47	39	32	24	17
660	670	115	101	88	74	63	55	48	41	33	26	19
670	680	118	104	90	77	64	57	50	42	35	27	20
680	690	121	107	93	79	66	58	51	44	36	29	22
690	700	123	110	96	82	68	60	53	45	38	30	23
700	710	126	112	99	85	71	61	54	47	39	32	25
710	720	129	115	102	88	74	63	56	48	41	33	26
720	730	132	118	104	91	77	64	57	50	42	35	28
730	740	135	121	107	93	80	66	59	51	44	36	29
740	750	137	124	110	96	82	69	60	53	45	38	31
750	760	140	126	113	99	85	72	62	54	47	39	32
760	770	143	129	116	102	88	74	63	56	48	41	34
770	780	146	132	118	105	91	77	65	57	50	42	35
780	790	149	135	121	107	94	80	66	59	51	44	37
790	800	151	138	124	110	96	83	69	60	53	45	38
800	810	154	140	127	113	99	86	72	62	54	47	40
810	820	157	143	130	116	102	88	75	63	56	48	41
820	830	160	146	132	119	105	91	77	65	57	50	43
830	840	163	149	135	121	108	94	80	66	59	51	44
840	850	165	152	138	124	110	97	83	69	60	53	46
850	860	168	154	141	127	113	100	86	72	62	54	47
860	870	171	157	144	130	116	102	89	75	63	56	49
870	880	174	160	146	133	119	105	91	78	65	57	50
880	890	177	163	149	135	122	108	94	80	67	59	52
890	900	179	166	152	138	124	111	97	83	70	60	53
900	910	182	168	155	141	127	114	100	86	72	62	55
910	920	185	171	158	144	130	116	103	89	75	63	56
920	930	188	174	160	147	133	119	105	92	78	65	58
930	940	191	177	163	149	136	122	108	94	81	67	59
940	950	193	180	166	152	138	125	111	97	84	70	61
950	960	196	182	169	155	141	128	114	100	86	73	62
960	970	199	185	172	158	144	130	117	103	89	75	64
970	980	202	188	174	161	147	133	119	106	92	78	65
980	990	205	191	177	163	150	136	122	108	95	81	67
990	1,000	207	194	180	166	152	139	125	111	98	84	70
1,000	1,010	210	196	183	169	155	142	128	114	100	87	73
1,010	1,020	213	199	186	172	158	144	131	117	103	89	76
1,020	1,030	216	202	188	175	161	147	133	120	106	92	78
1,030	1,040	219	205	191	177	164	150	136	122	109	95	81
1,040	1,050	222	208	194	180	166	153	139	125	112	98	84
1,050	1,060	225	210	197	183	169	156	142	128	114	101	87
1,060	1,070	228	213	200	186	172	158	145	131	117	103	90
1,070	1,080	231	216	202	189	175	161	147	134	120	106	92
1,080	1,090	234	219	205	191	178	164	150	136	123	109	95
1,090	1,100	237	222	208	194	180	167	153	139	126	112	98
1,100	1,110	240	225	211	197	183	170	156	142	128	115	101
1,110	1,120	243	228	214	200	186	172	159	145	131	117	104
1,120	1,130	247	231	216	203	189	175	161	148	134	120	106
1,130	1,140	250	234	219	205	192	178	164	150	137	123	109
1,140	1,150	253	238	222	208	194	181	167	153	140	126	112
1,150	1,160	256	241	225	211	197	184	170	156	142	129	115
1,160	1,170	259	244	229	214	200	186	173	159	145	131	118
1,170	1,180	262	247	232	217	203	189	175	162	148	134	120
1,180	1,190	265	250	235	220	206	192	178	164	151	137	123
1,190	1,200	268	253	238	223	208	195	181	167	154	140	126
1,200	1,210	271	256	241	226	211	198	184	170	156	143	129
1,210	1,220	274	259	244	229	214	200	187	173	159	145	132
1,220	1,230	278	262	247	232	217	203	189	176	162	148	134
1,230	1,240	281	265	250	235	220	206	192	178	165	151	137
1,240	1,250	284	269	253	238	223	209	195	181	168	154	140

Figure 15-4: Raoul's tax deductions stuff.

And about Betty? Remember that Betty's pay is $400 a week. If Betty's filing status is married filing jointly and with three personal exemptions, you would flip to the page that resembles Figure 15-5. Again, I circled the number in the table in Figure 15-5 that shows what Betty is supposed to pay.

MARRIED Persons—WEEKLY Payroll Period
(For Wages Paid in 1996)

If the wages are—		And the number of withholding allowances claimed is—										
At least	But less than	0	1	2	3	4	5	6	7	8	9	10
		The amount of income tax to be withheld is—										
$0	$125	0	0	0	0	0	0	0	0	0	0	0
125	130	1	0	0	0	0	0	0	0	0	0	0
130	135	1	0	0	0	0	0	0	0	0	0	0
135	140	2	0	0	0	0	0	0	0	0	0	0
140	145	3	0	0	0	0	0	0	0	0	0	0
145	150	4	0	0	0	0	0	0	0	0	0	0
150	155	4	0	0	0	0	0	0	0	0	0	0
155	160	5	0	0	0	0	0	0	0	0	0	0
160	165	6	0	0	0	0	0	0	0	0	0	0
165	170	7	0	0	0	0	0	0	0	0	0	0
170	175	7	0	0	0	0	0	0	0	0	0	0
175	180	8	1	0	0	0	0	0	0	0	0	0
180	185	9	1	0	0	0	0	0	0	0	0	0
185	190	10	2	0	0	0	0	0	0	0	0	0
190	195	10	3	0	0	0	0	0	0	0	0	0
195	200	11	4	0	0	0	0	0	0	0	0	0
200	210	12	5	0	0	0	0	0	0	0	0	0
210	220	14	6	0	0	0	0	0	0	0	0	0
220	230	15	8	1	0	0	0	0	0	0	0	0
230	240	17	9	2	0	0	0	0	0	0	0	0
240	250	18	11	4	0	0	0	0	0	0	0	0
250	260	20	12	5	0	0	0	0	0	0	0	0
260	270	21	14	7	0	0	0	0	0	0	0	0
270	280	23	15	8	1	0	0	0	0	0	0	0
280	290	24	17	10	2	0	0	0	0	0	0	0
290	300	26	18	11	4	0	0	0	0	0	0	0
300	310	27	20	13	5	0	0	0	0	0	0	0
310	320	29	21	14	7	0	0	0	0	0	0	0
320	330	30	23	16	8	1	0	0	0	0	0	0
330	340	32	24	17	10	2	0	0	0	0	0	0
340	350	33	26	19	11	4	0	0	0	0	0	0
350	360	35	27	20	13	5	0	0	0	0	0	0
360	370	36	29	22	14	7	0	0	0	0	0	0
370	380	38	30	23	16	8	1	0	0	0	0	0
380	390	39	32	25	17	10	2	0	0	0	0	0
390	400	41	33	26	19	11	4	0	0	0	0	0
400	410	42	35	28	20	13	5	0	0	0	0	0
410	420	44	36	29	22	14	7	0	0	0	0	0
420	430	45	38	31	23	16	8	1	0	0	0	0
430	440	47	39	32	25	17	10	3	0	0	0	0
440	450	48	41	34	26	19	11	4	0	0	0	0
450	460	50	42	35	28	20	13	6	0	0	0	0
460	470	51	44	37	29	22	14	7	0	0	0	0
470	480	53	45	38	31	23	16	9	1	0	0	0
480	490	54	47	40	32	25	17	10	3	0	0	0
490	500	56	48	41	34	26	19	12	4	0	0	0
500	510	57	50	43	35	28	20	13	6	0	0	0
510	520	59	51	44	37	29	22	15	7	0	0	0
520	530	60	53	46	38	31	23	16	9	1	0	0
530	540	62	54	47	40	32	25	18	10	3	0	0
540	550	63	56	49	41	34	26	19	12	4	0	0
550	560	65	57	50	43	35	28	21	13	6	0	0
560	570	66	59	52	44	37	29	22	15	7	0	0
570	580	68	60	53	46	38	31	24	16	9	2	0
580	590	69	62	55	47	40	32	25	18	10	3	0
590	600	71	63	56	49	41	34	27	19	12	5	0
600	610	72	65	58	50	43	35	28	21	13	6	0
610	620	74	66	59	52	44	37	30	22	15	8	0
620	630	75	68	61	53	46	38	31	24	16	9	2
630	640	77	69	62	55	47	40	33	25	18	11	3
640	650	78	71	64	56	49	41	34	27	19	12	5
650	660	80	72	65	58	50	43	36	28	21	14	6
660	670	81	74	67	59	52	44	37	30	22	15	8
670	680	83	75	68	61	53	46	39	31	24	17	9
680	690	84	77	70	62	55	47	40	33	25	18	11
690	700	86	78	71	64	56	49	42	34	27	20	12
700	710	87	80	73	65	58	50	43	36	28	21	14
710	720	89	81	74	67	59	52	45	37	30	23	15
720	730	90	83	76	68	61	53	46	39	31	24	17
730	740	92	84	77	70	62	55	48	40	33	26	18

Figure 15-5: Betty's tax deduction stuff.

Always use up-to-date information. The numbers you use for federal income tax withholding change annually. Therefore, don't use the tables shown in Figures 15-4 and 15-5. They will be long out-of-date by the time you read this.

Social Security and Medicare amounts are figured by multiplying the gross wage figure by a set percentage. Social Security is 6.2 percent of the gross wages up to a specified limit — roughly $63,000 in 1996. The Medicare tax is 1.45 percent of the gross wages. Be sure to check your faithful Circular E if you think limits come into play for a particular employee. Note, too, that as I'm writing this, Congress is fiddle-faddling with the tax laws again. But, of course, Congress is always fiddle-faddling with the tax laws.

Figuring out someone's net wages

Table 15-1 summarizes the payroll calculations shown in Figures 15-4 and 15-5.

Does Table 15-1 make sense? If it doesn't, take another look at the marked information in Figures 15-4 and 15-5 and read my earlier discussion of how to figure out deductions stuff. All I've really done in the table is reorganize some information, calculate the Social Security and Medicare taxes, and show how Raoul's and Betty's gross pay gets nickeled and dimed by the various taxes they owe.

Table 15-1	Payroll for Raoul and Betty		
Item	*Raoul*	*Betty*	*Explanation*
Gross wages	$600.00	$400.00	Hey, it's their pay.
Withholding	$084.00	$020.00	From Circular E.
Social Security	$037.20	$024.80	6.2 percent of gross wages.
Medicare	$008.70	$005.80	1.45 percent of gross wages.
Net Wages	$470.10	$349.40	What's left over.

What about other taxes and deductions?

If you have other taxes and deductions and you understand how the federal income taxes, Social Security taxes, and Medicare taxes work, you won't have any problem working with the other taxes — no matter what they are.

State income tax withholding, for example, works like the federal income tax withholding. (Of course, you need to get the state's equivalent to the Circular E guide.)

In general, other taxes and amounts paid by the employee get treated similarly.

In fact, the only thing that you need to be careful about is what affects your employees' gross pay for income taxes but not their Social Security taxes — things such as 401(k) deductions and certain fringe benefits. If you have these kinds of things to deal with and you need help, just ask your accountant. (It's just too difficult — and actually kind of dangerous, too — for me to provide general answers that will work for everyone who reads this paragraph. Sorry.)

Recording a payroll check

After you make the tax deduction and net wages calculation, you're ready to record the check. This is a little bit complicated, but stick with me, partner. We'll get through it in no time.

If Raoul and Betty are milling around your computer, whining and saying things like, "Gee, Boss, how much longer? I want to get to the bank before it closes," tell them to cool their heels for about three minutes.

Suppose that you're going to record the check using the register window for your checking account (see Figure 15-6). (As you know, recording the check into the Write Checks window works the same basic way. The difference is that by using the Write Checks window, you can print the payroll check.)

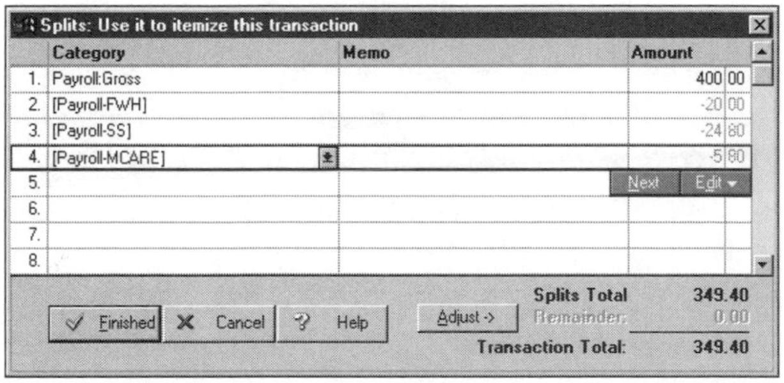

Figure 15-6:
The Split Transaction Window recording Betty's $400 wages and her $349.40 paycheck.

After you display the checking account register window and highlight the first empty row of the register, follow these steps.

1. **Enter the date of the payroll check in the Date field.**

2. **Enter the payroll check number in the Num field.**

3. **Enter the employee name in the Payee field.**

4. **Enter the net wages amount in the Payment field.**

5. **Open the Split Transaction Window (refer to Figure 15-7).**

   You can do this by clicking the Split button.

6. **In the first row of the Split Transaction Window, enter the category and gross wages amount in the correct fields.**

   Enter the category **Payroll:Gross**. The amount, of course, should be the gross wages figure (**400.00** in the example).

7. **Enter the employee's Federal withholding tax and account in the second row of the Split Transaction Window.** Instead of a category in the Category field, enter liability account [Payroll: FWH]. This amount of tax withheld comes from the Circular E form (20,000 in this example).

8. **Enter the employee's Social Security tax withheld and account in the row of the Split Transaction Window.**

   In the Category field, enter the liability account **[Payroll-SS]**. The amount of the Social Security tax withheld should be 6.2 percent of the employee's gross wages (**24.80** in this example). Type this in the Amount field.

9. **Enter the employee's Medicare tax withheld and account in the fourth row of the Split Transaction Window.**

   In the Category field, enter the liability account **[Payroll-MCARE]**. The amount of the Medicare tax withheld should be 1.45 percent of the employee's gross wages (**5.80** in this example).

   Figure 15-6 shows the Quicken register window and Splits dialog box filled out to record Betty's $400 of wages, the taxes poor Betty has to pay on these earnings, and the net wages figure of $349.40. If you have questions about any of these figures, take a peek again at Table 15-1.

10. **Optional, If you plan to print this paycheck on a payroll check that has a remittance advice or payroll stub, press the PgDn key twice.**

    (An *advice* is accounting jargon for the little slip of paper that's attached to the actual check form.)

    Only the first 16 lines of the Split Transaction Window information print on a payroll stub. So by using lines 17 and higher for the employer portions of the payroll tax, you won't confuse the employee about employee versus employer payroll taxes.

11. **On the next two empty lines of the Split Transaction Window, enter the employer's matching share of the Social Security tax that you have to pay.**

    If the employee pays $24.80 of Social Security tax, for example, use the first empty line to type **$24.80** of expense categorized to the Payroll:Comp FICA expense category. Type **24.80** in the Amount field and **Payroll:Comp SS** in the Category field.

    Then use the second empty line to record $24.80 of payroll SS tax liability using the [Payroll-SS] account. Type **–24.80** in the Amount field and **[Payroll-SS]** in the Category field.

12. **On the next two empty lines of the Split Transaction Window, enter the employer's matching share of the Medicare tax that you have to pay.**

If the employer pays $5.80 of Medicare, for example, use the first empty line to type **$5.80** of expense categorized to the Payroll: MCARE expense category. Type **–5.80** in the Amount field and **Payroll: CompMCARE** in the Category field.

Then use the second empty line to record $5.80 of payroll FICA tax liability using the [Payroll-MCARE] account. Type **–5.80** in the Amount section and **[Payroll-MCARE]** in the Category section.

Figure 15-7 shows the Social Security and Medicare payroll tax information.

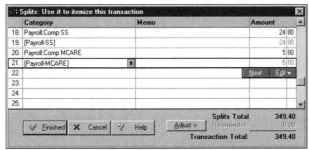

The accounts you use to show the payroll taxes withheld and owed are liability accounts. By looking at the account balances of these accounts, you can easily see how much you owe the government.

13. **If you have other employer-paid payroll taxes, record these following the employer's matching share of the Social Security and Medicare taxes.**

You can use this same basic approach to record federal and state unemployment taxes.

14. **After you finish entering the employer-paid payroll taxes, click Finished to close the Split Transaction Window.**

15. **To record the payroll check and related employer-paid payroll tax information, click Enter.**

You did it! You recorded a payroll check and the related payroll taxes. Maybe it wasn't all that much fun. But at least it wasn't very difficult.

Tax Deposits

Make no mistake. Big Brother wants the money you withhold from an employee's payroll check for federal income taxes, for Social Security, and for Medicare. Big Brother also wants the payroll taxes you owe — the matching Social Security and Medicare taxes, federal unemployment taxes, and so on.

Every so often, then, you need to pay Big Brother the amounts you owe.

Making this payment is actually simple. Just write a check payable for the account balances shown in the payroll tax liability accounts. If you have written only the one check to Betty (as shown in Figures 15-6 and 15-7), for example, your payroll liability accounts would show balances as follows:

Liability Account	Amount
Payroll-SS	$49.60
Payroll-MCARE	$11.90
Payroll-FWH	$20.00
Total	$81.50

Notice that the Payroll-SS account balance and the Payroll-MCARE account balance include both the employee's and the employer's Social Security and Medicare taxes.

Then you write a check for the $81.50 you owe (see Figure 15-8). The only tricky thing about this transaction is that you're transferring the check amount to the payroll liability accounts rather than assigning the check amount to a payroll tax category. In effect, you're transferring money from your checking account to the government to pay off the payroll taxes you owe.

Figure 15-8: The Split Transaction Window for paying Betty's payroll taxes.

The first time you see this sort of transfer, it can be a little confusing. So take a minute to think about this. If you write the check to the government, your checking account doesn't have the money in it anymore, and you don't owe them the money anymore. Therefore, the checking account balance and the liability account balance both need to be decreased. In Quicken, the way you do this is with an account transfer.

When do you make payroll tax deposits? Good question. Fortunately, it's not one you have to answer. The Internal Revenue Service will tell you when you're supposed to deposit your money. In my business, for example, I have to deposit payroll taxes within a couple of days of doing payroll. Some businesses have to deposit more frequently or quickly. And some businesses get to deposit less quickly or less frequently.

Since we're on the subject of federal payroll tax deposits, I should talk about another general rule related to when you need to make the deposit: If your accumulated payroll taxes are less than $500, you can just pay the taxes the next time you're supposed to remit payroll taxes: the next payroll date, the next month, or whatever. (This is called the De Minimis rule — named after the Congresswoman Dee Minimis, I think.) Don't rely on this rule, however, without first checking either the Internal Revenue Service or your tax advisor.

To make a payroll tax deposit, just run your check with a federal tax deposit coupon to a financial institution qualified as a depository for federal taxes or to the Federal Reserve bank serving your geographical area. (This is probably your local bank.) The IRS should have already sent you a book of coupons as a result of your asking for an employer ID number. And one other thing: Make your check payable to the depository or to the Federal Reserve.

Some businesses are either now or will shortly be required to electronically remit payroll tax deposits directly to the U.S. Treasury. The IRS should tell you when this is the case.

Filing Quarterly Payroll Tax Returns

At the end of every quarter, you need to file a quarterly payroll tax return. (By *quarters* here, I'm referring to calendar quarters. You don't do this four times on a Sunday afternoon as you or your couch-potato spouse watch football.)

If you're a business, for example, you must file a Form 941 — which is just a form you fill out to say how much you paid in gross wages, how much you withheld in federal taxes, and how much you owe for employer payroll taxes.

If you're not a business but you have household employees — such as a nanny — you must file a Form 942. Again, this is just a form you fill out to say how much you paid in gross wages, withheld in federal taxes, and owe in payroll taxes.

To get the gross wages totals and the balances in each of the payroll tax liability accounts, print the Business Payroll report. To do this, choose Reports➪Business➪Payroll. Quicken displays the Create Report dialog box, as shown in Figure 15-9.

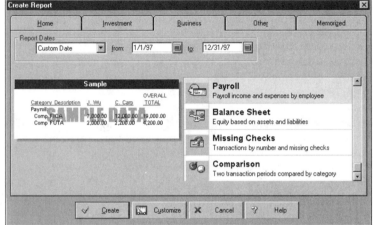

Figure 15-9:
The Create
Report
dialog box.

Specify the range of dates as the start and end of the quarter for which you're preparing a quarterly report. Then click Create. Quicken produces a payroll report, which you can easily use to fill out the quarterly payroll tax return. Figure 15-10 shows the Payroll report. As I mentioned earlier, this report summarizes all the transactions categorized as falling into the Payroll expense category or transferred to an account named Payroll (something).

The Gross amount in the Payroll Expenses section — $400 in the example — is the gross wages upon which employer payroll taxes are calculated.

The company Social Security contribution and Medicare contributions are the amounts you recorded to date for the employer Social Security and Medicare taxes — so you need to double these figures to get the actual Social Security and Medicare taxes owed.

The `Total Transfers` line in the Payroll report represents the federal tax deposits you paid.

By the way, if your accountant is the person who will fill out the 941 or 942, you don't even need to read this stuff. Your accountant won't have any problem completing the quarterly payroll tax return using the Quicken Payroll report and, in fact, — I kid you not — will probably even enjoy it.

Payroll Report

1/1/97 Through 12/31/97

Category Description	Betty Ready	Opening Balance	OVERALL TOTAL
EXPENSES			
Payroll:			
Gross	400.00	0.00	400.00
Comp SS	24.80	0.00	24.80
Comp ...	5.80	0.00	5.80
TOTAL Payroll	430.60	0.00	430.60
TOTAL EXPENSES	430.60	0.00	430.60
TOTAL INCOME LESS EXPEN...	-430.60	0.00	-430.60
TRANSFERS			
FROM Payroll-FWH	20.00	0.00	20.00
FROM Payroll-MCARE	11.60	0.00	11.60
FROM Payroll-SS	49.60	0.00	49.60
TOTAL TRANSFERS	81.20	0.00	81.20
Balance Forward			
Payroll-FWH	0.00	0.00	0.00
Payroll-MCARE	0.00	0.00	0.00
Payroll-SS	0.00	0.00	0.00
TOTAL Balance Forward	0.00	0.00	0.00
OVERALL TOTAL	-349.40	0.00	-349.40

Figure 15-10:
The Payroll
report.

Annual Returns and Wage Statements

At the end of the year, you'll need to file some annual returns — like the 940 federal unemployment tax return — and the W-2 and W-3 wages statements.

As a practical matter, the only thing that's different about filling out these reports is that you need to use a payroll report that covers the entire year — not just a single quarter. So you need to enter the range of dates in the Payroll Report dialog box as January 1 and December 31.

The 940 annual return is darn easy if you've been wrestling with the 941 or 942 quarterly returns. The 940 annual return works the same basic way as those more difficult quarterly tax returns. You print the old payroll report, enter a few numbers, and then write a check for the amount you owe.

Note that you need to prepare any state unemployment annual summary before preparing the 940, because the 940 requires information from the state returns.

For the W-2 statements and the summary W-3 (which summarizes your W-2s), you just print the old payroll report and then, carefully following directions, enter the gross wages, the Social Security and Medicare taxes withheld, and the federal income taxes withheld into the appropriate blanks.

If you have a little trouble, call the IRS. If you have a lot of trouble, splurge and have someone else do it for you. It doesn't take a rocket scientist to fill out these forms, by the way. Any experienced bookkeeper can do it for you.

Please don't construe my "rocket scientist" comment as personal criticism if this payroll taxes business seems terribly complicated. My experience is that some people — and you may very well be one of them — just don't have an interest in things such as payroll accounting. If, on the other hand, you're a "numbers-are-my-friend" kind of person, you'll have no trouble at all once you learn the ropes.

Doing the State Payroll Taxes Thing

Yeah. I haven't talked about state payroll taxes — at least not in any great detail. I wish I could provide this sort of detailed, state-specific help to you. Unfortunately, doing so would make this chapter about 150 pages long. It would also cause me to go stark, raving mad.

My sanity and laziness aside, however, you still need to deal with the state payroll taxes. Let me say, however, that you apply to state payroll taxes the same basic mechanics you apply to the federal payroll taxes. For example, a state income tax works the same way the federal income tax works, employer-paid state unemployment taxes work the same way the employer-paid federal taxes work, and employee-paid state taxes work the same way the employee-paid Social Security and Medicare taxes work.

If you've tuned in to how federal payroll taxes work in Quicken, you really shouldn't have a problem with the state payroll taxes — at least, not in terms of the mechanics.

Chapter 16

Receivables and Payables

● ●

In This Chapter

▶ Setting up an account to track customer receivables

▶ Recording customer invoices

▶ Recording customer payments

▶ Tracking amounts your customers owe

▶ Handling customer receivables: a problem

▶ Describing vendor payables

▶ Handling vendor payables

▶ Tracking vendor payables

▶ Using the Billminder utility

● ●

*Q*uicken, as a checkbook program, isn't really built for tracking the amounts that clients and customers owe you or that you owe your vendors, but you can do both if you don't have a long list of receivables or payables. This chapter describes how you can handle both situations.

Customer Receivables

To track customer receivables, you must set up an asset account just for tracking customer receivables. If you know how to set up an asset account, just do it. If you don't, follow these steps:

1. **Click the My Accounts icon on the Activity Bar to display the My Accounts menu.**

2. **Choose Create A New Account from the menu.**

   Quicken asks you to choose the type of account you want to create.

3. **Click the Asset button.**

   This tells Quicken that you're setting up a catch-all asset account to track something besides a bank account, cash, or your investments.

4. Click Next.

Quicken displays the Asset Account Setup dialog box.

5. Click the Summary tab.

Quicken displays the Summary tab, of course. And that's nice, because the Summary tab provides everything you need to set up an asset account. Figure 16-1 shows the Summary tab of the Asset Account Setup dialog box.

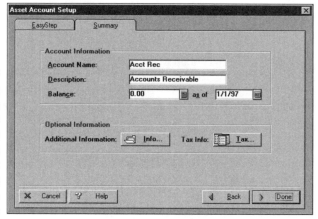

Figure 16-1:
The
Summary
tab of the
Asset
Account
Setup dialog
box.

6. Name the account.

Move the cursor to the Account Name text box and type a name, such as Acct Rec, to identify the account as the one that holds your accounts receivable. But one of the fun things about being in your own business is that *you* get to make the decisions about what you name your accounts — so go for it, dude, and be creative.

7. (Optional) Enter a description for the account.

I don't know — how about something creative, like *Accounts Receivable?* Of course, if the name you choose is descriptive enough you don't need to use this optional description.

8. Enter the starting balance as zero.

9. Accept the default date.

You don't need to enter a date because you aren't entering a starting balance.

10. Click Done.

Quicken redisplays the Account List window. But, magically, the window now lists an additional account — the accounts receivable account you just created. (Actually, this isn't really magic — but you know that.)

To tell Quicken which account you want to work with, use the Account List window. Display the Account List window, select the account you want by using the arrow keys or the mouse, and then press Enter. Quicken selects the account and displays the register window.

Customer Invoices and Payments

Because Quicken isn't designed to keep track of lots of receivables and doesn't generate its own invoices (see Chapter 2 for a refresher on what Quicken does and doesn't do), I think that the easiest approach to setting up an account is just to use Quicken to keep a list of your unpaid customer invoices. You could use a Quicken Other account to bill customers and track their invoices, but this approach requires Rube Goldbergesque complexity. What's more, if you do want to do all this complex stuff, you're really better off with a real small-business accounting system, such as QuickBooks by Intuit.

Now, back to the chase. . . .

Recording customer invoices

When you bill a customer, you just enter a transaction for the invoice amount in your Accounts Receivable register. You can follow these steps for recording a customer invoice in the next empty slot in the Accounts Receivable register:

1. **Open the register window for the Accounts Receivable account.**

   To display the register window, click the Accounts tab to display the Accounts List and double-click the Accounts Receivable account.

2. **Enter the invoice date — the date you bill your customer or client — in the Date field.**

3. **Enter the invoice number in the Ref field.**

   The invoice number you enter is the number of the invoice you create yourself.

4. **Enter the customer or client name in the Payee field.**

   After the transaction has been recorded, the name now appears in the Payee drop-down list box, and you can select the name from the list box any time you activate the list.

   Make sure that you use the same spelling of the customer's name every time you enter it because Quicken summarizes accounts receivable information by payee name; Quicken interprets *John Doe* and *Jonh Doe* as two different customers. In addition, you must take care with names because Quicken's QuickFill works quickly in assuming that you mean a particular account name. If you first enter a customer name as *Mowgli's Lawn Service,* for example, and then later you type **Mowg** as an account name, Quicken assumes that you're entering another transaction for *Mowgli's Lawn Service* and fills the Payee field with the complete name. You can avoid trouble in both these instances by activating the Payee drop-down list and selecting the payee name from the list.

5. **Enter the invoice amount in the Increase field.**

6. **Click Enter to record the transaction.**

   If Quicken reminds you to enter a category, click No. You don't want to use a category in this step because you later categorize the invoice by using an income category when you record the customer deposit.

Figure 16-2 shows a register entry for a $750 invoice to Mowgli's Lawn Service. The ending balance, shown in the lower-right corner, is actually the sum of all the transactions shown in the register.

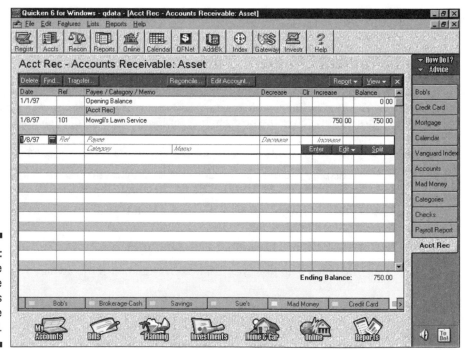

Figure 16-2:
An invoice entry in the Accounts Receivable register.

Recording customer payments

When you work with customer payments in Quicken, you actually need to do two things. First, you record the customer check as a deposit in your bank account and categorize it as falling into one of your income categories. Because you probably can record this information with your eyes closed and one hand tied behind your back, I won't describe the process again here.

Second, you must update your accounts receivable list for the customer's payment. To update the list, display the Accounts Receivable account in the register window and mark the existing invoice the customer has paid by putting a c in the Clr (or cleared) field. (You can do this simply by clicking the Clr field.) Figure 16-3 shows that the first $750 invoice to Mowgli's Lawn Service has been paid.

Notice that I've gotten pretty crazy and entered some other invoices, too. It's my job.

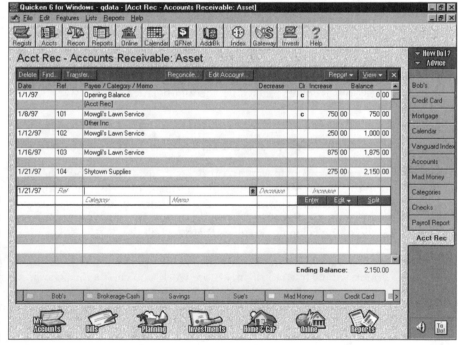

Figure 16-3:
The Accounts Receivable register with invoice #101 marked as cleared.

Tracking Your Receivables

When you look at the Accounts Receivable register at this point, you can't tell the total of what your customers owe you. In Figure 16-3, for example, even though I've marked invoice 101 as paid, the account balance still shows $2,150 (the balance of all four invoices shown).

Discovering a dirty little secret about A/R reporting in Quicken

You have just discovered an unfortunate quirk in the way Quicken handles accounts receivable: The account balance for an asset account includes all the transactions entered in the register — even those you mark as being cleared. This quirk causes some problems. For example, you can't print an accurate balance sheet report because Quicken uses the account balance from an asset account on the balance sheet report, and this balance is not accurate.

Oh m' gosh — does this mean that you can't track receivables this way? — naw. It does mean, however, that you can't use the accounts receivable account balance for anything because the balance is really a meaningless number. What's more, the accounts receivable, total assets, and net worth figures on the balance sheet reports are also meaningless numbers because the report uses the goofy accounts receivable account balances, too.

Producing an accurate balance sheet

Suppose that you do want to produce an accurate balance sheet. What do you do? You simply strip out the cleared transactions in a receivables register by deleting them one by one. Before you begin your deletions, however, print a copy of the Customer Receivables register. You may want to have a record some place of the customer invoices that you billed.

What's that? You don't like the idea of stripping out the transactions? Okay. If you're willing to go to slightly more work, you can fix the accounts receivable balance in another way. Using the Split Transaction Window (see Chapter 14), go through and add split transaction information showing a reduction in the invoice total that results when the customer makes a payment.

For a $750 invoice on which the customer pays the $400, for example, the Split Transaction Window includes one line that records a positive number for the initial $750 invoice and another line that records a negative number for the $400 customer payment. So what you're left with is a transaction that equals $350 — the open balance on the invoice — because that's what the split transaction amounts add up to. Figure 16-4 shows an example of this.

Figure 16-4:
The Split
Transaction
Window can
be used to
show
payments
on an
invoice.

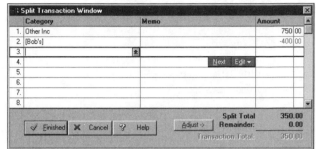

If you use the Split Transaction Window to show invoices being paid, don't
mark partially paid invoices as cleared. If you do, they won't show up on the
A/R by Customer report. I'll talk a bit more about this report in the next section.

Getting a list of what customers owe you

You could also mitigate the problem of the inaccurate balance sheet by printing
an A/R by Customer business report to summarize who owes you and how
much they owe. (This won't suddenly make an inaccurate balance sheet
accurate, of course. But it will let you know exactly who owes you what.)

The A/R by Customer report summarizes all uncleared transactions. To
Quicken, however, the first transaction in this register, Opening Balance, looks
like a customer — even though it is not a real account. So that this phantom
customer doesn't appear on your report, either delete it or mark it as cleared.

To print the A/R by Customer business report, follow these simple steps:

1. **Choose Reports⇨Business to display the Business Reports menu.**

2. **Choose A/R by Customer.**

   Quicken displays the standard Create Report dialog box. (Refer to
   Chapter 6 if you have questions about this dialog box.)

3. **Select Customize if you've already created other asset accounts.**

   Quicken displays the Customize A/R by Customer dialog box. Click
   the Accounts tab. Your dialog box should look like the one you see in
   Figure 16-5.

4. **Select which accounts with uncleared transactions you want on the
   accounts receivable report.**

   Then to select an account, click the mouse or press the spacebar. (By the
   way, if you have only one asset account — the Accounts Receivable
   account — the initial selection Quicken makes is correct.)

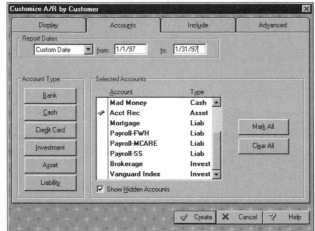

Figure 16-5:
The
Customize
A/R by
Customer
dialog box.

5. Click Create.

Quicken produces a report that summarizes the uncleared transactions by payee names. Figure 16-6 shows the A/R by Customer report based on the three uncleared invoices shown in Figure 16-3.

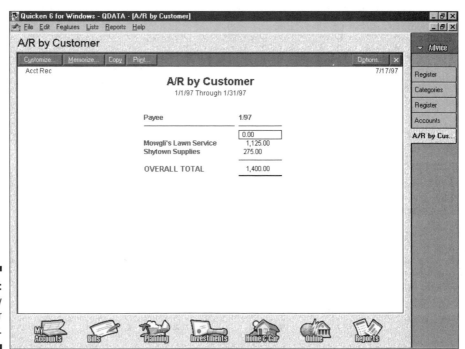

Figure 16-6:
The A/R by
Customer
report.

Preparing to Track Vendor Payables

You really don't have to do anything special to begin tracking the amounts you know that you'll pay; however, you do need to have a bank account already set up. (I'm assuming that you already have a bank account set up. If you don't — and it's almost impossible to believe that you don't — refer to Chapters 1 and 2.)

Describing your vendor payables

You describe your vendor payables by filling in the checks you use to pay a vendor's bills in the Write Checks window. Don't print the checks, though. Quicken tracks these unprinted checks because they represent your unpaid vendor invoices. That's it.

I'm super tempted to describe how you fill out the blanks of the Write Checks window — the result of the first tenet in the boring old computer writer's code of honor, "When in doubt, describe in detail." But really — and you probably know this — filling out the Write Checks window is darn easy.

If you're not sure about how to fill out the Write Checks window, don't feel that you're stupid or that the process requires an advanced degree. After all, you're still getting your feet wet. So if you feel unsure of yourself, peruse Chapter 5 and then go ahead and wail away at your keyboard.

Tracking vendor payables

Whenever you want to know how much money you owe someone, just print a report that summarizes the unprinted checks by payee name. Pretty easy, huh? All you have to do is print the A/P by Vendor business report. If you know how to print the report, go ahead. If you need a little help, here's a blow-by-blow account of the steps you need to follow:

1. **Choose Reports⇨Business to display the Business Reports menu.**

2. **Choose A/P by Vendor.**

   Quicken displays the Create Report dialog box, already filled out so that Quicken can print an A/P (Unprinted Chks) by Vendor report. Because I have explained this dialog box in Chapter 6, I didn't include it as a figure in this chapter.

3. **Click Create.**

   Quicken summarizes the unprinted checks in your bank, cash, and credit card accounts. Figure 16-7 shows an example of this cute little report.

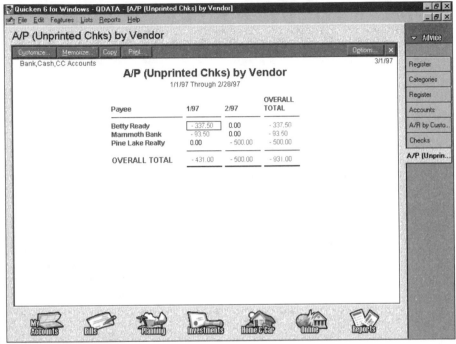

Figure 16-7:
The A/P
(Unprinted
Chks) by
Vendor by
Month
report.

How Quicken identifies an unprinted check

Here's a little tidbit of information you may (or may not) find useful. When you describe a check you want to print by using the Write Checks window, Quicken records the check in the register but uses the word *Print* in place of the check number. The word *Print* identifies the check as the one that you want to print and signals Quicken to look at the check and say to itself, "Aha! — an unprinted check!" *Print* is, to say the least, an important word.

If you're someone who's decided to get truly wild and crazy and use Quicken's electronic bill-paying feature, untransmitted payments show up in the register, too. This time, Quicken uses the word *XMIT* to look at and say, "Aha! — an untransmitted electronic payment!" Untransmitted payments, however, don't appear on the A/P (Unprinted Chks) by Vendor report. Go figure.

Electronic payments can be wild and crazy? What a concept! Yes, the entire Quicken program can be just that, if it means being fun and adventurous. You know, wild and crazy — as in ordering Thai food and saying, "Make that four stars, please." Or wild and crazy — as in not wearing any underwear. You understand.

Explaining how Quicken handles payables

Before I conclude this wonderfully interesting, terribly exciting discussion about how you track unpaid bills in Quicken, let me make one final, quick point: An unprinted check gets counted as an expense only after you print it. Does this news sound like much ado about nothing? It probably is.

But let's take a minute to explain the accounting system that Quicken uses. For example, if you record a $1,000 check to your landlord on December 31 but you don't print the check until January, Quicken doesn't count the $1,000 as an expense in December. It instead counts the $1,000 as an expense in January of the next year.

By the way, the Quicken register will show two balances: the current balance, which shows, well, the current balance (the balance that's in your account even as you read this sentence) and the ending balance, which shows the unprinted checks.

If you know a little about cash-basis accounting versus accrual-basis accounting, you've probably already said to yourself, "Hey, man, Quicken uses cash-basis accounting." And you're right, of course.

This little subtlety between the two accounting systems can cause confusion, especially if you've already been working with a regular, full-featured accounting system that uses an accounts payable module with accrual-basis accounting. In one of these systems, the $1,000 check to your landlord probably gets counted as an expense as soon as you enter it in the system.

Billminder

Bill, my affectionate nickname for Billminder, is a separate program in Quicken that will soon become a good friend of yours, too. You can tell Quicken to fix your computer so that the Billminder program runs every time you turn on your computer — a nice feature.

What Bill does is simple: He looks through your unprinted checks for any checks with dates falling on or before the current date. If Bill finds a check with such a date, he displays a message that says, "Hey, dude, you have checks that you need to print." Or, in the case where you have overdue checks, Bill displays a message that says, "Dude, the situation is getting gnarly — you've got some seriously overdue checks." (The messages don't use these exact words, by the way.)

To tell Bill you want him reminding you of the checks you need to print, follow these steps:

1. Choose Edit⇨Options⇨Reminders.

In a surprising move, Quicken displays the Reminder Options dialog box, where all the action happens — at least from Bill's perspective. Figure 16-8 shows the Reminder Options dialog box.

Figure 16-8:
The
Reminder
Options
dialog box.

2. Turn on the Billminder reminder feature by selecting the Turn on Billminder check box.

Billminder also keeps its eyes open for scheduled transactions, investment reminder messages, and notes you've posted on the Financial Calendar.

3. Enter a value in the Days in Advance text box on the dialog box.

This value tells Bill how many days in advance you want to be reminded of unprinted checks. The value also tells Quicken how many days in advance you want to be queried about scheduled transactions and investment reminder messages.

4. Select the Show Reminders on Startup check box.

Selecting this box tells Bill that you want to be reminded of the checks after you start up Quicken. If you don't select this box, by the way, Bill checks whether you've got checks to print, but he doesn't come right out and say whether you've got checks to print. To find out about unprinted checks, you need to click the Reminder tab — assuming that you check the Show Reminders on Startup.

5. Click OK.

When you start Quicken the next time, you'll see a screen like the one shown in Figure 16-9. It'll tell you whether you've got checks to print, scheduled transactions that need to be entered, and any calendar notes you should probably be reading.

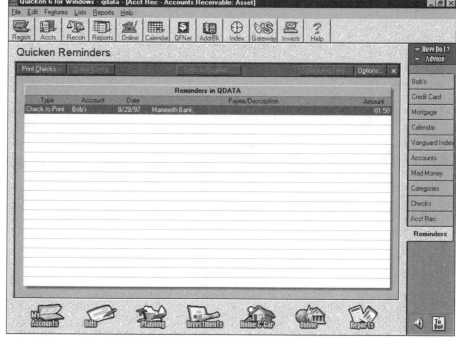

To actually see the checks that should be printed or the scheduled transactions that should be entered, you just click the Print Checks button or the Record Transactions button. Any calendar notes you've created will show in the list.

Well, that about wraps up the main part of tonight's show. If you're thinking that it's still a little too early to go to bed, flip through the following chapters. They provide lists of a bunch of eclectic topics: ten things to do when you visit Acapulco, ten things you should never do during a commercial airline flight, and so on. Time flies when you're having fun, doesn't it?

Part V
The Part of Tens

In this part . . .

As a writing tool, laundry lists aren't something that high school English teachers encourage. But you know what? The old laundry list format is pretty handy for certain sorts of information.

With this idea in mind (and, of course, deepest apologies to my high school English teacher, Mrs. O'Rourke), the next and final part simply provides you with lists of information about Quicken: answers to ten commonly asked questions about Quicken, ten things every business owner using Quicken should know, ten things you should (or should not) do if you are audited, and so on.

Chapter 17

Ten Questions I'm Frequently Asked about Quicken

*W*hen people find out that I've written a book about Quicken, they always ask a question or two. In this chapter, I list the most common questions and their answers.

Does Quicken Work for a Corporation?

Sure. But let me talk for a minute about what's unique — at least from an accountant's perspective — about a corporation.

In addition to recording assets (such as bank accounts and receivables) and liabilities (such as mortgages and trade payables), a corporation needs to *track*, or keep records for, the stockholders' equity.

Stockholders' equity includes the amount people originally paid for their stock, any earnings the corporation has retained, cumulative income for the current year, and sometimes other stuff, too.

"Ugh," you're probably saying to yourself. "Ugh" is right. Accounting for stockholders' equity of a corporation is mighty complicated at times. So complicated, in fact, that Quicken can't track a corporation's stockholders' equity.

I'm not saying that you can't use Quicken if you're a corporation, and I'm not saying that you shouldn't. (I do business as a corporation, and I use Quicken.) Just remember that someone — probably your poor accountant — periodically needs to calculate your stockholders' equity.

Fortunately, the financial information you collect with Quicken provides, in rough form, much of the information that your poor accountant needs in order to do things manually.

What Happens to Stockholders' Equity in Quicken?

Quicken doesn't exactly ignore a corporation's stockholders' equity. In an Account Balances report, the difference between the total assets and the total liabilities actually represents the total stockholders' equity. (Quicken labels this total Net Worth. So, to the extent that your total assets and total liabilities figures are correct, you know your total stockholders' equity.)

Does Quicken Work for a Partnership?

Yep, it does. But a partnership that uses Quicken faces the same basic problem as a corporation that uses Quicken. In a partnership, the partners want to track their partnership capital accounts (or at least they should). A partnership capital account simply shows what a partner has put into and taken out of a business.

As noted in the preceding section, Quicken calculates a net worth figure for you by subtracting total liabilities from total assets. So, to the extent that your total assets and total liabilities are accurately accounted for in Quicken, you know roughly the total partnership capital.

To solve this problem, you — or someone else — will need to track what each partner puts into the business, earns as a partner in the business, and then takes out of the business.

Can I Use Quicken for More Than One Business?

Yeah, but be very careful. *Very* careful. You must be especially diligent in keeping the two businesses' financial records separate.

Quicken provides a handy tool for keeping them straight: you can work with more than one file. Each file, in effect, is like a separate set of financial records. You can't record automatic transfers between accounts in different files; instead, you must record each side of the transaction separately. You can, however, keep truly separate business records.

To create a separate file, choose the File⇨New command.

If you've been using Quicken for a while, you can probably figure out for yourself how the File⇨New command works. If you need help, refer to my discussion of this command in Chapter 8.

Separate bank accounts are usually a must. If you keep separate records for two distinct businesses in Quicken, you need to set up separate bank accounts for them. In fact, my attorney tells me that in the case of a corporation, you must set up a separate corporate bank account for the corporation to be truly considered as an independent legal entity. Talk to your attorney if you have questions; attorneys can tell you the specifics that apply to a particular state and situation.

What Kind of Businesses Shouldn't Use Quicken?

You're probably saying to yourself, "Quicken works for corporations (sort of), and it works for partnerships (sort of). Does that mean that it works for just about any kind of business?"

The answer is no. Quicken is a darn good product. In fact, for many small businesses, it's a great product. But it doesn't work in every situation.

Here's a three-part test that you can use to determine whether your business should use Quicken. If you answer yes to two or three of the questions, you should seriously consider moving up to a full-featured small-business accounting system.

✔ *Do you regularly need to produce business forms other than checks?*

If you answer no to this question, you're in good shape with Quicken, which produces checks easily. And if all you need is an occasional invoice, you can create it easily enough on your computer. I, for example, produce a handful of invoices a month. I do them on my word processing program and never have any problems.

If you do produce a lot of forms besides checks, you should probably consider moving up to a small-business accounting system that produces the forms you want. If you've been using Quicken, for example, take a look at QuickBooks for Windows, another Intuit product. Another more powerful but wonderfully designed product you might try is Peachtree Accounting for Windows from Peachtree Software. You should be able to get either program at the local software store. You can certainly get either program by calling one of the mail order places.

✔ *Do you need to track assets other than cash or investments?*

For example, do you have a long list of customer receivables that you need to monitor? Or do you buy and resell inventory? An accounting system is usually helpful in tracking these items. Quicken doesn't do a very good job of tracking these other assets, so you may want to look at one of the other small-business accounting products — QuickBooks, for example.

✔ *Are you having problems measuring your profits with cash-basis accounting?*

I'm not going to get into a big, tangled discussion of cash-basis versus accrual-basis accounting. It wouldn't be any fun for you. It wouldn't be any fun for me, either. Nevertheless, you should know that if you can't accurately measure your business profits by using cash-basis accounting (which is what Quicken uses), you may be able to more accurately measure your business profits by using accrual-basis accounting. To do so, use an accounting system that supports accrual-basis accounting. I should be totally honest with you and tell you that to measure your profits the right way, you (or your accountant) need to use — horror of horrors — double-entry bookkeeping.

If you are a Quicken user but realize that you're outgrowing the checkbook-on-a-computer scene, check out QuickBooks. (No, I don't get a kickback from Intuit.) Here's the deal: QuickBooks looks and feels a lot like Quicken. Plus, it uses the data that you've already collected with Quicken. So you'll find that moving from Quicken to QuickBooks is only slightly more complicated than rolling off a log.

Can I Use Quicken Retroactively?

Yeah. And the idea is better than it might seem at first.

It doesn't take long to enter a year's worth of transactions in Quicken (as long as you have decent records to work with). If you're, like, a millionaire, it might take you a couple of days. (Of course, in this case you can probably hire someone to do it for you.) If you're a regular, ordinary person, I bet you can get it done on a rainy Saturday afternoon.

After you enter all the information into a Quicken register, you can easily monitor your spending in various categories, track your income and outgo, and reconcile your bank accounts. I know one professional who uses Quicken records to do these things every year. Hey, it's not the most efficient way to do things. And it's not a very good way to manage business or personal financial affairs. But it works. Sort of.

Can I Do Payroll with Quicken?

Yes. See Chapter 15 for more details.

You can also use a handy payroll utility called QuickPay to do payroll in Quicken. If you've got only one or two salaried employees who always earn the same amount — a nanny, for example — then you don't need QuickPay. But if you have a bunch of employees or even a single hourly employee, QuickPay saves you a great deal of time.

Intuit makes and sells QuickPay, as you might guess by its name. You can get QuickPay from the local software store, from one of the mail order places, or by calling Intuit.

Can I Prepare Invoices?

No. This is a good example of when you should consider moving up to a full-featured small-business accounting system.

Wait until the new year to switch programs

If you're moving to Quicken, your transaction volumes probably aren't so incredibly mammoth that you have gazillions of transactions to enter, anyway. Given this assumption, it probably makes sense to convert, or switch, programs at the beginning of your fiscal, or accounting, year — usually January 1. By waiting until the next fiscal year, the only data you absolutely have to load into Quicken are the asset and liability account balances. And you can do so easily enough when you set up the accounts.

Can I Import Data from an Old Accounting System?

Someone had to ask this question, I guess. (Imagine me taking a deep breath here.) Yes, you can import data from your old accounting system. To do so, export the old system's data into a file that matches the Quicken Interchange Format, or QIF, specification. Then import this file into an empty Quicken file.

- ✔ This process isn't for the timid or faint-hearted.
- ✔ I would also claim that it isn't for people who have better things to do with their time.
- ✔ My advice to you? Go to a movie. Mow your lawn. Read a trashy novel. Forget all about this importing business.

What Do You Think about Quicken?

I think it's great. But I bet your question isn't really whether Quicken is good or not. Heck, the package sells something like two million copies a year. So we both know that the package is pretty good, right? My guess is that what you really want is my opinion about using Quicken in particular business or personal situations.

It's tough to answer this question in a one-way conversation. Even so, let me give you some of the best reasons for using Quicken:

- ✔ You always know your bank account balances, so you won't ever have to wonder whether you have enough money to pay a bill or charge a purchase.

- ✔ Reconciling your account takes about two minutes. (I'm not joking. It really does take a couple of minutes.)

- ✔ You get a firm handle on what you're really making and spending.

- ✔ You can budget your spending and then track your spending against your budget.

- ✔ If you're a business, you can measure your profits as often as you want by using cash-basis accounting.

- ✔ If you're an investor, you can monitor your investments and measure their actual returns.

I hope these answers help. My guess is that if you think a program like Quicken will help you better manage your financial affairs, then it probably will.

Chapter 18

Ten Tips for Bookkeepers Who Use Quicken (And Anyone Else, Too)

An amazing number of people use Quicken for small-business accounting: dentists, contractors, lawyers, and so on. And, not surprisingly, many bookkeepers use Quicken.

If you're jumping up and down, waving your hands, saying, "I do, I do, I do," this chapter is for you. I tell you here what you need to know to make your use of Quicken smooth and sure.

Tricks for Learning Quicken If You're New on the Job

First of all, let me congratulate you on your new job. Let me also remind you how thankful you should be that you'll be using Quicken and not one of the super-powerful-but-frightening, complex accounting packages.

If you're new to computers, you need to know a thing or two about them. Don't worry. This task isn't as difficult as you may think. (Remember that a bunch of anxious folks have gone before you.)

Turning on the computer

Before you use the computer, you need to:

1. **Find and flip on the computer's power switch (usually a button labled "Power").**

2. **Push a switch to turn on your monitor (the television-like screen).**

3. **Flip a switch to turn on the printer.**

Even if you're a little timid, go ahead and ask your boss how to turn on the computer and its peripherals. This won't be considered a stupid question. Different computers get turned on in different ways. For example, the computer and its peripherals may already be on and plugged into a fancy-schmancy extension cord called a *power strip* — but this power strip thing is turned off.

By the way, the word *peripherals* refers to things that work with the computer, such as the printer.

Starting Windows 95 and Quicken

After you turn on the computer, Windows 95 starts automatically. (Unlike with the previous versions of Windows, you don't have to type the **WIN** command at the DOS prompt to get Windows 95 to start.)

You use Windows 95 to start Quicken. If you don't "do" Windows 95, refer to Appendix A for a quick and dirty overview.

If you're using a computer that doesn't have Windows 95, you start Windows and Quicken slightly differently. First, turn on the computer. Then, when you see the DOS prompt — it'll look like C:\> or something like that — type **win**. This tells DOS to start Windows. After Windows starts and you see the Program

Manager window on your screen, double-click the Quicken program group (it'll be a little square picture labeled Quicken). And then, after Windows displays the Quicken program group, double-click the Quicken program item (it'll be the little Quicken icon thingamajig). If this all seems too complicated, I have two suggestions. First, get Windows 95 (or beg your boss to get it). Windows 95 makes it much, much easier to start and stop programs. Plus, you don't have to do anything special to start Windows 95. It starts itself. Second, if you can't get Windows 95, find a copy of IDG Books Worldwide's *Windows 3.11 for Dummies,* 3rd Edition.

Learning Quicken

When you know how to turn on the computer and how to start Quicken, you're ready to rock. Give Part II of this book a quick read. Then carefully read those chapters in Part IV that apply to your daily work.

One last thing. Remember when you learned how to drive a car? Sure, it was confusing at first: all those gauges and meters . . . the tremendous power at your fingertips . . . traffic. After you gained some experience though, you loosened your death grip on the wheel. Heck, you even started driving in the left lane.

Give yourself a little time. Before long, you'll be zipping around Quicken, changing lanes three at a time.

Cross-Reference and File Source Documents

Be sure to cross-reference and file (neatly!) the source documents (checks, deposit slips, and so on) that you use to enter transactions. I won't tell you how to set up a document filing system. There's a pretty good chance you can do this better than I — in fact, I usually use a crude, alphabetical scheme.

Check forms (the check source documents) are numbered, so you can cross-reference checks simply by entering check numbers when recording a check transaction. But be sure to do the same for deposits and other withdrawals, too.

Cross-referencing enables you to answer any questions about a transaction that appears in a register. All you have to do is find the source document that you used to enter the transaction.

Always Categorize

Always categorize a transaction. In an account transfer, specify the account to which an amount has been transferred.

A favorite but sloppy accounting trick is to assign funny transactions to a *"suspense" account.* Suspense accounts, however, often become financial garbage dumps where you (and anyone else using Quicken) dump transactions that you don't know what to do with.

The suspense grows and grows. And pretty soon, it's a huge mess, and no one has the energy to clean it up.

By the way, you can tell Quicken to remind you to enter a category every time you enter a transaction. Here's how to get this reminder:

1. **Choose Edit⇨Options⇨Register.**

   Quicken displays the Register Options dialog box.

2. **Specify that you want Quicken to warn you if a transaction has no category.**

   Click the Miscellaneous tab of the Register Options dialog box. Then move the selection cursor to the When Recording Uncategorized Transactions check box and press the spacebar. Or just select the check box by using the mouse.

3. **Click OK.**

Reconcile Promptly

This is a pet peeve, so bear with me if I get a little huffy.

I think you should always reconcile, or balance, a business's bank accounts within a day or two after you get the bank statement. You'll catch any errors that either you or the bank has made.

You also minimize the chance that you'll suffer financial losses from check forgery. Here's why: If a business or individual promptly alerts a bank about a check forgery, the bank, rather than the business, suffers the loss in most cases. (I have to tell you that one day, after I wrote these paragraphs, I was reconciling my account and I discovered that an employee of mine had forged checks. Weird, huh?)

Reconciling in Quicken is fast and easy, so there's no good excuse not to reconcile promptly. Chapter 7 describes how to reconcile accounts in Quicken.

Things You Should Do Every Month

In a business, everyone has some routine tasks: Go through the In basket. Return phone messages. Clean the coffee machine.

Here are six bookkeeping chores that you should probably do at the end of every month:

- If the business uses a petty cash system, replenish the petty cash fund. Make sure that you have receipts for all withdrawals.
- Reconcile the bank and credit card accounts.
- If you're preparing payroll, be sure to remit any payroll tax deposit money owed. (You may need to remit payroll taxes more frequently than once a month. The Internal Revenue Service will tell you how often you must remit payroll tax desposit money.)
- Print a copy of each of the account registers for the month.

  Set these copies aside as permanent financial records. Chapter 5 describes how to print reports, including the account registers.
- Print two copies of the monthly cash flow statement and the P&L statement.

  Give one copy to the business's owner or manager. Put the other copy with the permanent financial records.
- If you haven't done so already during the month, back up the file containing the Quicken accounts to a floppy disk.

  You can reuse the floppy disk every other month. Chapter 8 describes how to back up files.

Don't view the preceding list as all-inclusive. There may be other things you need to do. I'd hate for people to say, "Well, it doesn't appear on Nelson's list, so I don't have to do it." Yikes!

Things You Should Do Every Year

Here are the things I think you should do at the end of every year:

✔ Do all the usual month-end chores for the last month in the year.

See the list in the preceding section.

✔ Prepare and file any state and federal end-of-year payroll tax returns.

Businesses in the United States, for example, need to prepare the annual federal unemployment tax return (Form 940).

✔ Print two copies of the annual cash flow statement and the annual P&L statement.

Give one copy to the business's owner or manager. Put the other copy with the permanent financial records.

✔ If the business is a corporation, print a copy of the Business Balance Sheet report.

This report will help whoever prepares the corporate tax return.

✔ Back up the file containing the Quicken accounts to a floppy disk.

Store the floppy disk as a permanent archive copy.

✔ If the business's accounts are full — you notice that Quicken runs more slowly — use Quicken's Year End Copy command to shrink the file.

Quicken creates a new version of the file, keeping only the current year's transactions. See Chapter 8.

Again, don't view the preceding list as all-inclusive. If you think of other things to do, do them.

Debits and Credits (If You're Used to These)

If you've worked with a regular small-business accounting system, you may have missed your old friends, debit and credit.

Quicken is a single-entry accounting system and, as a result, doesn't really have debits and credits. Double-entry systems have debits and credits. (As you may know, the two entries in a double-entry system are your old friends: debit and credit. For every debit, you have equal credit.)

Quicken does supply a sort of chart of accounts, which you can use to describe accounting transactions. The Category & Transfer List window (which you can usually display by pressing Ctrl+C) actually parallels a regular accounting system's chart of accounts.

Accordingly, when you record a transaction that increases or decreases one account, you record the offsetting debit or credit when you categorize or transfer the account.

Converting to Quicken

If you're converting to Quicken from a manual system or from another more complicated small-business accounting system, here are two important tips:

- ✔ Start using Quicken at the beginning of a year.

  The year's financial records are then in one place — the Quicken registers.

- ✔ If it's not the beginning of the year, go back and enter the year's transactions.

  Again, the year's financial records are then in one place — the Quicken registers. (This task will take time if you have a bunch of transactions to enter. In fact, you may want to postpone your conversion to Quicken.)

Income Tax Evasion

A nice fellow wandered into my office the other day and told me that he had inadvertently gotten entangled in his employer's income tax evasion. He didn't know what to do. He had unwittingly helped his employer file fraudulent income tax returns. Then, already sucked into the tar pit, he had lied to the IRS during an audit.

I didn't have anything good to tell him.

I never did get the fellow's name, so I'll just call him *Chump*. It really didn't make any financial sense for Chump to help his employer steal. Chump didn't get a share of the loot; he just helped his employer commit a felony. For free. Although Chump didn't receive any of the booty, he probably still is in serious trouble with the IRS. The criminal penalties can be enormous. Prison, I understand, is not fun.

I'm not going to spend any more time talking about this. But I do have a piece of advice for you: Don't be a Chump.

Segregate Payroll Tax Money

While I'm on the subject of terrible things the IRS can do to you, let me touch on the problem of payroll tax deposits — the money you withhold from employee checks for federal income taxes, Social Security, and Medicare.

If you have the authority to spend the money you withhold, don't — even if the company will go out of business. If you can't repay the payroll tax money, the IRS will go after the business owners and also after *you*.

It doesn't matter that you're just the bookkeeper; it doesn't matter whether you regularly attend church. The IRS doesn't take kindly to those who take what belongs to the IRS.

By the way, I should mention that the IRS is more lenient in cases where you don't have any authority to dip into the payroll tax money while the business owner or your boss dips away. If you find yourself in this situation, however, be darn careful not to get involved. Start looking for a new job. And talk to an attorney if you have any legal questions.

Chapter 19

Ten Tips for Business Owners

1 f you run a business and you use Quicken, you need to know some accounting stuff. You can discover these things by sitting down with your certified public accountant over a cup of coffee at $100 an hour. Or you can read this chapter.

Sign All Your Own Checks

I have nothing against your bookkeeper. In a small business, however, it's just too darn easy for people — especially full-charge bookkeepers — to bamboozle you. By signing all the checks yourself, you keep your fingers on the pulse of your cash outflow.

Yeah, I know this can be a hassle. I know this means you can't easily spend three months in Hawaii. I know this means you have to wade through paperwork every time you sign a stack of checks.

By the way, if you're in a partnership, I think you should have at least a couple of the partners co-sign checks.

Don't Sign a Check the Wrong Way

If you sign many checks, you may be tempted to use a movie-star autograph signature: You know, something really quick and dirty. Although this makes great sense if you're autographing 5 x 7 publicity portraits or baseballs, don't do it when you're signing checks. A wavy line with a cross and a couple of dots is really easy to forge.

Which leads me to my next tip . . .

Review Canceled Checks before Your Bookkeeper Does

Be sure you review your canceled checks — before anybody else sees the monthly bank statement.

This chapter isn't about browbeating bookkeepers. But a business owner will discover whether someone is forging signatures on checks only by being the first to open the bank statement and reviewing each of the canceled check signatures.

If you don't take this precaution, unscrupulous employees — especially bookkeepers who can update the bank account records — can forge your signature with impunity. And they won't get caught if they never overdraw the account.

Another thing: If you don't follow these procedures, *you*, not the bank, will probably eat the losses.

By the way, I should probably tell you — just for the fun of it — that the very first employee I hired for my business forged checks on one of my business accounts. And the way I caught him was by reviewing the canceled checks as I was reconciling the bank account. (Just in case you're interested, he stole around $700 — which the bank immediately reimbursed — and was arrested, convicted, and sentenced to four months of home detention.)

How to Choose a Bookkeeper If You Use Quicken

Don't worry. You don't need to request an FBI background check.

In fact, if you use Quicken, you don't need to hire only people who are familiar with small-business accounting systems. Just find people who know how to keep a checkbook and work with a computer; you shouldn't have a problem getting them to understand Quicken.

Of course, you don't want someone who just fell off the turnip truck. But even if you do hire someone who rode into town on the truck, you're not going to have much trouble getting him or her up to speed with Quicken.

But when you hire someone, find someone who knows how to do payroll — not just the federal payroll tax stuff (see Chapter 15), but also the state payroll tax monkey business.

Get Smart about Passwords

In Chapter 8, I get all hot and bothered about passwords. Let me add here that I suggest you use a password to keep your financial records confidential if you use Quicken in a business and it's you who does the Quicken *thang*. (Especially if you have employees who know how to operate a PC and have access to the PC you use for Quicken.)

Keep Your Password Record at Home

To assign a file password, see Chapter 8. But be sure that you don't lose your financial records by forgetting your password. (I think it's a good idea to keep *at home* a record of the password that you use for the computer at work.)

Cash-Basis Accounting Doesn't Work for All Businesses

When you use Quicken, you employ an accounting convention called *cash-basis accounting* to measure your profits. When money comes in, you count it as revenue. When money goes out, you count it as expense.

Cash-basis accounting is fine when a business's cash inflow mirrors its sales and its cash outflow mirrors its expenses. This isn't the case, however, in many businesses. A single-family home contractor, for example, may have cash coming in (by borrowing from banks) but may not make any money. A pawn-shop owner who loans money at 22 percent may make scads of money even if cash pours out of the business daily. As a rule of thumb, when you're buying and selling inventory, accrual-basis accounting works better than cash-basis accounting.

So this news isn't earthshaking. It's still something you should think about.

When to Switch to Accrual-Basis Accounting

If tracking cash flows doesn't indicate whether your business is making a profit or a loss, then you probably need to switch to accrual-basis accounting. Almost certainly you need to switch accounting systems.

What to Do If Quicken Doesn't Work for Your Business

Quicken is a great checkbook program.

However, if Quicken doesn't seem to fit your needs — for example, you need accrual-basis accounting (see the preceding section) — you may want one of the more complicated but also more powerful small-business accounting packages.

If you like using Quicken, look at QuickBooks for Windows, also made by Intuit, the maker of Quicken.

You also should look at other more powerful programs, such as the full-featured Windows accounting programs — Peachtree Accounting for Windows from Peachtree Software, for example.

I am amazed that PC accounting software remains so affordable. You can buy a great accounting package — one you can use to manage a $5 million or a $25 million business — for a few hundred bucks. This deal is truly one of the great bargains.

Keep Things Simple

Let me share one last comment about managing small-business financial affairs. *Keep things as simple as possible.* In fact, keep your business affairs simple enough that it's easy to tell if you're making money and if the business is healthy.

This advice may sound strange, but as a CPA I've seen some very bright people build monstrously complex financial structures for their businesses, including complicated leasing arrangements, labyrinth-like partnership and corporate structures, and sophisticated profit-sharing and cost-sharing arrangements with other businesses.

I can offer only anecdotal evidence, of course, but I strongly believe that these super-sophisticated financial arrangements don't produce a profit when you consider all the costs. What's more, these super-sophisticated arrangements almost always turn into management and record-keeping headaches. Especially for small businesses.

Chapter 20

Ten Things You Should Do If You're Audited

*B*ecause you may use Quicken to track things like your income tax deductions, I want to mention some of the things that you should do if you get audited.

Leave Quicken at Home

Don't take Quicken with you to an IRS audit. Even if you're really proud of that new laptop.

Here's the problem: Quicken's reporting capabilities are incredibly powerful. If you've been using Quicken diligently, you own a rich database describing almost all your financial affairs. If you take Quicken (and your Quicken file) to the IRS, you're essentially spilling your financial guts.

Now I'm not one who recommends sneaking stuff by the IRS. But it is dumb to give an IRS agent the opportunity to go on a fishing expedition. Remember: The agent isn't going to be looking for additional deductions.

I know of a young woman who took Quicken to an audit. After the IRS agent asked a question, the business owner proudly tapped a few keys on the laptop, smiled broadly, and then showed the agent on-screen, for example, all the individual entertainment expenses claimed by the taxpayer in question.

Funny thing, though. The IRS agent also saw some other things. Such as money that should have been claimed as income. Reporting requirements the taxpayer failed to meet. Out-of-line deductions.

Print Summary Reports for Tax Deductions

Ol' Quicken can be your friend, though, if you're audited.

Before you go to the audit, find out what the IRS is questioning. Print a summary report of every questioned deduction: charitable giving, medical expenses, travel and entertainment, and so on. You'll have an easy-to-understand report explaining how you came up with every number the IRS wants to examine.

By the way, I know a very clever tax attorney who used Quicken in this manner. The audit lasted half an hour.

Collect All Source Documents

After you print a summary report of every questioned deduction, collect all the source documents — usually canceled checks — that prove or indicate a transaction in question.

For example, if you claim $600 in charitable giving, the report summarizing this deduction may show 12 $50 checks written to your church or to the local United Way agency. To verify this report, find the 12 canceled checks.

Call a Tax Attorney If the Agent Is "Special"

An IRS *special agent* isn't an agent endorsed by Mr. Rogers. Internal Revenue Service special agents investigate criminal tax code violations. If a special agent is auditing your return, you may be in a heap of trouble. So get a tax attorney.

In my mind, being audited by a special agent is like being arrested for murder. Call me a scaredy-cat, but I'd want legal representation even if I were innocent.

Don't Volunteer Information

Loose lips sink ships. Don't volunteer any information — even if it seems innocuous. Just answer the questions you're asked.

Again, I'm not suggesting that you lie. The agent, however, is looking for income you forgot or deductions you overstated. The more information you provide, the more likely you'll reveal something damaging.

For example, if you offhandedly tell the agent about your other business — where you knit socks for golf clubs — you may wind up debating whether that cute little business is really a business (and not a hobby) and whether knitting golf socks entitles you to deduct those country club dues and green fees.

Consider Using a Pinch Hitter

I don't think an audit should terrify you. And I'm someone who's scared of everything: dinner parties where I don't know anyone, stormy nights when the neighborhood seems particularly deserted, driving on bald tires. You get the idea. Nonetheless, if you used a paid preparer, think about sending that person in your place.

You'll pay for this service, of course. But it may help if the person who prepared your return does the talking.

Understand Everything on Your Return

Make sure that you understand everything on your return. You won't help yourself if you tell an agent that you don't have a clue about some number on your return.

Be Friendly

Be nice to the IRS. Remember, the agents actually work for you. In fact, the more taxes that the agents collect from people who owe the federal government, the less the rest of us have to pay. (An article in *Money* magazine a few years ago suggested that we end up paying several hundred dollars more a year in income taxes because so many people cheat.)

Don't Worry

If you've been honest and careful, you've got nothing to worry about. Sure, maybe you made a mistake. Maybe the agent will find the mistake. And maybe you'll have to pay some additional taxes.

If you haven't been honest and careful, I offer my condolences. Sorry.

Don't Lie

Don't lie; it may be perjury. You could go to jail and share a cell with someone named Skull Crusher.

You get the picture. And it's not pretty.

So don't lie.

Appendix A

Quick and Dirty Windows 95

● ●

1 f you're new to the Microsoft Windows 95 operating environment, you need to know a few things about Windows 95. Although this appendix doesn't reveal anything earthshaking, it provides a quick and dirty overview of what you need to know to get around.

If you've used other Windows 95 applications, you probably don't need to read this appendix because you already know the material it covers.

I won't bore you with technical details. The information here, though, will enable you not only to operate Quicken but also to converse easily about Windows 95 at cocktail parties, over lunch, or with the guy at the computer store.

If you want to find out more, read a good book such as Andy Rathbone's *Windows 95 For Dummies* (IDG Books Worldwide, Inc.).

What Is Windows 95?

Windows 95 is an operating environment that manages your *system resources* — things like memory, monitor, printer, and so on.

Applications (programs such as Quicken) run on top of Windows 95. In other words, you start Windows 95 first (by turning on your personal computer); then, after Windows 95 is running, you can start applications such as Quicken.

Windows 95 provides a standard graphical interface. In English, Windows 95 provides a common approach for using *visual elements* — icons, buttons, check boxes, and so on. (This appendix describes how the major pieces of this graphical interface work.)

Windows 95 enables you to run more than one application at a time. You may, for example, run Quicken, a tax preparation package, and even a Windows accessory program such as the Calendar. Sure, you don't need to do this stuff. But, hey, you can if you want.

Starting Windows 95

Starting Windows 95 is easy. You just turn on your personal computer. If you can find the on-off switch, you're set.

By the way, if for some reason you can't find the on-off switch or it doesn't seem to work, don't feel silly. Ask someone who's used the computer before. Sometimes the on-off switch is on the front of the computer and is labeled "on-off" (which makes good sense, of course). But all too frequently, I'm afraid, manufacturers stick the on-off switch on the back of the computer or label the switch something really stupid, such as 0 and 1. Sometimes, too, people plug a computer and all its peripherals (such as printers, modems, and all that junk) into a power strip that needs to be turned on to turn on the computer. So just ask someone. (If you bought the computer, of course, you can just telephone the place you bought it from.)

Just so you don't feel like a complete imbecile, I have to tell you something. I once had to call someone to learn how to click this stupid mouse that I got with my laptop computer.

Figure A-1 shows what a typical Windows 95 desktop looks like. The desktop is what you see after Windows 95 has started. Figure A-1 shows icons for programs that are not included in Windows 95, such as MS Word.

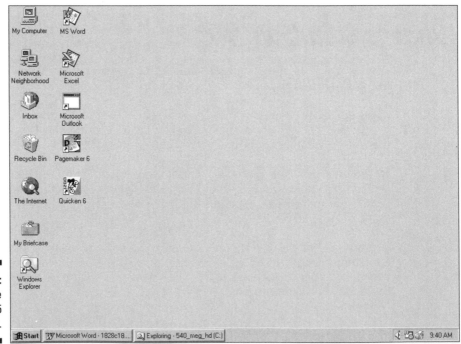

Figure A-1:
The
Windows 95
desktop.

Starting Programs

To start a program like Quicken, you click the Start button so that Windows 95 displays the Start menu. Then you click the Programs menu option so Windows 95 lists all the programs that you, Windows 95, or someone else has installed. And then you click one of the listed programs to start that program.

Some programs — such as Quicken — don't appear as options on the Programs menu. They appear on Programs submenus. If you click Start and then choose the Programs menu option, you'll see a Quicken item, for example. Choosing the Quicken item from the Programs menu displays the Quicken submenu, which lists a bunch of different options (which depend on the version of Quicken you've installed). To start Quicken, you choose Programs⇨Quicken⇨Quicken 6 For Windows.

To practice this starting business, try starting the WordPad application that comes with Windows 95 by following these steps:

1. **Click the Start button.**

2. **Choose <u>P</u>rograms⇨Accessories⇨WordPad.**

When you follow these steps, Windows 95 opens the WordPad program. Figure A-2 shows the WordPad application window. (An application window is just the window that a program like WordPad or Quicken displays.)

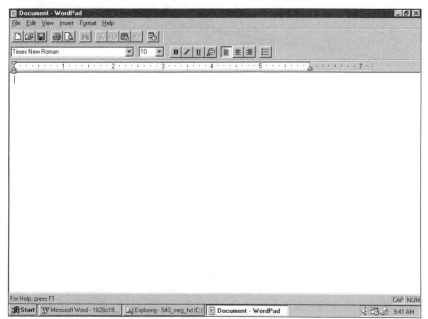

Figure A-2:
The
WordPad
application
window.

A tidbit about the taskbar

At the bottom of your screen, Windows 95 displays a *taskbar.* It provides the Start button, which I've already talked about, so you can start another program. (With Windows 95, you can run several programs at the same time.) And the taskbar provides buttons that you can click to move between the programs you're running. If you look closely at it while you're running WordPad, for example, you'll see a taskbar button for the WordPad program. You'll also see a taskbar button for any other program you're running at the same time. You probably will be glad to know that *multitasking,* which is what running multiple programs is called, is this easy to do — just click the buttons on the taskbar to switch from one running program to another.

Choosing Commands from Menus

To set in motion something in Windows 95, you usually need to choose *commands* from menus.

I don't know why they're called commands. Perhaps because you often (but not always) use them to command Windows 95 and Windows applications to do things. "Windows 95, I command thee to start this application," or "Quicken, I command thee to print this report."

Most application windows have a *menu bar* — a row of menus across the top of the window. Predictably, not every menu bar contains the same menus. But they're often darn similar. Some of the commands on the Quicken menus, for example, mirror commands on the WordPad menus.

This isn't some nefarious conspiracy. The common command sets make things easier for us.

As you read the next section, don't worry about what particular commands or menus do. Just focus on the mechanics of choosing commands.

Choosing commands with the furry little rodent

I think that the easiest way to choose a command is to use the mouse.

To select one of the menus using a mouse, move the *mouse pointer* — the small arrow that moves across your screen as you physically roll the mouse across your desk — so that it points to the name of the menu that you want to select. Then click the mouse's left button: Windows 95 or the Windows application displays the menu. (Pointing to some object like a menu name and then pressing the mouse's left button is called *clicking* the object.) Now click the command that you want to choose.

If you inadvertently display a menu, you can deselect it (that is, make it go away) by clicking anywhere outside the menu box.

Choosing commands by using the Alt+key combinations

Another way to choose a command is to use an *Alt* key (cleverly labeled Alt, these keys are usually at either end of the spacebar):

1. Press the Alt key.

This action tells Windows 95 or the Windows application that you want to choose a command.

2. Press the underlined letter of the menu that you want to choose.

This action tells Windows 95 or the Windows application which menu contains the command you want. For example, if you want to choose the WordPad application's File menu, you press the F key because that's the underlined letter. WordPad proudly displays the menu in question. Figure A-3 shows the File menu, for example.

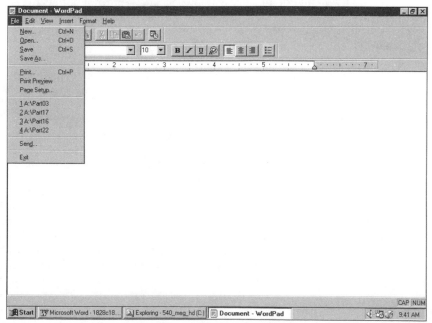

Figure A-3:
The
WordPad
File menu.

3. **Press the underlined letter of the command you want to choose.**

   Each of the commands on a menu is underlined, too, so you can tell the program which command you want to choose by pressing the underlined letter of that command. For example, if you've chosen the File menu, you can choose the last option, Exit, by pressing the letter *X*. (You can try choosing Exit if you want, but then restart WordPad so you can continue to follow along, okay?)

Windows 95 and Windows applications offer yet another way to choose menu commands. After you press the Alt key, use the left- and right-arrow keys to highlight the menu that you want. Then press Enter. Windows 95 or the Windows application displays the menu. Use the up- and down-arrow keys to highlight the command that you want to choose. Then press Enter.

For example, press Alt to activate the menu bar. Press the right-arrow key twice to highlight the Search menu. Press Enter to display the Search menu of commands. Press the down-arrow key once to highlight the Find command. Then press Enter.

If you want to deselect a menu but still leave the menu bar activated, press the Esc key once. To deselect the displayed menu and, at the same time, deactivate the menu bar, press the Esc key twice.

Using shortcut-key combinations

For many menu commands, Windows 95 and Windows applications offer shortcut-key combinations. When you press a shortcut-key combination, Windows 95 or the Windows application simultaneously activates the menu bar, chooses a menu, and chooses a command.

Windows (and Windows applications like WordPad and Quicken) display the shortcut-key combination that you can use for a command on the menu beside the command.

Using one of the menu selection techniques described earlier, activate the Edit menu (see Figure A-4). Do you see the rather cryptic codes, or whatever, that follow each of the command names? Following the Undo command, for example, you can just barely make out the code Ctrl+Z. And following the Paste command, you can see the code Ctrl+V. These are the shortcut-key combinations. If you simultaneously press the two or three keys listed — the Ctrl key and the Z key, for example — you choose the command. (Shortcut-key combinations often use funny keys such as Ctrl, Alt, and Shift in combination with letters or numbers. In case you're not familiar with some of these keys' locations, take a minute to look over your keyboard.)

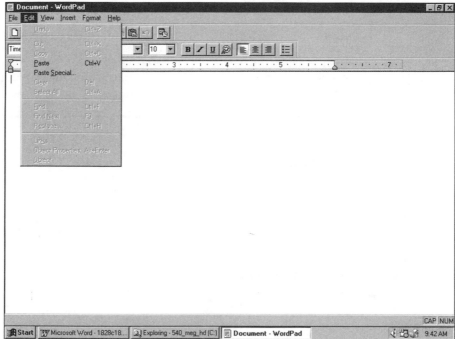

Figure A-4:
The
WordPad
Edit menu.

Disabled commands

Oh, jeepers. There's something I almost forgot to tell you. Not every menu command makes sense in every situation. So Windows 95 and Windows applications disable commands that would be just plain kooky to choose. To show you when a command has been disabled, the program displays disabled commands in gray letters. In comparison, commands you can choose show up in black letters. Take another look at Figure A-4. Several of the commands on that menu are disabled. That's why you can barely read some of their names.

Working with Dialog Boxes

Windows 95 (and Windows applications like Quicken) use a special type of window, called a *dialog box,* to communicate with you. In fact, after you choose a command, Windows 95 and Windows applications often display a dialog box to get the information they need to carry out the command.

Dialog boxes have five unique design elements: text boxes, option buttons, check boxes, list boxes, and command buttons.

Which commands display dialog boxes

Seeing which menu commands display dialog boxes is easy: Command names that prompt dialog boxes are followed by an ellipsis, as shown in the File menu in Figure A-3, after Open, Save As, and Page Setup. Choosing these commands always opens a dialog box.

Text boxes

Text boxes provide a space into which you can enter text. To see what a text box looks like, start WordPad (if you haven't already) type *Steve,* and choose Edit⇨Find. WordPad, responding nicely to your deft touch, displays the Find dialog box (as shown in Figure A-5). The text box is the box to the right of Find what.

Figure A-5:
The Find
dialog box.

To use a text box, move the *selection cursor* — the flashing line or outline that selects the active element of a dialog box — to the text box. Then type in the text. If this "active element" mumbo jumbo seems too technical, just press Tab a bunch of times and watch the dialog box. See that thing that moves around from box to button to box? It selects the active element.

You can move the selection cursor several ways:

- ✔ Click the text box.
- ✔ Press Tab or Shift+Tab until the selection cursor is in the text box (pressing Tab moves the selection cursor to the next element; pressing Shift+Tab moves the selection cursor to the preceding element).
- ✔ Press the Alt+key combination (for example, press Alt+N to move the selection cursor to the Find what text box).

If you make a mistake typing in the text box, use the Backspace key to erase incorrect characters. There are some other editing tricks, but I won't describe them here. Remember that this is just a quick and dirty overview of Windows 95.

You also can move the *insertion bar* — the vertical line that shows where what you type gets placed — using the left- and right-arrow keys. The left-arrow key moves the insertion bar one character to the left without deleting any characters. The right-arrow key moves the insertion bar one character to the right without deleting any characters.

Figure A-6 shows the Find what text box after I typed some text.

Check boxes

Check boxes work like on-off switches. A check box is "on" if the box is selected with an X. A check box is "off" if the box is empty (Figure A-6 shows the Match case check box turned off).

To turn a check box on or off with the mouse, click the check box. If the check box is on, your click turns the check box off. If the check box is off, your click turns the switch on.

You also can use the spacebar to select and deselect a check box. After you move the selection cursor to the check box, press the spacebar to alternatively select and deselect the check box. Toggle, toggle, toggle.

Option buttons

Option buttons are sets of buttons representing mutually exclusive choices. The Options dialog box, which appears when you choose the WordPad View⇨Options command, uses one set of option buttons, the Measurement units buttons: Inches, Points, Centimeters, and Picas (see Figure A-7).

You can select only one button in a set. Windows 95 or the Windows application identifies the selected button by putting a *bullet,* or darkened circle, inside the button. In Figure A-7, for example, the Inches button is selected. The easiest way to select an option button is to click the button you want.

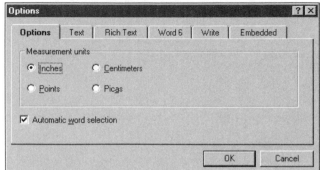

Figure A-7:
A dialog box
with some
option
buttons.

Command buttons

Every dialog box includes command buttons. *Command buttons* tell Windows 95 or a Windows application what you want to do after you finish with a dialog box.

Figure A-7, for example, shows two command buttons: OK and Cancel. If you use the Options dialog box to make some changes, you click OK after completing the rest of the dialog box. If you don't want to use the Options dialog box after all, you choose Cancel.

To choose a command button, either click it or move the selection cursor to a command button and press Enter.

List boxes

List boxes list a series of possible choices. To see an example of a list box, choose the File⇨Open command. Windows 95 or the Windows application displays the Open dialog box (as shown in Figure A-8).

Windows 95 and Windows applications use two types of list boxes: a regular list box, which is always displayed, and a *drop-down* list box, which Windows won't display until you tell it to. Drop-down list boxes look like text boxes with a down-arrow button at the right end of the box.

If you exit Quicken the wrong way

If you exit Quicken by turning off (or resetting) your computer, the index file Quicken uses to organize your financial records gets, well, wasted. Quicken will rebuild the index when you restart, but this process takes a few seconds.

Don't exit Quicken or Windows by turning off your computer. This action may not cause serious problems (let me say, though, that Windows 95 isn't as forgiving as Quicken), but it is bad form — akin to eating the last potato chip or leaving the gas tank empty in your spouse's car.

To open a drop-down list box — such as the Files of Type list box shown in Figure A-8 — click the down-arrow button (or you can move the selection cursor to the list box and then press Alt+↓ key).

Figure A-8:
The Open
dialog box.

Once opened, a drop-down list box works the same as a regular list box. After you select an item from the list box (using the mouse or the arrow keys), press Enter.

Unfortunately, a list is sometimes too long to be completely displayed in the list box. When this minor tragedy occurs, you can use the PgUp and PgDn keys to page through the list.

You also can use the *scrollbar* — the vertical bar with arrows at either end. Just drag the square scrollbar selector up or down. You also can click the arrows at either end of the scrollbar, or you can click the scrollbar itself (this last trick moves the scrollbar selector toward the place where you clicked).

Stopping Quicken for Windows

To stop a Windows application, either click the application's Close box — the button with the X in it that appears in the top-right corner of the application window — or choose File⇨Exit.

A Yelp for Help

Help, a separate application within Windows 95, has a number of powerful tools to help you learn about Windows 95 and Windows applications such as WordPad and Quicken. To access Help, select the Help menu or click the ? icon.

The Help menu (see Figure A-9) lists nine commands: Contents, Index, Help On This Window, Introduction, QuickTours, Quicken Tips, Show Qcards, Load Sample Data, and About Quicken. In the following paragraphs, I briefly describe how each command works.

Figure A-9:
The Quicken
Deluxe Help
menu.

Note: The other versions of Quicken use slightly different commands on the Help menu. If you know how the Quicken Deluxe Help menu and its commands work, however, you won't have any trouble using the Help menus for other versions of Quicken.

Contents command

Choosing the Help command starts the Help program and loads the Quicken Help file. The Help program displays a dialog-box-like window (see Figure A-10) that lists three tabs: Contents, Index, and Find. The Contents tab shows a list of the major help topic categories.

If you want to see the topics that fall within a particular category, click the help topic category. Help expands the list shown on the Contents tab so that it shows the topics within each category (see Figure A-11).

Figure A-10:
Select the Help menu's Contents command to display a list of Quicken's major help topic categories.

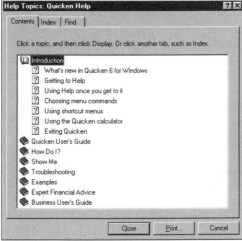

Figure A-11:
After you select one of the major topic categories, Help lists other related topics and provides information.

Finally, pick the specific Help topic for which you want more information. For example, if you want more information on the new features in Quicken 6, click that topic. Help displays the first page of help information on the selected topic (see Figure A-12).

Often there's more than a single page, or window, of help information on a particular topic. To page through a Help topic, use the PgDn and PgUp keys. (You also can use the mouse and scrollbars.)

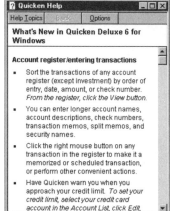

Figure A-12:
The first
page of help
information
on the new
features of
Quicken 6.

Index command

You can also choose the Help⇨Index command to start the Help program.
When you do, Quicken starts the Help program and it displays the same
window shown in Figure A-10 — except the window shows the Index tab instead
of the Contents tab (see Figure A-13).

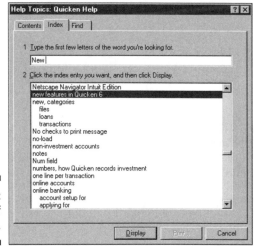

Figure A-13:
The index of
Help topics.

To use the index, type the first few letters of the topic you're interested in or curious about into the text box. (If you want to learn more about the new features in Quicken 6, for example, you might type in the word **new**.) Then review the list of help topics shown on the Index tab's list box. If you see one that matches the topic you have questions about, double-click it. Help next displays a dialog box that lists the specific help topics related to the index entry. You double-click the one you want. And that's that.

Note: You can also use the Index tab by scrolling through its (lengthy!) alphabetical list of all of Quicken's Help topics until you find the one you want. If you have the time.

Help On This Window command

You can also get help information specifically related to the active window (the window that appears on top of any others). To do this, choose the Help➪Help on this Window command to start the Help program. There's not really any reason to say more than this about this command. If you have questions about it, just try it.

Introduction command

The Introduction command starts an online introduction to Quicken 6. You can view this, if you want. But there's a good chance you already saw it if you installed Quicken yourself and paid attention the first time you started Quicken.

The QuickTour command

The QuickTour command displays a window with a bunch of buttons you can click to start online tutorials and tours that describe how Quicken works (in general terms) and how you can use it. The tours are pretty neat, although they don't provide a whole lot of detailed, background information. They're sort of like watching CNN's Headline News.

You don't need that stuff, though. You should find out what you need to know in this book.

The Quicken Tips command

The Quicken Tips command tells Quicken to display its Quicken Tips window (see Figure A-14). This window, which you typically see whenever you start Quicken, displays some useful bits of information about using Quicken. Although the Quicken Tips window shows only one tip at a time, you can read through all of its tips by repeatedly clicking the Next Tip button.

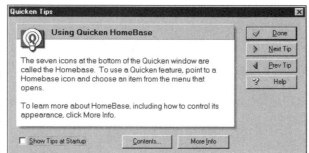

Figure A-14:
The Quicken
Tips
window.

The Show Qcards command

The Show Qcards command turns Quicken's Qcards on and off. "What are Qcards?" you ask. Good question. There are actually two answers. *Answer #1:* If you're a new user and like the idea of a bit of hand-holding, Qcards are these truly nifty pop-up boxes that display helpful information and useful nuggets about the Quicken window or dialog box you're using. *Answer #2:* If you're already comfortable with Quicken and pretty much know your way around town, Qcards are these really irritating pop-up boxes that hide portions of the Quicken window and tell you a bunch of obvious things you already know.

If you start to get irritated by a Qcard that you see for one of Quicken's windows, you can click its Close box (the box with an *X* in the corner of the Qcard box). This is like a secret message to Quicken saying, "I pretty much know everything I need to know about what I'm doing right now. Give me a break, will you?" If you do the clicking thing for a Qcard displayed with the account register window, for example, Quicken won't display Qcards with the account register window anymore — but it will display them for other stuff, like the Investment Portfolio window.

If you get truly irritated by each and every Qcard you see, you should, however, use the Show Qcards command to turn them all off. Doing so tells Quicken enough is enough.

If the Show Qcards command is checked with a check mark, Quicken's Qcards are on. If the command isn't checked with a check mark, all the Qcards are off.

By the way, if you turn off the Qcards for a particular window and then later decide that the backseat driving they do isn't such a bad thing, you can turn them back on. Here's how: First, turn off all the Qcards by choosing the Show Qcards command. Then turn on all the Qcards by choosing the Show Qcards command again.

Load Sample Data command

You can choose the Load Sample Data command to grab a rich, sample data Quicken file from your hard disk or the Quicken CD. And you might want to do this. By fooling around with sample data (instead of your own) you can experiment, noodle around, and even goof off — all without having to worry about damaging or destroying your own, real data. By the way, when you want to reload your own data, you'll need to use the File⇨Open command. Chapter 8 describes how to do that.

The About Quicken command

The About Quicken command displays a dialog box that gives the application's complete name, Quicken for Windows. To remove the About Quicken dialog box, press Esc.

Quitting Windows 95

To quit Windows 95, click the Start button and choose the Shut Down command. Then wait until Windows 95 says it's okay for you to turn off your computer. When it is okay, flip the power switch.

Appendix B

Online Banking and Online Bill Payment

● ●

*B*anks are moving toward offering electronic banking services in a big, big way. It's an exciting area, a step toward providing a pretty impressive variety of online services to the general consumer. Still, I'm not really sure what to think about it. On one hand, you can take care of all your banking in the privacy of your own closet or kitchen or wherever you found room for your computer. On the other hand, it's not all that hard to stop by an ATM (or even — gasp! — a bank with a real, live teller). But maybe you're the type who is so pressed for time that you find yourself waiting in the bank lines and simultaneously trying to read the latest Sue Grafton novel, eat your lunch, and talk to your office on your cell phone. In that case, Online Banking and Online Bill Payment, Quicken's entries in the electronic banking arena, may be for you.

Online Banking helps you to keep track of your banking transactions. You call your bank via a *modem*, a gizmo that allows you to send and receive information over the phone lines. The bank then sends up-to-date information regarding your transactions to your computer — which checks have cleared, deposits you've made, service charges, and so on — and Quicken uses that information to update your Quicken accounts. You can also transfer money between accounts, as long as they are at the same bank. For example, you can pay your credit card bill by transferring money from your checking account to your credit card account.

Online Bill Payment runs along much the same lines, but it's an electronic bill-paying service. You start Quicken and then ask Online Bill Payment to send payments to certain vendors. Quicken has made arrangements with many vendors to make electronic payments directly to them, so the whole process can be accomplished without a single piece of paper changing hands. If your particular vendor isn't one of them, Online Bill Payment will write a real, live check and send it to them.

Wise Whys and Wherefores

Before you hasten down to Electronic Ed's to buy a modem, however, you should consider a few other points before signing up for Quicken's online services:

- ✔ Your bank must be a part of Quicken's Online Banking program. (See the next section for directions on how to find out whether your bank qualifies.)

- ✔ You should be fairly comfortable with Quicken, especially with account transactions and transferring money between accounts.

- ✔ Your records should be completely up to date, reconciled with the last statements you've received from the bank.

One other consideration — and this is the one you've probably been waiting for me to bring up — this stuff ain't free. It's impossible for me to tell you how much they cost because your bank sets the charges. You probably shouldn't pay much more for Online Bill Payment than you pay for postage. However, in making a decision about Online Banking, consider all the hidden costs of the normal way of banking and paying bills. Gasoline, time, and postage can all add up, and it may make the costs of the online services appear more reasonable. (Besides, you won't have to deal with all that nasty glue on your tongue from licking envelopes.)

Let me say one final thing before I start describing these services. If you've worked with Quicken even a little bit, you'll find electronic banking to be a cakewalk. But since I'm covering the basics here, I will cover only the most important features of these online service.

Banking on Online Banking and Online Bill Payment

The first step to using Online Banking and Online Bill Payment is to sign up with your bank. As I mentioned before, your bank must be part of Quicken's Online Banking program The easiest way to find out if your bank qualifies is to call your local branch and ask.

The Quicken Financial Network (QFN) on the World Wide Web also has a list of service providers, as well as additional information on Online Banking and Online Bill Payment services. You have two ways to access the Quicken Financial Network:

✔ If you installed the Netscape Navigator that comes with Quicken, you can choose Features➪Online➪Quicken Financial Network.

✔ If you have other World Wide Web Access, the URL for the Quicken Financial Network is `http://www.qfn.com`.

When you get to the Quicken Financial Network home page, click Banking. When that page appears, scroll down to the Intuit Financial Partners section and select "your financial institution." The next page which appears will display a table of participating banks.

If your bank is part of Quicken's online services, you must contact the bank to register for the service. When you've completed the materials and sent it back, the bank will soon send you a welcome packet containing all the data you will need to complete the sign-up process.

Setting up your Quicken accounts

After you've received the welcome packet, you're ready to prepare your Quicken accounts for Online Banking and Online Bill Payment.

1. **Click the Accts button on the iconbar.**

2. **Select the first account you will set up and click Edit.**

3. **When Quicken displays the Edit Bank Account dialog box, click the Enable Online Banking check box and/or the Online Bill Payment check box.**

4. **Click Next, and Quicken displays the dialog box shown in Figure B-1.**

5. **Open the Financial Institution drop-down list box and choose your financial institution.**

Figure B-1:
The Edit
Bank
Account
dialog box.

6. **Type the routing number the bank gave you for this account in the Routing Number text box. (You should find this information in the welcome packet they sent.)**

7. **Type the account number the bank gave you in the Account Number text box.**

8. **Open the Account Type drop-down list box and choose the appropriate account type.**

9. **Type your Social Security number in the Social Security Number text box.**

10. **Click Done.**

I guess this is probably obvious, but you need to repeat this process for every account that you want to use for Online Banking and/or Online Bill Payment. When you're finished, the hardest part is over.

A Bank where only the telephones have long lines

Using Online Banking and Online Bill Payment is surprisingly easy. Choose Features⇨Online⇨Online Banking/Investments, and Quicken opens the Online Banking/Investment Centers window. If it isn't showing, click the Transactions tab, and you'll see a window with information similar to Figure B-2.

Using the online services is a two-step process. First, you type your transactions into the computer. But here's the important point: Nothing is actually transferred to or from the bank until you click the Go Online button shown in Figure B-2. That's when the bank actually receives your transactions for processing.

Updating your Quicken accounts

One major advantage of Online Banking is that you can get the most up-to-date information regarding your accounts. Click the Go Online button, and the bank automatically sends current transactions to your computer. They are not loaded immediately into your Quicken registers. Quicken gives you a chance to examine them before they go into your records. With the Transactions tab of the Online Banking/Investments Center window showing, select an account from the list box at the upper-left of the window tab, and the new transactions for that account appear in the lower half of the tab window. (Figure B-2 shows this window.)

Note: You can see one of the disadvantages of Online Banking from Figure B-2 if you're observant. Since the bank doesn't keep track of the check's payee, every check is simply labeled "Check." Once you accept all the transactions into your

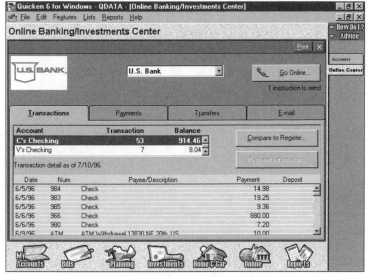

Figure B-2:
The
Transactions
tab of the
Online
Banking/
Investments
Center.

Quicken accounts, you have to go back and type in the Payees. However, since you have to categorize each check anyway, this may not be so bad.

To add the transaction you've downloaded from the bank to your account register, click Compare to Register button, and Quicken displays the appropriate register in the top half of the window, and the list of new transactions in the bottom half, as in Figure B-3. You can accept each new transaction one at a time by clicking it and then clicking Accept. If you're the daring sort, you can click Accept All, and Quicken places all the new transactions in your register. Click Done to close the window.

Using Online Bill Payment

Online Bill Payment pays your bills electronically if the company you're paying is set up to handle electronic transactions. If not, Online Payment will write out a check and send it to them.

To use Online Bill Payment, choose Features⇨Online⇨Online Payments to open the Payments tab of the Online Banking/Investments Center window, shown in Figure B-4. (If the window is already open, you can always just click the Payments tab.)

Before you make an online payment, you should compile a list of the vendors which you will pay. Quicken calls this list Online Payees. To add someone to this list, click the Online Payees button, and the Online Payee List appears. (I haven't shown it here because it is so similar to all the other Quicken lists.) Click its New button, however, and the Set Up Online Payee dialog box appears (see Figure B-5).

Figure B-3:
Quicken
displays this
version of
the account
register so
you can
compare the
new
transactions
to your
Quicken
register.

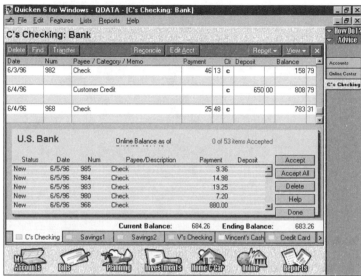

Figure B-4:
The
Payments
tab of the
Online
Banking/
Investments
Center
window.

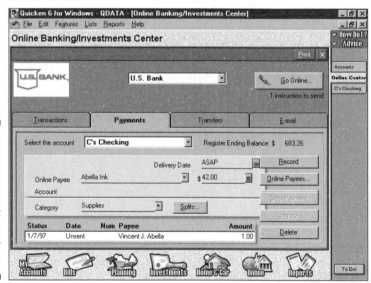

To describe an online payee, just click the text boxes and then fill in the appropriate information. (The Account # text box is for the number the vendor uses to identify you. You probably won't have any problems with the rest.) After you're done, click OK. Quicken returns you to the Online Payee List, which now includes your new entry.

Figure B-5:
The Set Up
Online
Payee
dialog box.

After you've compiled your list, making an online payment is very simple. Just follow these steps:

1. **Make sure that the Payments tab of the Online Banking/Investments Center window is showing. (Figure B-4 shows the window, in case you'd like to follow along.)**

2. **Open the drop-down list box at the top of the Payments area to indicate the account to pay the bill from.**

3. **Open the Online Payee drop-down list box and choose the vendor to pay.**

4. **Click to the right of the dollar sign ($) and type in the amount to pay.**

5. **Open the Category drop-down list box and categorize this payment, or press the Split button if the payment should be divided into more than one category. The Split button works the same way it works when you're categorizing checks.**

6. **Click Record**.

Quicken adds the new Online Payment to the list in the text box under Status. This payment will be sent to your bank the next time you click the Go Online button.

Whatever happened to CheckFree?

CheckFree, which closely resembles Online Bill Payment, used to be highly touted by Intuit, the makers of Quicken. Although Intuit still lets Quicken users use CheckFree, Intuit says they believe Online Bill Payment is a better bargain for their customers. This means that Quicken will strongly support Online Bill Payment and that it will probably be integrated more smoothly than CheckFree. In the interests of full disclosure, I should mention that Online Bill Payment is an Intuit service.

Transferring money between online accounts

If you have more than one Online Banking account, you can easily transfer money from one account to another. If one is a credit card account, you can even make your payments by transferring money into the credit card account, without having to go through Online Bill Payment.

To transfer money between accounts, click the Transfers tab of the Online Banking/Investments Center window (see Figure B-6).

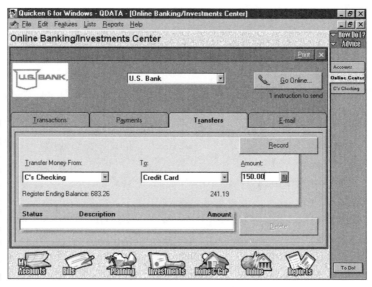

Figure B-6: The Transfers tab of the Online Banking/ Investments Center window.

Then use the Transfer Money From drop-down list box to indicate the account you're transferring money from and the To drop-down list box to indicate the account you're transferring money to. Type the amount you want to transfer in the Amount box. After you're done, click Record, and Quicken adds the transaction to the text box under Status. Just like the other online features, your bank won't actually receive the transfer until you click the Go Online button.

I was recently shocked — shocked, I tell you — to find out that not all online transfers are handled electronically. In some cases, my financial institution sends the information on to a department where it is entered manually. This meant that my transfer was not instantaneous, and I had to make a slight change in my planning.

If you want to delete a transfer that has not been sent to the bank yet, click the transaction in the Status text box and then press Delete.

Communicating online with the bank

Quicken also provides a means of sending and receiving e-mail from your bank. Click the E-mail tab of the Online Banking/Investments Center window, and you'll see something similar to Figure B-7.

Figure B-7:
The E-mail tab of the Online Banking/ Investments Center window.

Quicken sends and receives E-mail with any transactions when you click the Go Online button and then lists any messages which are received in the text box in the middle of the E-mail tab. In order to read a message, you just highlight it by clicking it and then clicking Read. Click Close after you're done, and Quicken returns you to the Online Banking/Investments Center window. If you don't want to save the message, click it to highlight it and click Delete to remove it from the list.

If you want to send your bank a message, click Create. Quicken opens a dialog box similar to the one in Figure B-8.

Quicken automatically fills in the date and the To text box. Fill in the other text boxes by clicking them and then typing the necessary information. Open the Regarding Account drop-down list box by clicking the down arrow and then choosing the appropriate account.

After you've completed your message, click OK, and Online Banking records your message and forwards it to the bank the next time you click Go Online.

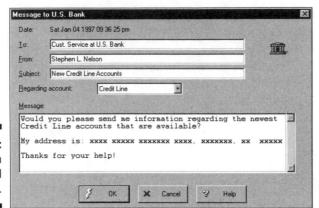

Figure B-8:
Creating an
e-mail
message.

Appendix C
Glossary of Business, Financial, and Computer Terms

1-2-3

The Lotus 1-2-3 spreadsheet program. The original "killer" application, 1-2-3 almost single-handedly turned IBM-compatible personal computers into standard business and financial management tools.

940 Payroll Tax Form

The annual federal unemployment tax return. There's also a 940EZ version that is supposed to be EZ-er to fill out.

941 Payroll Tax Form

The quarterly federal payroll tax form that tells the IRS what federal employee payroll taxes (Social Security and Medicare) you've collected and remitted.

942 Payroll Tax Form

The quarterly payroll tax form that tells the IRS what domestic employee payroll taxes an employer has collected and remitted.

Account

In Quicken, a list of the increases and decreases in an asset's value or in a liability's balance.

Account Balance

The value of an asset or the outstanding principal owed for a liability. For example, the value of a checking account is the cash value of the account. The balance of a mortgage liability is the principal you still owe.

Account Transfer

An amount you move from one account (such as a checking account) to another (such as a savings account).

Account Type

Quicken provides several versions, or types, of accounts: six for keeping records of the things you own and two for keeping records of the amounts you owe.

- **Checking accounts:** For tracking checking accounts
- **Savings accounts:** For tracking savings accounts
- **Cash accounts:** For tracking the cash in your pocket or wallet
- **Money market accounts:** For tracking money market accounts
- **Investment accounts:** For tracking mutual funds and brokerage accounts
- **Other asset accounts:** For tracking anything else you own
- **Credit card accounts:** For tracking your plastic
- **Other liability accounts:** For tracking everything else you owe

Accounts Payable

In a business, the amounts you owe your trade creditors — your landlord, the office supplies store, the distributor from whom you purchase your inventory, and so on. People who prefer monosyllabic speech often refer to accounts payable as *A/P*.

Accounts Receivable

In a business, the amounts your customers or clients owe you. People who prefer monosyllabic speech often refer to accounts receivable as *A/R*.

Activity Bar

The Activity Bar amounts to a table of contents (displayed as icons) that you use to move to the Quicken windows that you'll commonly use.

Amortization

The itsy-bitsy principal payments you make over the course of repaying a loan. Eventually, these principal reductions pay off the loan.

ASCII

An acronym standing for the American Standard Code for Information Interchange. People usually use the term to refer to files — in other words, ASCII files — that contain just regular old text: letters, numbers, symbols from the keyboard, and so on.

Backing Up

Making a copy. If something terrible happens — fire, hard disk failure, thermonuclear exchange — you still have a copy on floppy disk.

Balancing an Account

The steps you take to explain the difference between what your records show as a balance and what the bank's records (statement) show. Also referred to as *reconciling an account.*

Billminder

A program that comes with Quicken, Billminder looks through your postdated checks whenever you start your computer. If there's a check that needs to be paid, Billminder tells you.

Bookkeeper

Someone who keeps the "books," or financial records.

Brokerage Account

An account specifically set up to track a brokerage account that you use to invest in securities. Unlike a mutual fund account, a brokerage account includes a cash element.

Budget

A plan that says how you will make and spend money.

Capital Accounts

The money a sole proprietor leaves in or contributes to the sole proprietorship. Also, the money a partner leaves in or contributes to a partnership.

Capital Gain

What you earn by selling an investment for more than you paid for it.

Capital Loss

What you lose by selling an investment for less than you paid.

Category

In Quicken, how you summarize income and outgo. For example, you may use a category such as Wages to summarize your payroll check deposits. And you may use categories such as Housing, Food, and Fun to summarize your checks.

Category List

The list of categories you can use. While setting up the first account in a file, Quicken suggests category lists for home users and for business users.

Certified Public Accountant

Someone who's taken a bunch of undergraduate or graduate accounting courses, passed a rather challenging two-and-a-half-day test, and worked for at least a year or two under a CPA doing things like auditing, tax planning and preparation, and consulting.

Chart

A picture that shows numbers. In Quicken, you can produce pie charts, bar charts, line charts, and so on.

Check Date

The date you write your payment instructions, or check. Technically, the check date is the date on which your payment instructions to the bank become valid.

Check Form

The preprinted form that you use to provide payment instructions to your bank: "Okay, Mammoth National, pay Joe Shmoe $32 from my account, 00704-844." Theoretically, you could use just about anything as a check form — a scrap of paper, a block of wood, and so on. In fact, rumor has it that someone once used a cowhide. It's easier for your poor bank, though, if you use check forms that follow the usual style and provide OCR characters along the form's bottom edge.

Circular E

Instructions from the IRS to employers. This publication tells how much federal income tax to withhold and other stuff like that. Call the IRS and request a copy if you need one.

Cleared

When a check or deposit has been received by the bank. An *uncleared* transaction hasn't been received by the bank.

Click

The process of pointing to something on a screen with a mouse and then pressing the mouse's left button. Occasional secondary usage (spelled "clique") refers to a snobbish group of adolescents.

Commands

What you use to tell Quicken what it should do. For example, "Quicken, I command thee to print a report."

Controller

A business's chief accountant — and usually the brunt of most accountant jokes. Also known as a *comptroller.*

Corporation

A legal business entity created by state law, owned by shareholders, and managed by directors and officers. As a business entity, a corporation has unique advantages and some disadvantages. Ask your attorney for more information.

Credit Card Account

A Quicken account specifically set up to track credit card charges, payments, and balances.

Cursor

Someone who uses vulgar language habitually. Also, the little blinking line or square (mouse pointer) that shows where what you type will go.

Deleted Transaction

A transaction that Quicken has removed from the register. *See also* **Voided Transaction.**

Directory

Basically, a drawer (like a filing cabinet drawer) that DOS uses to organize your hard disk. *See also* **Folder.**

Disk

The thingamajig in your computer on which DOS stores your programs (such as Quicken) and your data files (such as the Quicken file for your financial records). A hard disk (inside your computer) can store a great deal of information; floppy disks (5 ¼-inch or 3 ½-inch), which can be removed, store less data than a hard disk.

DOS

An acronym standing for the Microsoft *Disk Operating System*. DOS isn't all that germane to Quicken for Windows users — especially if you're using Quicken with Windows 95. Nonetheless, since you're already reading here, I'll tell you that even if you're running Windows 95, a version of DOS still hangs around on your computer and does some stuff for Windows 95. Because this book is about financial stuff, I should also mention that DOS is one reason why Bill Gates became America's richest man.

Double-Click

Two clicks of the mouse in quick succession.

Exit

To shut down, terminate, or stop a program.

Field

Where bunnies hop around. Also, input blanks on a screen.

File

Where data is stored. Your Quicken financial records, for example, are stored in a file.

Filename

The name of a file in which Quicken stores data. Actually, what Quicken calls a filename is actually the name used for several files.

Financial Wizards

People who believe that they know so much about the world of finance that it is actually their God-given duty to share their expertise with you.

Find

A tremendous bargain, as in: "At $22,000, the five-bedroom house was a real find." In Quicken, also an <u>E</u>dit menu command that you can use to locate transactions. *See also **Search Criteria.***

Fiscal Year

A fiscal year is just the annual budgeting year. Most of the time, a fiscal year is the same as the calendar year, starting on January 1 and ending on December 31. But some businesses use a different fiscal year. (Why they do that is way, way beyond the scope of this book.)

Folder

What Windows 95 uses to organize your hard disk. DOS calls folders "directories."

Formatting

Hey, this word is too complicated for a book like this, isn't it? Let me just say that formatting means doing some things to a disk so that you can write files to that disk. It can also mean setting up some nice typesetting "looks" in your printed documents.

Graphics Adapter Cards

A chunk of circuitry inside your computer that Quicken and other programs need to draw pictures on your monitor. The acronyms EGA, VGA, CGA, and SVGA all refer to graphics adapter cards. But you really shouldn't have to worry about this stuff. Heck, you really don't need to know the difference between an EGA and the PTA (as in Harper Valley — get it?). Also needed for playing neat computer games.

Help

A program's on-line documentation — which can almost always be accessed by pressing F1. Also, a verbalized cry for assistance.

Internal Rate of Return

An investment's profit expressed as a percentage of the investment. If you go down to the bank and buy a certificate of deposit earning 7 percent interest, for example, 7 percent is the CD's internal rate of return. I don't want to give you the heebie-jeebies, but internal rates of return can get really complicated really fast.

Liability Accounts

An account specifically set up for tracking loans, payments, the principal and interest portions of these payments, and the outstanding balance.

Memo

A brief description of a transaction. Because you also give the payee and category for a transaction, it usually makes sense to use the Memo field to record some other bit of information about a check or deposit.

Menu

In Quicken, a list of commands. In a restaurant, a list of things you can order from the kitchen.

Menu Bar

Although it sounds like a place where menus go after work for a drink, a menu bar is a horizontally arranged row, or bar, of menus.

Missing Check

A gap in the check numbers. For example, if your register shows a check 101 and a check 103, check 102 is a missing check.

Mouse

A furry little rodent. Also, a pointing device you can use to select menu commands and fields.

Mutual Fund Account

A Quicken account specifically set up to track a mutual fund investment.

Partnership

A business entity that combines two or more former friends. In general, each partner is liable for the entire debts of the partnership.

Password

A word you have to give Quicken before Quicken gives you access to a file. The original password "Open sesame" was used by Ali Baba.

Payee

The person to whom a check is made payable. (If you write a check to me, Steve Nelson, for example, I'm the payee.) In Quicken, however, you can fill in a Payee field for deposits and for account transfers.

Power User

Someone who's spent far more time than is healthy fooling around with a computer. Power users are good people to have as friends, though, because they can often solve your worst technical nightmares. However, note that most people who describe themselves as power users aren't.

QIF

An acronym standing for *Quicken Interchange Format.* Basically, QIF is a set of rules that prescribes how an ASCII file must look if you want Quicken to read it. If you're a clever sort, you can import category lists and even transactions from ASCII files that follow the QIF rules.

Quicken

The name of the checkbook-on-a-computer program that this book is about. You didn't really need to look this up, did you?

Quicken Quotes

Quicken Quotes is an on-line service that you can use to grab up-to-date price information on stocks and bonds. This book doesn't talk much about Quicken Quotes.

QuickFill

A clever little feature. If Quicken can guess what you're going to type next in a field, it types, or *QuickFills,* the field for you. QuickFill types in transactions, payee names, and category names.

QuickPay

An extra program that you can buy from Intuit, the maker of Quicken, to make payroll a snap.

QuickTabs

QuickTabs are the little pages that appear along the right edge of the Quicken application window. You can click a QuickTab to move to its window.

QuickZoom

A clever, big feature. If you have a question about a figure in an on-screen report, double-click the figure. Quicken then lists all the individual transactions that go together to make the figure.

Register

The list of increases and decreases in an account balance. Quicken displays a register in a window that looks remarkably similar to a crummy old paper register — your checkbook. To print a copy of the register that you see on your screen, press Ctrl+P and then press the Enter key.

Report

An on-screen or printed summary of financial information from one or more registers.

Restore

Replace the current version of a file with the backup version. You may want to do this after a fire, hard disk failure, or thermonuclear exchange. *See also Backing Up.*

Savings Goal Accounts

Quicken includes this pseudo-account called a *savings goal account.* In effect, a savings goal account is a compartment in a banking account where you can "hide" or set aside money that you're saving for a special purpose: A new car. A boat. A trip to Montana. Whatever.

Scroll Bars

The vertical bars along the window's right edge and the horizontal bars along the window's bottom edge. Use them to scroll, or page, through your view of something that's too big to fit on one page.

Search Criteria

A description of the transaction that you want to locate. *See also* **Find.**

Sole Proprietorship

A business that's owned by just one person and that doesn't have a separate legal identity. In general, businesses are sole proprietorships, partnerships, or corporations.

Spacebar

An intergalactic cocktail lounge. Also, the big long key on your keyboard that produces a blank space.

Split Transactions

A transaction assigned to more than one category or transferred to more than one account. A split check transaction, for example, might show a $50 check to the grocery store paying for both groceries and automobile expenses.

Stockholders' Equity

The money that shareholders have contributed to a corporation or allowed to be retained in the corporation. You can't track stockholders' equity with Quicken.

Subcategory

A category within a category. For example, the suggested Quicken home categories list breaks down utilities spending into a Gas and Electric subcategory and a Water subcategory.

Supercategory

A group of categories that you monitor as a group. You create supercategories so that you can monitor them using a progress bar.

Tax Deduction

For an individual, an amount that can be deducted from total income (such as alimony or Individual Retirement Account contributions) or used as an itemized deduction and deducted from adjusted gross income (such as home mortgage interest or charitable contributions). For a business, any amount that represents an ordinary and necessary business expense. Be sure, however, to consult with your tax advisor if you have any questions about what is or isn't a vaild tax deduction.

Tax-Deferred Account

Some accounts aren't taxable — Individual Retirement Accounts, for one example, and 401(k) Plans for another. To deal with this real-life complexity, Quicken lets you tag any account as being tax-deferred. As a practical matter, however, it'll probably be only investment accounts and the occasional bank account that are tax-deferred.

Techno-Geek

Someone who believes that fooling around with a computer is more fun than anything else in the world.

Transposition

Flip-flopped numbers — for example, 23.45 entered as **24.35** (the 3 and 4 are flip-flopped as 4 and 3). These common little mistakes have caused many bookkeepers and accountants to go insane.

Voided Transaction

A transaction that Quicken has marked as void (using the Payee field), marked as cleared, and set to zero. Voided transactions appear in a register, but because they are set to zero, they don't affect the account balance. *See also **Deleted Transaction.***

W-2 and W-3

A W-2 is the annual wages statement that employers use to tell employees what they made and to tell the IRS what employees made. When employers send a stack of W-2s to the IRS, they also fill out a W-3 form that summarizes all the individual W-2s. W-2s and W-3s aren't much fun, but they're not hard to fill out.

Windows

The Microsoft Windows operating system. Quicken 6 for Windows relies on Windows to do a bunch of system stuff, such as print. Refer to Appendix A for more information.

Zen Buddhism

A Chinese and Japanese religion that says enlightenment comes from things such as meditation, self-contemplation, and intuition — not from faith, devotion, or material things. I don't really know very much about Zen Buddhism. I did need a Z entry for the glossary, though.

Index

••

Note: Page numbers in *italics* refer to
   illustrations.

NUMBERS
1-2-3, Lotus, 327
940, 941, 942 Payroll Tax Forms,
   defined, 327

• A •

account files, 126–132
   Checking Account Setup dialog box, *129*
   Create New Account dialog box, *128*
   Create Quicken File dialog box, *128*
   defined, 129, 334
   passwords, 133–135
   setting up, 127–129
   shrinking, 130–132
   switching between, 130
Account List window
   credit cards, *157*, 159
   reconciliations, 107, *108*
   setting up additional accounts, *27*, 30
account registers
   printing, 86–90
   restoring data after backing up, 124–125
   window, *19*, 20
account transfers, 63–65, *66*
   cash, 224–225
   categories, 64
   credit card, 162–163
   defined, 328
   editing, 65
   mutual fund, 197
   online transactions, 324
   split categories, 69–70

accounting
   See also bookkeepers
   cash-basis and accrual-basis, 292
accounts
   balancing. *See* reconciliations
   cash, 231–236
   Create New Account dialog box, *27*,
      128, *157*
   credit card, *157*, 333
   defined, 328
   destination, 127
   files. *See* account files
   finding, 55–56
   investment, 199–201
   liability, 336
   setting up additional, 26–30
   setting up credit card, 156–159
   setting up first, 14–16
   source, 127
   types of, 328
accounts payable, 265–269
   Billminder program, 267–269
   defined, 329
   reports, 265, *266*
   tracking vendors, 265, *266*
   Write Checks window, 265
accounts receivable, 257–264
   customer lists, 263–264
   defined, 329
   inaccuracies in, 262
   recording invoices, 259–260
   recording payments, 261
   reports, 263–264
   setting up asset accounts, 257–259
   Split Transaction window, 262–263
   tracking, 262–264
accrual-basis accounting, switching to, 292
Activity Bar, 18, 329

equity, stockholders', 274, 340
escrow. *See* mortgage escrow accounts
exemptions, Tax Planner, 151–152
exiting
  defined, 334
  Quicken, 309
  Windows 95, 315
expense categories, setting up for payroll,
    242–243

• F •

FAQs (frequently asked questions),
    273–279
fields, defined, 334
File Copied Successfully dialog box,
    shrinking files, *132*
File Open command, setting up Quicken if
    used before, 20–21
file source documents, cross-reference
    and, 283
filenames, defined, 334
files, account. *See* account files
filing quarterly tax returns, 253–254
Financial Calendar, 189–192
  Note button, 192
  View button, 192
  window, *190*
financial wizards, defined, 334
Find command, defined, 334
Find/Replace command, transactions,
    74–75
finding
  accounts, 55–56
  reports, 98–99
  transactions, 72–75
Finish Later button, credit card
    reconciliations, 168
fiscal years, defined, 335
floppy disks, formatting, 119–121
folders, defined, 335
formatting
  defined, 335

floppy disks, 119–121
forms, check, 331
frequently asked questions (FAQs),
    273–279

• G •

goals
  mutual fund, 198
  stock and bond, 223
graphics adapter cards, defined, 335
graphs, 103–104
  Create Graph dialog box, *103*
  Easy Answer Reports & Graphs, 98–99
  Income and Expense, *104*

• H •

Help menu, 310–315
  Contents command, 310–311
  Help On This Window command, 313
  Index command, 312–313
  Introduction command, 313
  Load Sample Data command, 315
  Quicken Tips command, 314
  QuickTour command, 313
  Show Qcards command, 314–315
Home Cash Flow reports, 93, *94*
home category lists, *31–32*
Home reports, *95–96*
  printing, 92
housekeeping functions, 119–135
  account files, 126–132
  backing up, 121–126
  formatting floppy disks, 119–121
  passwords, 133–135

• I •

iconbar, 18–19
icons in this book, 6–7
importing data, 278
income changes and budgets, 42–44
Income and Expense graphs, *104*
income taxes. *See* taxes

• Q •

document, 17, *18*
WordPad, Windows 95, 301
Write Checks window. *See* printing checks

• *Y* •

Year-End Copy dialog box, shrinking
    files, *131*

• *Z* •

Zen Buddhism, defined, 342
zooming reports, QuickZoom, 100